Psychiatric Rehabilitation Programs

The Johns Hopkins Series in Contemporary Medicine and Public Health

Also of interest in this series:

Work and Mental Illness: Transitions to Employment, Bertram J. Black

Vocational Rehabilitation of Persons with Prolonged Psychiatric Disorders, edited by Jean A. Ciardiello and Morris D. Bell

Family Management of Schizophrenia: A Study of Clinical, Social, Family, and Economic Benefits, Ian R. Falloon, M.D., and others

Psychiatric Rehabilitation Programs

Putting Theory into Practice

EDITED BY

Marianne D. Farkas
CENTER FOR PSYCHIATRIC REHABILITATION, BOSTON UNIVERSITY

and William A. Anthony
CENTER FOR PSYCHIATRIC REHABILITATION, BOSTON UNIVERSITY

The Johns Hopkins University Press   Baltimore and London

The Johns Hopkins University Press
701 West 40th Street
Baltimore, Maryland 21211
The Johns Hopkins Press Ltd., London

The paper used in this publication meets the minimum requirements of the
American National Standard for Information Sciences—Permanence of Paper for
Printed Library Materials, ANSI Z39.48–1984.

LIBRARY OF CONGRESS CATALOGING-IN-PUBLICATION DATA
Psychiatric rehabilitation programs.

(The Johns Hopkins series in contemporary medicine and public health)
Bibliography: p.
Includes index.
  1. Mentally ill—Rehabilitation. 2. Mentally ill—Services for. I. Farkas,
Marianne D., 1948– . II. Anthony, William Alan, 1942– . III. Series.
[DNLM: 1. Mental Disorders—rehabilitation. 2. Mental Health Services—
organization & administration.
WM 29.1 P9742]
RC439.5.P78 1989   362.2   88-8360
ISBN 0-8018-3724-3 (alk. paper)

Contents

Acknowledgments

A multiauthor text, about an approach that has evolved over the years, is the result of the efforts of many more people than could possibly be listed in an Acknowledgments section. Therefore, first, we thank all of you who have been involved in our ability to "put theory into practice." There are some, however, whose contributions must be individually acknowledged.

The seminal work of Robert Carkhuff and his colleagues in developing the technology of interpersonal skills and human resource development is the basic foundation upon which psychiatric rehabilitation is built. Many of us involved in the development of the psychiatric rehabilitation approach were once students or colleagues of Dr. Carkhuff and his associates.

The unfailing support of Sam Silverstein at the National Institute of Mental Health (NIMH) made it possible for us to develop the training technology and dissemination strategies necessary to allow those in the field to actually use the approach. His personal support and grant support from the NIMH over the past decade also made it possible for us to have the luxury, at times, of spending years with programs in our wish to teach the techniques. Dr. Silverstein most recently further supported our efforts to disseminate the technology of the approach to university graduate programs in psychiatry, psychology, nursing, and social work. Without his faith in our ability to develop a new approach to inservice and preservice training, psychiatric rehabilitation might never have been put into practice by the programs in this book.

We wish to acknowledge the National Institute on Disability and Rehabilitation Research, whose grant support, along with that of the NIMH, created the Center for Psychiatric Rehabilitation in 1979. The backing of the institute allowed us to develop materials to support those who wished to train their staff in psychiatric rehabilitation, and a methodology to train program consultants to support those administrators who wished to introduce the approach, at a program level. It also allowed us to do the research needed to identify the needs of the field.

Boston University's Sargent College of Allied Health Professions, Department of Rehabilitation Counseling, has been our home base. The editors of this book are faculty members in the department, which is chaired by Dr. Arthur Dell Orto. Some of those who wrote the case studies in this book graduated from Dr. Dell Orto's department. He imbued them with the notion that they were the kind of committed professionals who surely would make contributions to the field.

Barry Cohen, Bill Kennard, Rick Forbess, Bill O'Brien, and Sue McNamara, along with the rest of the staff who are not mentioned elsewhere in this book, provided the training and consultation to the people, programs, and systems in the field that in fact made the theoretical practical and possible. Great ideas are lost without those willing to put in the long hours of detailed work necessary to disseminate them.

We wish to acknowledge the help of Jennifer Tratnyek, Cindilee Jope, Darlene Beckwith, Arlene Branniff, Susan Dickinson, Bob Mac-Williams, and the other support staff of the Center for Psychiatric Rehabilitation who often must have wondered if their work on this book would ever end. Yumi Yamamoto painstakingly proofed and reproofed this work with a professionalism that goes well beyond her role as student-assistant. Katharine Wall helped with the final proofreading of the galleys. Aurora Wilber-Leach kept everyone going, often staying overtime to ensure that the manuscript would actually be typed and delivered.

Wendy Harris, science editor of the Johns Hopkins University Press, has the patience of Job.

Finally, we wish to acknowledge all those consumers and their families who were willing to participate with us and the programs described in this text, in developing these applications of psychiatric rehabilitation. Their participation ranged, for example, from directly giving us input on what they felt was important to include, sitting through endless hours of audiotaped sessions so that practitioners could get feedback on their skills, to allowing themselves to become subjects for research. Without their involvement, psychiatric rehabilitation would be a meaningless set of intellectual concepts.

Introduction

Many mental health settings have begun developing psychiatric rehabilitation programs to enhance or replace existing, more traditional programs (Allen & Velasco, 1980; Bachrach, 1982a; Beard, Propst & Malamud, 1982; Cannady, 1982; Hume & Marshall, 1980; Heffner & Gill, 1982; Rogan, 1980; Witheridge, Dincin & Appleby, 1982). Some are adopting a rehabilitation approach as a complement to existing services (Anthony, Buell, Sharatt & Althoff, 1972), while others are moving from no services for severely psychiatrically disabled persons to a psychiatric rehabilitation approach (Lamb, 1982).

This volume presents the recent advances in psychiatric rehabilitation practice and the ways in which they are being translated into program services. Its intended audience includes program administrators interested in developing rehabilitation-oriented mental health programs; systems administrators interested in supporting such programs; and students of mental health, rehabilitation, or administration.

There are three main domains through which rehabilitation services are delivered: people, programs, and systems. The *people* include any professional or laypersons (e.g., families or consumers themselves) who interact with those who are severely psychiatrically disabled. Rehabilitation personnel, regardless of their position, require the knowledge, positive attitudes, and skills to involve disabled persons in psychiatric rehabilitation. *Programs*, regardless of where they are located, require certain environments and operating structures to support people using psychiatric rehabilitation techniques. The *system* of services supports the people and programs by providing financial, legislative, political, and technical resources.

Essentially, the book contains two sections. Its focus is on service delivery at a program level (chapters 1–4). Personnel and systems domains are discussed as they relate to the ability of the program to deliver its services (chapters 5 and 6).

Chapter 1 explains the concepts of psychiatric rehabilitation as the term is used throughout the book. The explanation includes the elements of a psychiatric rehabilitation program and the methods used to implement it. The next three chapters describe psychiatric rehabilitation programs in residential (chapter 2), vocational (chapter 3), and educational settings (chapter 4). Chapter 5 addresses system-level support for program services. Chapter 6 discusses critical support services provided by professional and lay personnel.

Each program chapter is divided into three parts. The general focus of the first part is an overview of the historical and current issues in the chapter's specific area of concern. The second part of each chapter is a collection of case studies written by administrators and practitioners in the field. The case studies describe, within a variety of settings, the introduction of the principles and methodology of psychiatric rehabilitation into their programs. The final portion of the chapter presents the emerging concepts, principles, or models for future service delivery.

The case studies incorporated within each of the program chapters (chapters 2, 3, and 4) are formated in a similar way. Each case study first introduces the agency that is its subject and, where appropriate, includes a profile that summarizes basic information about that agency's program. Second, the program is described in terms of the manner in which it implements the psychiatric rehabilitation process. Next, the case study describes the strategies for and barriers to the full implementation of a psychiatric rehabilitation approach. Last, program evaluation information relevant to the implementation effort is provided. While the program case studies are organized in a similar manner, because each setting is unique, the case studies naturally vary in terms of the detail provided. For example, some case studies use client illustrations to describe their program. Some case studies describe their program outcomes with anecdotal data, others with more formal data, while others are currently involved in research studies.

Chapters 5 and 6 also contain sections written by those in current practice. Chapter 5 describes how to integrate the psychiatric rehabilitation approach into a mental health system, and chapter 6 focuses on supports for psychiatrically disabled persons. Each case study or practical article is preceded by an overview of the topic and is followed by an analysis of emerging concepts, principles, or models. However, because of the wide variety of topics included in these chapters, the articles themselves are not organized in an identical manner.

The book concludes with a brief look at the future of psychiatric rehabilitation programs given the level of today's learning and the client needs that are projected.

1
Psychiatric Rehabilitation:
The Approach and Its Programs

MARIANNE D. FARKAS, SC.D.; WILLIAM A.
ANTHONY, PH.D.; AND MIKAL R. COHEN, PH.D.

Finding ways to enable persons with severe or chronic psychiatric disabilities to live more satisfying lives has been a difficult goal to achieve. The problems in achieving this goal have become particularly acute over the past twenty years. The public policy of transferring large numbers of state hospital residents to "the community" was instituted as one means of realizing this goal. While many agree that the philosophy of what came to be known as "deinstitutionalization" was one that was worthy of advocacy, its implementation became entangled in the politics and economics of the 1970s and early 1980s (Bachrach, 1983). The result was that those who should have benefited from a policy to release them from what could only be termed civil incarceration often suffered other forms of deprivation in the "community" (Bachrach, 1986a; Sheper-Hughes, 1981; Stelovich, 1979). Problems in achieving deinstitutionalization included the lack of organized adequate services, the lack of housing, the lack of support systems, and a general lack of public awareness (Bachrach, 1986b; Kiesler, McGuire, Mechanic, Mosher, Nelson, Newman, Rich & Schulberg, 1983; Talbott, 1979). These difficulties left many questioning the implementation of the deinstitutionalization policy and even the wisdom of the policy itself.

The issue confronting practitioners, social planners, and concerned citizens remained clear, although its articulation was often confused. What was the best way to help people with severe and varied limitations achieve a satisfying life? For some, reacting to the problems that came to light because of deinstitutionalization, the answer seemed to be "reinstitutionalization." At least in the hospital, the argument went, people would be taken care of. For others, this response was a civil outrage, "Close the hospitals! Keep them in the community!" Providing a solution too often became an argument about the *location* for treatment of disabled persons (Anthony, 1979a). While the discussion may be important because of the severe stigma society places upon those it tries to keep out of the mainstream, the question of what can be done effectively, in either place, remains the heart of the problem.

Another response was to call for biological cures. While advances in understanding the biochemistry and the electrophysiology of the brain have been made, most researchers feel a "cure" is, if at all possible, many years into the future. The question remains—what can be done in the meantime?

The field of rehabilitation has emerged as a promising direction for those professionals, consumers, and family members concerned with the future of individuals with severe psychiatric disabilities (Farkas & Anthony, 1981). The term *psychiatric rehabilitation* is becoming routinely used in the mental health field. It is a term used increasingly in both treatment professionals' jargon and administrators' program descriptions.

In 1977, Anthony characterized the field of psychiatric rehabilitation as a "concept in need of a method" (Anthony, 1977). In subsequent years, the methods for developing psychiatric rehabilitation services have begun to be understood, taught, and researched.

The overall aim of psychiatric rehabilitation is to help persons with psychiatric disabilities increase their ability to function, so that they are more successful and satisfied in their environment of choice, with the least amount of ongoing professional intervention (Anthony, 1979; Anthony, Cohen & Cohen, 1984; Anthony, Cohen & Farkas, 1987a; Anthony & Nemec, 1984). The main methods of achieving this aim are through the development of client skills and environmental supports.

This chapter discusses general psychiatric rehabilitation programs. First, it explains the psychiatric rehabilitation approach. Second, it discusses what psychiatric rehabilitation programs are, and last it describes some strategies for introducing the approach into service delivery.

The Psychiatric Rehabilitation Approach

The psychiatric rehabilitation approach to treating persons with severe psychiatric disabilities consists of a conceptual model, values, principles, and a process. This section traces the rationale for the approach, identifies the roots of the model, describes the model and its principles, outlines the process, and, last, defines the population for whom it is intended.

THE ROOTS OF THE PSYCHIATRIC REHABILITATION MODEL

Psychiatric rehabilitation programs evolved out of a number of previous responses to the problems of the psychiatrically disabled. Each development contributed to the shaping of or acceptance of psychiatric rehabilitation programs. These developments include: (1) the moral therapy era; (2) the inclusion of the psychiatrically disabled into the state vocational rehabilitation program; (3) the development of community mental health centers; (4) the psychosocial rehabilitation center movement; and, more recently, (5) the community support system (Anthony & Liberman, 1986).

The moral therapy era, as a response to the perceived inhumanity of previous treatment, stressed the need for a comprehensive assessment of the psychiatrically disabled. A pragmatic approach, moral therapy also contributed the notion that structured activity in a person's work, play, and social life can be valuable. Today, psychiatric rehabilitation practice emphasizes a comprehensive approach to helping people *function* differently, in their work, home, and school life, using activity-oriented interventions.

State vocational rehabilitation programs were initially designed for the rehabilitation of the physically disabled. In 1943, changes in the vocational rehabilitation legislation helped to make vocational interventions for psychiatrically disabled persons a legitimate service. Vocational interventions have become an integral part of the rehabilitation process for psychiatrically disabled persons (Beard, Propst & Malamud, 1982; Grob, 1983; Lamb, 1982).

The Community Mental Health Centers (CMHC) Act of 1963 introduced the concept that persons could be treated and supported outside the hospital and near their homes and workplaces. Unfortunately, the CMHCs were none too eager to provide the comprehensive services needed by the more severely psychiatrically disabled (Braun, Kochansky, Shapiro, Greenburg, Gudeman, Johnson & Shore, 1981). There is evidence to suggest that their staff members were not well prepared to work with severely disabled persons (Liberman, King & DeRisi, 1976) and consequently were more inclined to work on primary prevention or with a fairly verbal, insight-oriented clientele. Psychiatric rehabilitation programs did, however, incorporate the CMHC idea of immediately intervening in person's crises without removing them from their environment for long periods of time.

Rehabilitation centers such as Fountain House and Horizon House were founded initially by groups of ex-patients for the purpose of mutual aid and support. Comprehensive, multiservice centers such as Fellowship House, in Miami; Hill House, in Cleveland; Center Club, in Boston; Thresholds, in Chicago; and the Social Rehabilitation Center, in Fairfax, Virginia, to name but a few, evolved from the early simple clubhouse model. From the very beginning, these centers have emphasized strategies that are today at the core of psychiatric rehabilitation philosophy and practice (Anthony & Liberman, 1986). Psychosocial rehabilitation centers help people to improve their ability to *do* something in a specific environment rather than *succumb* to it (Grob, 1983; Wright, 1960). They focus on health induction rather than on symptom reduction (Leitner & Drasgow, 1972). Dincin (1981) pointed out that the centers' orientation did not value the development of therapeutic insights, but rather the development of reality-oriented factors. The fundamental message of these centers is the belief in the potential productivity of the most severely disabled person (Beard et al., 1982).

In 1977, in direct response to the problems occasioned by deinstitutionalization, the National Institute of Mental Health created the concept of a Community Support System (CSS) (Turner & TenHoor, 1978). Both the rehabilitation approach and the CSS approach share a common philosophy and set of principles. The CSS emphasized "people," "their needs," and "their potential" rather than "patients" and "pathology." The CSS further made the task of supporting the disabled person the business of *people* in the *community*, rather than simply that of paid professionals in specific agencies. The components of the CSS provided for a comprehensive array of services, including housing and vocational services, and supports to help people function within the community. It made it quite clear that mental health services were not enough and incorporated many ingredients of a psychiatric rehabilitation approach (Mosher, 1984). With the advent of CSS, the field of mental health further incorporated a belief in the need for a comprehensive array of supports (which included any person who cared); an attention to environmental barriers rather than just individual functioning; and a belief that meeting basic needs, such as housing, employment, and education, were legitimate goals for psychiatrically disabled persons. The development of a rehabilitation process and technology added to the ability of CSS to implement these concepts.

In summary, the moral therapy era, the state vocational rehabilitation system, community mental health centers, psychosocial rehabilitation centers, and community support systems each contributed to psychiatric rehabilitation's emergence as a legitimate, credible field of study and practice.

THE PSYCHIATRIC REHABILITATION MODEL

The psychiatric rehabilitation approach integrates the values, philosophy, and principles of physical rehabilitation with various techniques common to psychotherapeutic approaches. The rehabilitation model, as practiced with severely physically disabled persons (e.g., people with quadriplegia, blindness, etc.) serves as a conceptual model for the basic goals and treatment process of psychiatric rehabilitation (Anthony, 1980). The basic philosophy of physical rehabilitation provides direction to the psychiatric rehabilitation process: i.e., disabled people need skills and support to function in the living, learning, and working environments of their choice. Despite the obvious differences between severe psychiatric disabilities and physical disabilities, there are similarities as well. Both groups of service recipients require a wide range of services, exhibit limitations in their role performance, may receive services for a long period of time, and often do not experience complete recovery from their disabilities (Anthony, 1982).

Table 1–1 illustrates the concepts of impairment, disability, and handicap that are applicable to both physical and psychiatric rehabilitation. As presented in Table 1–1, the impairment of structure or function can lead to decreased ability to perform certain skills and activities that, in turn, can limit the person's fulfillment of certain roles. For example, an impairment might be a damaged spinal cord for someone with quadriplegia, or the incapacity of the body to produce insulin for someone with diabetes. This impairment leads to a decreased ability to perform physical skills, in the case of the person with quadriplegia, but may not necessarily lead to a decreased functional capacity for the person with diabetes. Limited functional mobility *may* handicap the person with a spinal cord injury, by preventing that person from holding a job, or going to school, or living on his or her own. Again, this is not necessarily true for the person with diabetes.

Typically, mental health treatment has tried to develop interventions at the impairment stage. Somatic and psychological treatment efforts have attempted to alleviate the signs and symptoms of the pathology, such as thought disorder or loss of concentration. In general, treatment attempts are directed more toward minimizing sickness whereas rehabilitation is directed more toward maximizing health (Leitner & Drasgow, 1972). Eliminating or suppressing impairments, however, does not lead automatically to more functional behaviors. For example, chemotherapy may decrease a person's hallucinations, but this may not allow the person to perform the skills necessary to hold a job—particularly if he or she never had those skills. Likewise, a decrease in disability does not lead to reductions in impairment.

TABLE 1-1   The Focus of Rehabilitation

Stage	Impairment	Disability	Handicap
Definition	Any loss or abnormality of psychological, physiological, or anatomical function (resulting from underlying pathology)	Any restriction or lack (resulting from an impairment) of the ability to perform an activity in the manner or within the range considered normal	A disadvantage for a given individual that limits or prevents the fulfillment of a role that is normal (depending on age, sex, social, cultural factors) for that individual
Example:	Positive or negative symptoms of schizophrenia	Inability to follow directions on the job	Homelessness Job discrimination
Interventions:	Clinical treatment (e.g., psychopharmacology)	Clinical rehabilitation (e.g., functional assessment; skills training; support)	Societal rehabilitation (e.g., community support; consumer advocacy; vocational rehabilitation policies

Adapted from: Center for Psychiatric Rehabilitation, 1984 (with permission)

Learning the skills necessary to hold a job does not automatically lead to a reduction in hallucinations. Furthermore, chronic or severe impairment does *not* always mean a chronic disability or handicap. The impairment simply increases the risk of chronic disability and handicap (Anthony & Liberman, 1986).

Clinical rehabilitation is comprised of two intervention strategies: (1) skill development and (2) environmental resource development. The assumption of clinical rehabilitation is that by changing a psychiatrically disabled person's skills or supports in the immediate environment, he or she will be more able to perform those activities necessary to function in the specific roles of choice (Anthony, Cohen & Cohen, 1984).

With respect to barriers that originate in the environment, psychiatrically disabled persons can be helped to overcome their handicaps through societal rehabilitation interventions (Anthony, Buell et al., 1972). Societal rehabilitation is designed to change the system in which the psychiatrically disabled person must function. Examples of this type of system intervention are the changes in the Social Security Work Incentives program; the development of alternative funding to create new housing for disabled and nondisabled persons; the development of regulations which mandate that educational institutions make reasonable accommodations to allow disabled students to participate in their classrooms. Clinical rehabilitation and societal rehabilitation interventions are not mutually exclusive (Stubbins, 1982). The 1973 amendments to the Vocational Rehabilitation Act, for example (which mandates clinical types of interventions), established the principle of affirmative action by contractors who do business with the federal government (Stubbins, 1982). A person who suffers severe psychiatric problems is often in need of both assistance with society's economic and social limitations on his or her participation as a full citizen and skill development and support to overcome the psychiatric disability.

In addition to the concepts borrowed from physical rehabilitation, psychiatric rehabilitation has incorporated techniques of various psychotherapeutic approaches. The core of the approach uses elements of Rogerian client-centered techniques (Rogers, 1951) and human resource development (see, e.g., Carkhuff, 1969, 1983a,b; Carkhuff & Berenson, 1976; Carkhuff, Berenson & Pierce, 1976) to involve the person in making choices and increasing the likelihood of learning to act on those choices.

Contributions to an understanding of assessment and skill development techniques were drawn from behavioral analysis (see, e.g., Bandura, 1969a; Lovaas, 1964) together with the additions made by social learning theory (see, e.g., Bandura, 1969b; Meichenbaum, 1966; Miller 1959) and lifespan developmental psychology (see, e.g., Erickson, 1968; Kohlberg, 1969).

PSYCHIATRIC REHABILITATION VALUES AND PRINCIPLES

The philosophical emphasis in the various historical developments that contributed to psychiatric rehabilitation helped to root the approach in a number of values (summarized in Table 1–2). Since the rehabilitation model focuses on overcoming disability (Table 1–1), psychiatric rehabilitation values *functioning* or competency above verbal insights alone. Out of its historical concern with practical issues, rehabilitation developed a further belief in the intrinsic worth of focusing on activities related to the "real world" concerns of *working, living, and learning* environments. The focus on environments extended to the idea that rehabilitation worked to help the client live, learn, or work in the most natural environment possible. The focus on functioning and

TABLE 1-2   Definition of Rehabilitation Values

Functioning	A focus on competency or the performance of every-day activities.
Environment	A focus on the "real world" context of where a person lives, learns, or works.
Outcome Orientation	A focus on evaluating client success; on accountability of the rehabilitation deliverer; on judging the usefulness of a technique by its impact on client outcome.
Client Involvement Choice	A focus on participation by the client in selecting his or her own criteria or goals for success and satisfaction; in choosing the methods of the rehabilitation process, and participation in conducting the rehabilitation process.
Comprehensiveness	A focus on including factors relating to as many aspects of the person and his or her surroundings as needed; a holistic view.
Support	A focus on providing assistance and reinforcement as long as needed.
Growth Potential	A focus on the inherent capacity of any person to improve or grow, given opportunity and resources; on the possibilities for change; an attitude of hope.
Individualization	A focus on respecting a person's unique differences; on developing specificity as a means of distinguishing among people.

real world activities, both of which are easily observed and therefore can be evaluated, contributed to a strong *outcome orientation*. The focus on outcomes asks each practitioner to evaluate the effectiveness of his or her own practice, with the understanding that every interaction is an opportunity to learn more about the methods of delivery. It further implies that the determination of what can be considered "good practice" should be based more on evidence of "real world" results than on adherence to "good" theory. Proponents of rehabilitation value the *involvement of consumers* in their own rehabilitation and the development of a *comprehensive approach* to the needs of people for *support* services and environmental change. They believe in people's *potential for growth*, regardless of their disability. One implication of this value is that rehabilitation does not prejudge the degree of independence a person may achieve given the appropriate resources and opportunity. The value placed on consumer involvement and a commitment to people's potential for growth naturally implies a value on the uniqueness of each individual or *individualization*. Techniques that allow specific descriptions of individuals, rather than categories of behaviors or traits, are emphasized as one important means of respecting individual differences.

Basic to the philosophy of rehabilitation and integrated into the rehabilitation process itself are a number of rehabilitation principles. While this section only summarizes the principles, others (Anthony, Cohen & Cohen 1983; Anthony & Nemec, 1984) have described these principles at length. The principles are based on the rehabilitation values (Table 1–2) as well as on research (Anthony, Cohen & Vitalo, 1978). They guide rehabilitation treatment and are reflected in programs that provide rehabilitation services.

Principle 1. Client involvement is necessary in all phases of rehabilitation treatment.

Rehabilitation practitioners constantly work to demystify the process. The principle that client involvement is necessary leads to a commitment to doing rehabilitation *with* clients and not *to* clients.

Principle 2. Newly learned skill behaviors are situation specific.

Since psychiatric rehabilitation values "real world" outcomes, it is necessary to insure that skills are not only learned but also used in the environment of need. Efforts have to be made either to teach the needed skills in the natural environment or to plan how generalization is to occur.

Principle 3. Each client must have individualized skill goals.

Since not every client has the same history and the same skill experiences, not every client needs to learn the same skills. A value on individualization leads to the notion, verified by research (Cohen, Ridley & Cohen, 1983), that skills teaching must be tailored to an assessment of what clients actually need to know how to do in relation to a specific arena in which they would like to succeed.

Principle 4. The reduction of a client's personal and environmental discomfort does not automatically result in improved client skills.

Reducing the impairment may not decrease the disability. For example, if symptoms are reduced, a person does not necessarily know how to hold a job better (Anthony & Jansen, 1984). Similarly, reducing the dysfunction in the environment, or the handicap, does not automatically mean that the person can perform more skills. An emphasis on functioning implies a direct approach to increasing skills.

Principle 5. The restrictiveness of the environment is a function of the characteristics of both the environment and the client.

The difficulties presented by a particular setting are experienced differently by different people. A person in a wheelchair may find his own home (presumably the "least restrictive environment") more restrictive of his mobility than a barrier-free Center for Independent

Living. Consequently, it is important to understand both the unique individual and the individual's unique environment.

Principle 6. Increased client dependency can produce improved client functioning.

Since rehabilitation values the concept of support, "client dependency" upon the support of people, places, or things is seen as a normal state of affairs. Interventions that allow for a certain degree of dependence upon some support system can, at times, increase a person's ability to function elsewhere. Again, physical rehabilitation accepts the fact that dependence upon (or support of) personal care attendants may allow a person with quadriplegia to hold a job.

Principle 7. Hope is an essential ingredient of the practice of psychiatric rehabilitation.

Rehabilitation believes in each person's potential for growth, regardless of his or her disability. In fact, empirical evidence exists to confirm this belief. Currently, the field's inability to correctly predict who will and who will not benefit from a psychiatric rehabilitation intervention (Anthony, 1979) prevents us from ruling out the possibility of improvement for any one client.

THE CLIENT POPULATION

The target population of psychiatric rehabilitation is those persons who have become disabled due to psychiatric illness. There are several definitions of severe psychiatric disability that characterize this population. The most common definitions are those used by the National Institute of Mental Health's Community Support Program (CSP), the Rehabilitation Services Administration's (RSA) definition of severe disability, and Goldman's definition of the "chronically mentally ill" (Goldman, Gattozzi & Taube, 1981). Each of these three definitions (CSP, RSA, Goldman) shares common elements. These elements are: a *diagnosis* of mental illness of prolonged *duration*, with resultant severe *disability* or role incapacity. It has been estimated that there are between 1.7 to 2.4 million severely psychiatrically disabled persons in the United States (Goldman, Gattozzi & Taube, 1981).

Whereas in 1955 there were approximately 560,000 patients living in state mental hospitals (Goldman, Adams & Taube, 1983), current estimates from the National Institute of Mental Health place the number of state hospital residents at 120,000 (Bachrach, 1986). Unfortunately, there is no specific residential data which are comparable across studies. Thus, no accurate estimates exist as to the typical degree of independent living status of severely psychiatrically disabled persons (Anthony & Dion, 1986). The National Plan for the Chronically Mentally Ill (U.S. Department of Health and Human Services, 1980) estimated that 38–50 percent of those persons living in the community were in board and care homes, and 19–21 percent lived with their families. A nationwide survey of family members of severely psychiatrically disabled persons who were also members of the National Alliance of the Mentally Ill (NAMI) reported that approximately 30 percent lived at home with their families, 15 percent lived in a community residence, and 18 percent were hospitalized (Spaniol, Zipple & Fitzgerald, 1984).

Studies containing data on the competitive employment rate of persons discharged from psychiatric hospitals have been surveyed periodically by Anthony and his colleagues (Anthony, Buell et al., 1972; Anthony, Cohen & Vitalo, 1978; Anthony, Danley & Howell, 1984). The data have been fairly consistent, suggesting full-time competitive employment figures of 20–25 percent for *all* persons discharged from psychiatric hospitals. However, if just *severely* psychiatrically disabled persons are studied, the full-time and part-time competitive employment figure drops to approximately 15 percent and below. For example, the NAMI survey data of well-educated, severely psychiatrically disabled persons from middle to upper income families reported a full-time employment rate of only 6 percent (Spaniol, Zipple & Fitzgerald, 1984). Farkas, Rogers & Thurer (1987) followed up 54 long-term state hospital patients who had been targeted for deinstitutionalization in 1979. Over a five-year period, none obtained competitive employment. Goering and her colleagues reported that 11 percent of their hospitalized sample were employed prior to admission (Goering, Wasylenki, Farkas, Lancee & Ballantyne, 1988).

Data with respect to the educational status of severely psychiatrically disabled persons have received little attention. The available data, however, serve as a reminder of the advanced educational status of many severely psychiatrically disabled persons. Depending, again, upon the sample taken, approximately 52–92 percent of severely psychiatrically disabled persons are high school graduates, and 15–60 percent of these graduates have attended college (Anthony & Dion, 1986). For example, the NAMI survey data indicated that of the total sample of middle to upper middle income families, 92 percent were high school graduates, 59 percent had also attended college, and 17 percent had graduated (Spaniol, Zipple & Fitzgerald, 1984). A study of Community Support Program clients reported 52 percent were high school graduates, with 19 percent having attended college (Tessler & Goldman, 1982). A study of 505 severely psychiatrically disabled persons discharged from hospitals in Toronto, Canada, reported that 72 percent were high school graduates, with 16 percent having attended college (Goering, Wasylenki, Lancee & Freeman, 1984).

Psychiatric Rehabilitation Programs

The articulation of the psychiatric rehabilitation approach has made it possible to specify what is needed to implement programs that will effectively impact on outcome for the severely psychiatrically disabled population. A number of both hospital based and community based programs call themselves rehabilitation programs. Many are considered modifications of the originators of psychiatric rehabilitation programing, such as Fountain House, Horizon House, Center Club, Thresholds, etc. Others seem to consider themselves rehabilitation programs because they serve the severely psychiatrically disabled person. At times, traditional modalities become relabeled with "rehabilitation names." For example, traditional group therapy sessions become labeled "communication skills groups"; arts and crafts sessions are renamed "socialization skills groups." As Anthony and Nemec (1984) commented, "it is often not clear whether the programs that these new settings provide are actually psychiatric rehabilitation programs, or simply variations of traditional inpatient treatment programs now offered in a community based setting" (p. 398).

A psychiatric rehabilitation *program,* on the other hand, consists of an overall rehabilitation *program mission* with a structure that promotes the *process* of rehabilitation to occur in specific *environments.* The program is based on rehabilitation values (Table 1–2) (Anthony, Cohen & Farkas, 1982; Farkas, Cohen & Nemec, 1988).

The next section of this chapter describes the characteristics of each of these program elements, that is, mission, process, and environments. By defining the characteristics of these elements, it is now possible to measure their presence or absence in the operational dimensions of a program, that is, in its operating guidelines, activities, and documentation (Center for Psychiatric Rehabilitation, in preparation). The operating guidelines consist of program policies and procedures that direct the provision of services. Activities are the events that occur during the day-to-day program operation. Documentation includes the records that describe the client's rehabilitation. Table 1–3 profiles the ingredients of psychiatric rehabilitation programs.

THE CHARACTERISTICS OF A REHABILITATION PROGRAM MISSION

The statement of the program mission gives overall direction to its activities. The psychiatric rehabilitation mission is: to help a person increase his or her ability to function so that he or she is successful and satisfied in the environment of choice with the least amount of ongoing professional intervention (Anthony, 1979a). The concepts of the mission statement are based on the rehabilitation values.

TABLE 1-3   Psychiatric Rehabilitation Program: A Profile

Program Elements   *Dimensions of Program Structure*

Mission		Policies	Procedures	Activities	Documentation
Process	Diagnosis				
	Planning				
	Intervention				
Environment	Network of Environments				
	Context of Environments				

The first key mission concept (client functioning) orients program activities toward the development of client competencies rather than toward the reduction of symptoms.

The second concept emphasizes the need to view the person in relationship to a particular living, learning, or working environment. For example, the phrase "successful and satisfied in the environment" demonstrates this concept.

The third mission concept is that of client involvement. Involvement is critical to the process of psychiatric rehabilitation. The overall mission statement emphasizes this perspective by making "client choice" a fundamental part of the process and "client satisfaction" an important outcome variable. The client, as a full partner in the rehabilitation process, has the right to work toward becoming successful and satisfied in an environment that he or she chooses, rather than in one in which he or she is placed.

The concept of outcome orientation in a rehabilitation mission statement orients the program toward a program goal beyond simply one of providing service. Often mission statements include phrases such as "to provide clients with assessment and counseling." Such program goals emphasize service provision. An evaluation of these programs would involve the number of assessments or counseling sessions that had been offered. The mission would not hold the program "accountable" for the degree of client success achieved as the outcome of those sessions. The rehabilitation mission focus on outcome, however, is contained in such phrases as "increase . . . function(ing)" and "so that . . . ."

Support is a concept that does appear in many missions. Most programs do view themselves as offering assistance or reinforcement to their clients. The potential for growth is the last critical concept of a psychiatric rehabilitation program mission. This concept, coupled with the principle of hopefulness, implies that the program believes its aim is to do more than simply maintain the client. This is not to deny the importance of stabilization. It does imply, however, that stabilization is not sufficient. While total independence might be an outcome for some clients, the most important outcome, from a psychiatric rehabilitation perspective, is for the person to "increase functioning" while decreasing professional intervention or support to the "least amount."

A psychiatric rehabilitation mission statement incorporates all of these concepts. In doing so, the mission integrates the various aspects of a program by giving the program one purpose, as well as by identifying the variables considered important for the evaluation of program effectiveness.

THE ELEMENTS OF A PROGRAM: PROCESS

The elements of a psychiatric rehabilitation program's structure reflect the mission. These elements include the rehabilitation process and the network and context of the environments in which the process occurs.

The psychiatric rehabilitation process consists of three phases: the diagnostic phase, the planning phase, and the intervention phase. Table 1–4 summarizes the rehabilitation process and its components. Simply put, the process of psychiatric rehabilitation seeks to help clients figure out where they might like to live, learn, or work and assesses what they are currently doing or what supports they currently have which will help them to succeed in that environment. Based on this rehabilitation diagnosis the process organizes the information and then helps clients to learn the skills which they do not have in their repertoire and which are critical to success and satisfaction in their chosen environment and to improve the ones they do have. It links them to the resources whose support they need to succeed, or modifies others to create new resources if what the clients need does not exist.

The Diagnostic Phase

The diagnostic phase lays the groundwork for the development of the rehabilitation plan. Unlike traditional psychiatric diagnoses, which describe symptoms, the rehabilitation diagnosis describes a client's current level of skill functioning in relation to a specific environment in which the client chooses to live, learn, or work within the subsequent

TABLE 1-4   Rehabilitation Process

Rehabilitation Diagnosis
   Setting the overall rehabilitation goal
   Conducting a functional assessment
   Conducting a resource assessment
Rehabilitation Plan
   Selecting priority skill or resource objectives
   Organizing responsibilities
   Projecting timelines
   Monitoring the plan
Rehabilitation Intervention
   Skill development
      Direct skill teaching
      Programming skill use
   Resource Development
      Resource coordination
      Resource modification

6–24 months (an Overall Rehabilitation Goal). The diagnostic process begins therefore with the client, the practitioner, and, if possible, relevant others agreeing upon a specific environment (e.g., "working in the Pine Valley Vocational Unit"). The assessed skills include the physical, emotional, and intellectual skills required for the client to be successful and satisfied in that setting (e.g., "organizing tasks" or "offering help" at work). The skill use descriptions and the skill functioning evaluations for "Joe" in Table 1–5 provide examples of how such skills are described behaviorally and evaluated in terms of the frequency of their use in the chosen environment.

The diagnosis also includes an assessment of the resources available to support the client in his chosen environment. The resources used can include people, places, or objects that will contribute to the client's success and satisfaction there. For example, Joe requires safety glasses to be successful in the Pine Valley Vocational Unit (see Table 1–6).

A psychiatric rehabilitation program's policies, procedures, activities, and documentation reflect the rehabilitation process (Anthony, Cohen & Farkas, 1987; Center for Psychiatric Rehabilitation, in preparation). Each component of the rehabilitation diagnosis can be included in policy statements in order to insure that such a diagnosis is implemented, regardless of the bias or orientation of individual practitioners. For example, in order to make sure that all clients at Joe's Pine Valley Vocational Unit have a reason for working in the specific unit

TABLE 1-5 Example: Functional Assessment Chart

Overall Rehabilitation Goal for Joe: I want to work in the Pine Valley Vocational unit for the next year.

+/-	Critical Skills *(Client agrees & initials)*	Skill Use Descriptions	Skill Functioning					
			Spontaneous Use		Prompted Use		Performance	
			Present Use	Needed Use	Yes	No	Yes	No
−	Organizing Tasks *(J.P.)	Number of weeks per month Joe writes a "task by timeline" list when he gets work for the week from his supervisor.	0	4	—	X	—	X
+	Scheduling Appointments *(J.P.)	Percentage of times per month Joe arranges a date and time to meet when his schedule indicates a service provider's visit is expected.	100%	95%	—	—	—	—
−	Requesting Social Contacts *(J.P.)	Percentage of times per week Joe asks someone to spend time with him, when he is doing nothing else during breaks.	0%	50%	X	—	—	—
−	Offering Help *(J.P.)	Percentage of times per month Joe asks if he can help when other workers request.	25%	75%	—	—	—	—

Adapted from: Cohen, Farkas & Cohen, 1986.

The client's skill level is evaluated in three different ways. Spontaneous Use indicates the highest present frequency of appropriate use in the chosen environment as compared to what is needed or required in that environment. Prompted Use indicates whether a client can (Yes) or cannot (No) perform the skill at least once in the chosen environment. Performance indicates whether a client can (Yes) or cannot (No) perform the skill in a simulated environment. These last two evaluations are only done if the present level of spontaneous functioning is 0.

TABLE 1-6   Example: Resource Assessment

Overall Rehabilitation Goal: Joe wants to work in the Vocational unit for the next year.

Assets/ Deficits (+/−)	Critical Resources	Resource Use Description	Resource Actual Use		Resource Evaluation			
					Resource Available		Resource Exist	
			Present Use	Needed Use	Yes	No	Yes	No
+	Empathic Supervisor	Percentage of times per week Joe's supervisor paraphrases Joe's feelings and the reasons for those feelings when Joe stops work and stares at the ceiling.	75%	75%				
−	Safety Glasses	Percentage of times per month the Vocational Unit supervisor issues Safety Glasses to Joe at 9:00 A.M.	0%	100%	X			

Resources are evaluated in three ways. Resource Use indicates the highest present level of spontaneous delivery to the client of the resource in the chosen environment as compared to what is needed or required in that environment. Resource Availability indicates whether a resource is willing or available (Yes) or not (No) to provide the described support in the chosen environment. Resource Existence indicates whether a resource exists at all (Yes) or not (No) to provide the described support in the chosen environment. These last two evaluations are done if the present level of resource use is 0.

they enter, Pine Valley *policy* may state that "all incoming clients will participate in establishing an overall rehabilitation goal for the subsequent 6–24 months, before they begin work in any specific unit." The *procedures* supporting the policy describe who in the organization will carry out the policy and how he or she will do it. One procedure might state that "the agency case manager will organize visits to various work sites to help clients begin to clarify for themselves what their work values might be, as a first step in establishing an overall rehabilitation goal." The *program activities* then translate each procedure into action. For example, work site visits by the case manager and new clients are scheduled into the program's regular activity list. Finally, the program's *documentation* or record-keeping system requires the information generated by all the assessment activities. For example, the chart in Table 1–5 may itself be included in the record. The client's notes on what he or she likes and dislikes about the various work sites, or values and criteria for choosing a work site, might be part of the record-keeping system. Staff typically complain about record keeping and often find it useless to their actual work with clients. This makes it less likely that they will do it on a regular basis. A program which ensures that the required record-keeping information is the information staff must collect in order to complete the procedures in their job description (for example, establishing an overall rehabilitation goal or a functional assessment) is more likely to have the support of staff in regularly and efficiently recording that information.

Planning Phase

The planning phase organizes the diagnostic information by selecting high-priority skill or resource objectives for intervention. Each objective is assigned a specific intervention, with specific persons responsible for the development, implementation, and monitoring within specific timelines. For example, based on the information from the functional assessment (Table 1–5), Joe's high-priority skill objective was to increase his ability to "organize tasks." The assessment revealed that Joe did not have this skill in his repertoire. The plan, therefore, was developed with Joe to specify that he would be taught the skill (Direct Skills Teaching) and that various personnel would develop, teach, and monitor his use of the skill. It also identified projected beginning and ending dates (Table 1–7).

One *policy statement* that the vocational unit might make with respect to planning might be: "All plans will be reviewed every 90 days with the client present." A regular review of plans helps to track changes in clients' performance which then might require a recycling of the planning process. One *procedure* for this might be: "A staff per-

TABLE 1-7 Example: Rehabilitation Plan

Overall Rehabilitation Goal: Joe wants to work in the Vocational Unit for the next year.

Priority Objectives	Skill/ Resource	Intervention	Person(s) Responsible	Starting Dates: Projected Dates	Starting Dates: Actual Dates	Completion Dates: Projected Dates	Completion Dates: Actual Dates
Organizing Tasks	Skill	Direct Skills Teaching	*Preparing Lesson:* Mrs. Jones OT (agreed M.J.)	Oct. 15		Dec. 2	
			Teaching: Mr. E. Smith Voc. Supervisor (agreed E.S.)	Jan. 2		Feb. 15	
			Programming Skills Use: Ms. R. Sargent Voc. Support Worker (agreed R.S.)	Feb. 17		March 20	
Safety Glasses	Resource	Resource Coordination	*Programming Resource Use:* Mr. E. Smith Voc. Unit (agreed E.S.)	Oct. 15		Feb. 15	

I helped to prepare this plan.
Client Signature: Joe P.

Practitioner: Mark Jones

son, assigned to be the 'primary coordinator,' will survey the client and each practitioner responsible for an intervention on a regular basis to ascertain the client's progress on each skill and resource objective. Progress will be recorded on the rehabilitation plan review sheet. This sheet will form the basis of the oral report and discussion among the client, the primary coordinator, and relevant staff once every 90 days." The *activity* required by this procedure would, again, have to be scheduled into the list of program activities for which space, time, and resources (such as secretarial support) would be allocated. *Documentation* might include a version of Table 1–7 as the chart filed in Joe's records along with a planning review sheet to record client progress on each skill or resource objective.

The Intervention Phase

The intervention phase implements the plan by conducting either skill development or resource development. Skill development directly teaches clients the skills they do not know or develops the skills that they do know, but don't use effectively (programming). If the plan calls for resource development, interventions include either coordination to link clients to existing needed resources or modification of the resources that have to be changed if they are to be useful to the client.

In Joe's vocational unit, a *policy statement* related to interventions might be: "All vocational unit clients who have been assessed as lacking a specific skill relevant to their personal vocational goal will have skill teaching activities designed to overcome those deficits." The policy statement makes it clear that clients will only be taught those skills which are evaluated as missing and which are also critical to the chosen goal. This policy statement implies that the program cannot, in general, develop skill classes without current functional assessments. Furthermore, it suggests that a client who does not have an individual overall rehabilitation goal or a subsequent functional assessment that indicates skill performance deficits cannot be simply placed in a skill teaching class as a way of "keeping him or her busy." Two *procedures* to begin to translate such a policy might be:

(1) After the planning meeting, the person assigned to develop the skill lesson will outline the skill content and will write up a lesson plan that incorporates didactic, modeling, and experiential techniques. The lesson will address those skill behaviors which the client(s) have demonstrated that they cannot perform even in simulated situations.

(2) All skill teaching activities will be followed by the development of a sequenced series of behavioral steps designed to help the client overcome the barriers to using the newly learned skill in the en-

vironment of need (the overall rehabilitation goal). Staff job descriptions would, again, need to reflect these procedures.

Skill interventions would require that *program activities* include sufficient time to allow a practitioner and a client to develop a skill use program. For example, Joe knows how to "offer help" at work (Table 1–6). He does not do it as often as he needs to do it. The practitioner and Joe need sufficient time to explore the barriers to Joe's use of this skill, devise a sequenced set of action steps to overcome each barrier, and develop a series of techniques to increase the likelihood that Joe will implement the program. If the program frowns on individual client attention, it is still possible, although much more difficult, to go through the process of programming skill use. *Documentation* of skill development activities might include notes on behavioral evidence of client progress in learning the skill and on the client's participation in the skill teaching activities. Implementation of the skill use program might also be documented. For example, Joe and his co-workers in the vocational unit might keep a record of how often Joe actually offers help when they request it during the course of a week.

Resource coordination involves the client and the practitioner selecting a preferred resource, arranging for a link to be made, and then systematically supporting the client's use of the selected resource (Cohen, Anthony, Pierce & Vitalo, 1980). This task is, in some systems, done by a case manager. In the example of the vocational unit, a *policy* statement relative to resource coordination might be: "All clients who are linking with another resource will have an assessment of both their potential problems in using the resource and the resource's problems in serving the client effectively." The implication of this policy statement is that the job of the vocational program is not considered completed when a simple referral to a resource is made. Clients are supported in making the link with the identified resource.

One *procedural* statement associated with this policy might be: "The liaison worker from the vocational program, together with the client and the case manager, will spend no more than three sessions conducting an assessment of the client's skill or support problems in using the selected resource, or the selected resource's problems in serving the client." The *program activity* might be a series of exploratory meetings with the client and the intended resource. For example, Joe, his vocational unit supervisor, and his case manager might discuss why the supervisor is currently not taking care of Joe's safety glasses without which he is not allowed to work (Table 1–6). It may be that Joe does not respond to the supervisor when he asks Joe to give up the glasses at the end of the day (a client-based problem). It may also be that the supervisor does not know how to ask Joe for the safety glasses without patronizing him, which in turn causes Joe to react and walk off (a resource-based problem). This particular resource use assessment would result in a plan to overcome each party's problems with the other to maximize the possibility that Joe can use his supervisor's support to keep track of his safety glasses and thus remain in the program or the resource's barriers to providing the service.

The program's *documentation* would have headings on the case record forms which required listing the "assessed skill or support barriers" to the client's use of the identified resource or the resource's barriers to providing the service.

Resource modification deals with developing resources that do not now exist in the form needed. This might involve negotiating with whatever service will be most appropriate. For example, if someone requires a social group in a church setting that provides extra support for psychiatrically disabled members, and none exists, the practitioner or the program administrator may negotiate with the administration of a church social group to modify its program to provide support for members who have disabilities. The modified resource might be to have the church social group assign volunteer "buddies" to team up with the member who has disabilities.

THE ELEMENTS OF A PROGRAM: ENVIRONMENT

A psychiatric rehabilitation program is also defined by its network of environments and the context of those environments (Center for Psychiatric Rehabilitation, in preparation). The range of settings for the rehabilitation program is the *network of environments*. The way in which the environment is organized is the *context* of the environment.

The environments may be residential/social, vocational, or educational/treatment settings. The settings may be formal mental health or rehabilitation settings (such as clinics or group homes), or informal settings (such as church basements or mobile trailers). The program's *network of environments* includes a range of types of settings that match both the psychiatrically disabled persons' preferences and the current level of client functioning in the specific environments available (Anthony, Cohen & Farkas, 1987). For instance, if most of the program's client population are young adults who prefer living in groups, then having a series of supervised individual apartments does not match client preferences. If these same young adults are college dropouts or liberal arts majors, then, having a number of sheltered workshops with manual labor tasks is not likely to match the program's population preferences. Further, if the vocational environments available are related not to manual labor but rather to more intellectual or interpersonal tasks that require consistent high levels of skill performance, they may not match the current level of functioning of the majority of the program's client population. "An ideal rehabilitation program has access to a sufficient variety of settings so that the client does not have to 'fit' or be placed in environments simply because they are available" (Anthony, Cohen & Farkas, 1987).

The environments included in the concept of a psychiatric rehabilitation program are those within the program's direct control. The physical settings may themselves be outside the professional system yet are supported by it. For example, an apartment that is leased directly by the client is outside the professional system. Program policy and procedures, however, may provide a structure for skill teaching activities to occur within that client's apartment.

Those settings to which the program has access, but are not within the program's direct control, are considered to be part of the system support necessary for effective program delivery. Such settings may include those in the control of another agency or program and may thus be part of the mental health service system. The program's clients may live, learn, or work in settings that are unsupported by that program or any other mental health program. Those settings belong to the overall general system. For example, the general subsidized housing system or public adult educational system of a region may serve clients of a psychiatric rehabilitation program, without being considered to be part of the program's network of environments. The program and its network of environments are usually connected to the larger system by means of interagency agreements, individual liaison practitioners, or, at times, by case managers.

Case management serves the function of reaching clients beyond any one specific program and creating a relationship with them. The case managers then help to identify the client's service needs (if any), linking the clients to rehabilitation programs and/or those that meet basic needs (Anthony, Cohen, Farkas & Cohen, 1988; Cohen, Nemec, Farkas & Forbess, 1988). The case managers' skills serve to integrate the system, while their ability to advocate for needed resources helps to keep the system responsive to client needs (Cohen et al., 1988).

A rehabilitation network of environments is integrated in that the functional exit criteria of one setting matches the entry criteria of the next most demanding setting. This does not mean that clients move systematically from a social club, to a day treatment center, to an outpatient facility, as is often implied in the concept of an environmental continuum. It does mean that a comprehensive program includes a range of options that intersect.

The *context* of the environment refers to the cultural or organizational beliefs, social mores, and physical settings in which the program activities occur (Center for Psychiatric Rehabilitation, in preparation). The cultural or organizational context might include generally accepted points of view about the importance of considering socioeconomic background when hiring new staff or about the best type of organizational chain of command, for example. Some programs take great care in matching staff demographics with those of the clients. In some organizations, the chain of command is very informal and is often superseded. In others, it is considered an affront if an employee speaks to someone above his or her direct supervisor. Another example of the organizational or cultural context might be the program's implicit or explicit expectations about when to arrive at work, how long the workday should be, or the acceptability of working weekends to "get the job done." The social context may include such items as the program's protocol for observing staff or client personal events (birthdays, marriages, etc.) or the desirability of making friends out of colleagues. Some programs expect staff to function as a quasi family. Others expect no personal interactions at all. The physical aspects of the environment include items such as decor, layout, and equipment.

Rehabilitation values determine the type of context developed in psychiatric rehabilitation programs (Farkas, Nemec & Taylor, 1989). For example, a program that valued *client involvement* might demonstrate this commitment in the organizational context of the program environment. The program might be open on weekends and in the evenings because of client requests for those hours. A contrasting organizational environment might result in a program that bases its hours on staff expectations only and is therefore open from 8:00 A.M. to 4:00 P.M., Monday through Friday. Placing a value on the physical support in the environment might be demonstrated by providing comfortable chairs for clients to wait in and magazines likely to interest them. A priority on the value of *individualization* might be demonstrated in the physical context of a program that made sure to have at least some private rooms or physical space to allow for individual attention. In contrast, the organizational context of another program might be created by a low staff-client ratio that left little possibility for individual attention.

The type of supervision that the staff is given can also reflect the program's values. An organizational value placed on *outcome* might result in expectations that supervisory sessions request reports on observable, behavioral changes in relation to a specific environmental goal. Supervisory sessions in which the focus is on "the number of units of service provided" or "the number of sessions clients attended" are more process-oriented than outcome-oriented in their methods of personnel evaluation. Programs may express a value on people's *potential for growth* by arranging for staff development as part of the ongoing program schedule. Along with "consumer involvement," the commitment to growth may be expressed in training consumers to be effective board members of the program.

In sum, staffing, hours of service, furniture, physical plant, and expectations about how staff are treated as well as how clients are treated are all part of the context of the program. The context, together with the network of available, integrated settings, serves to reinforce or to negate the psychiatric rehabilitation process.

IMPLEMENTING PSYCHIATRIC REHABILITATION PROGRAMS

Effective program service depends upon the support of systems and personnel. Programs are, therefore, in reality, implemented by changes in the programs themselves, the personnel, and/or the systems in which they operate. Some strategies, however, focus exclusively on the program domain, while others focus exclusively on one of the other two aspects. The strategies for changing programs involve assessing the readiness of the program for change, assessing how congruent the program already is with a psychiatric rehabilitation approach, developing a plan for change, and then changing the elements that are not congruent (Center for Psychiatric Rehabilitation, in preparation).

An assessment of the program is an important first step. Often the degree to which rehabilitation elements are already in place is not clear to program administrators. A recent study assessed forty agencies that viewed their programs as rehabilitation oriented. The assessment evaluated each element of the program by reviewing its congruence with the psychiatric rehabilitation approach and its readiness for change. A number of incongruities among the psychiatric rehabilitation approach and the programs emerged. For example, while all programs stated that they assessed skills as a part of their diagnostic workup, only 30 percent actually evaluated items that could be defined as skills. Further, 61 percent thought that their discussion groups or group therapy meetings were, in fact, structured behavioral skills training sessions (Farkas, Cohen & Nemec, 1988).

If such an assessment is conducted and recommendations are made, program administrators may still have difficulties planning and creating the needed changes. The emergence of a clearer understanding of the nature of psychiatric rehabilitation programs is relatively new. Many program leaders, while effective mental health administrators, lack the necessary knowledge to develop a new mission statement that reflects psychiatric rehabilitation concepts, for example, or to revise their record-keeping system to be congruent with a psychiatric rehabilitation approach. In this situation, a program consultant is helpful.

The most effective format for program consultation is usually a one-to-one, on-site relationship over time (Anthony, Cohen & Farkas, 1987; Bennis et al., 1976; Center for Psychiatric Rehabilitation, in preparation). Changing the daily practice of a program is a complex and lengthy undertaking. Conventional wisdom states that it requires about two to five years to implement a new program. Backer, Liberman & Kuehnel (1986) analyzed effective innovation efforts in rehabilitation programs and concluded that the following factors were critical: inter-personal contact with credible professional peers; outside consultation for the adoption process; organizational support for the innovation; persistent championship of the innovation; adaptability of the inno-vation; and credible evidence of success for the innovative program. Unfortunately, there are very few program consultants who have the knowledge, attitudes, and skills required to assist program adminis-trators to create psychiatric rehabilitation programs (Anthony, Cohen & Farkas, 1987). In response to this lack in the field, the Center for Psychiatric Rehabilitation has developed both a strategy and support-ing training materials for training program consultants (Center for Psy-chiatric Rehabilitation, in preparation). The strategy has been used in a number of states to train consultants who could support the develop-ment of local rehabilitation programs.

In addition to program change strategies, personnel change strate-gies are also necessary for comprehensive program service delivery. The specification of the rehabilitation process has made it possible to identify the knowledge, attitudes, and skills needed by practitioners to guide clients through the rehabilitation diagnosis, planning, and in-tervention phases of the process.

As a method of disseminating the skills of psychiatric rehabilita-tion, the Center for Psychiatric Rehabilitation developed a "training of trainers approach" which selected key staff in programs and trained them for a minimum of 60 hours of training and 8 months of super-vised practice to a maximum of 300 classroom hours with 16 months of supervised practice. Clearly, this method is not the usual two-day in-service model for training. The emphasis in such a training program is on what staff *do*, to train other staff to *do things differently* with clients, rather than on what they know or believe. Rogers and associates con-ducted a study on the effectiveness of the training of trainers strategy (Rogers, Cohen, Danley, Hutchinson & Anthony, 1986). Results indi-cate that staff from carefully selected programs can learn psychiatric rehabilitation skills and then learn how to teach their own staffs. In-service training of trainer programs is, therefore, a good means of developing staff to support psychiatric rehabilitation program delivery.

Very few university programs give graduate students the knowledge, attitudes, and skills necessary for psychiatric rehabilitation (Anthony, Cohen & Farkas, 1988; Farkas & Anthony, 1980). To support the ongoing development of psychiatric rehabilitation programs, more than in-service training of current staff is needed. Boston University offers master's degree on-campus and off-campus programs as well as a regular doctoral program in psychiatric rehabilitation (Farkas, O'Brien & Nemec, 1988). An initiative, funded by NIMH, has recently been made to disseminate this curriculum to graduate students in psychiatry, nursing, social work, and psychology as an attempt to increase the number of graduates trained to work with the severely psychiatrically disabled client (Farkas, Anthony, Cohen, Cohen & Danley, in preparation).

Strategies to change systems to be more supportive of psychiatric rehabilitation programs are only just emerging. Up to this point, they have focused on revising policies, funding mechanisms, and legislation, and providing opportunities for manpower development across a region or state. The systems change methods have included supporting advocacy groups, developing relationships with key political figures, testifying before legislative committees, as well as providing ongoing consultation and training to state level personnel, such as evaluators, planners, and trainers.

In summary, the emergence of specific program elements that define the psychiatric rehabilitation program, and the identification of strategies to change those programs, their practitioners, and the supporting systems set the stage to put theory into systematic practice.

2

A Psychiatric Rehabilitation
Approach to Housing

PAUL J. CARLING, PH.D., AND
PRISCILLA RIDGWAY, M.S.W.

Historical and Current Perspectives

This chapter presents an introduction to the current state of practice in the field of residential services. Several programs describe their attempts to shift from more traditional residential services to a rehabilitation approach. Finally, the critical emerging issues for the field are presented, in the context of a rehabilitation approach to meeting housing needs termed "Community Residential Rehabilitation." This approach is described in terms of its mission and principles, and the implications for implementing housing-related rehabilitation services are explored.

A STATEMENT OF THE PROBLEM

Adequate housing is an essential element of all people's well-being. Decent, affordable housing is an essential support to effective rehabilitation of all persons with long-term mental disabilities. In fact, without the appropriate range of housing options, the success of other treatment and rehabilitation approaches is seriously undermined. In spite of this obvious need, most people with psychiatric disabilities do not have stable, affordable housing, nor, in most instances, are they likely to secure it. This is a complex problem, and there are many factors that contribute to it:

- The psychiatric disability itself sometimes interferes with selecting and maintaining housing (Bachrach, 1982, 1984; Budson, 1981; Carling, 1978, 1984b, 1985; Carpenter & Bourestan, 1976; Chatetz D. Goldfinger, 1984; Coulton, Holland & Fitch, 1984).

- Our service systems have not been organized to provide the training and support needed to secure adequate housing (Carling, 1984b).
- Discrimination severely limits the housing options available (Avirom & Segal, 1973).
- Poverty is a major barrier, and affordable housing is growing increasingly scarce (Baxter & Hopper, 1981; Carling, 1984b).

The overall consequences of not responding to the housing and support needs of people with psychiatric disabilities have been profound. They include inappropriate use of hospital care (Braun et al., 1981; Chatetz & Goldfinger, 1984; DHHS, 1983); inappropriate transfer to other institutional or custodial settings (Carling, 1984b, 1984d; Kohen & Paul, 1976; Minkoff, 1978); lack of community integration (Carling, Daniels & Ridgway, 1984b; Cometa, Morrison & Zishoren, 1979; Segal & Aviram, 1978); inappropriate use of families as primary care providers (Hatfield, 1984; Wasow, 1982); homelessness (Bachrach, 1984; Baxter & Hopper, 1984; Lamb, 1984; Mowbray, 1985); revolving-door hospital readmissions and ineffective mental health interventions (Geller, 1982); community opposition to residential programs (Rutman & Piasecki, 1976); the call for reinstitutionalization (Talbott, 1979b); and consumer dissatisfaction (Chamberlin, 1978).

THE HOUSING NEEDS OF INDIVIDUALS WITH
PSYCHIATRIC DISABILITIES

In the last several decades, there have been many positive programmatic and conceptual developments within the mental health field in its attempts to meet the housing needs of people with psychiatric disabilities. These developments are briefly summarized below.

Residential settings, typically called "halfway houses," geared to easing the move from hospital to community living, began to proliferate in the early 1960s. Although the name "halfway house" implies a short-term or transitional program, in reality many of these programs have extended or even indefinite-term lengths of stay (Apte, 1968; Budson, 1981; Glasscote, Gudeman & Elpers, 1971; Rog & Raush, 1975; Rutman & Piasecki, 1976).

After experimentation with the halfway house as the only option between hospital and "independent living," service providers came to realize the need for a range of living environments termed a "residential continuum." The idea of a continuum implies not only that an array of options is available, but also that these options are organized developmentally, or functionally, to respond to various levels of need. This shift to a functionally based approach was a highly significant one for the field. Various elements in a "residential continuum" have been suggested by a variety of authors and have included:

- *"Quarterway Houses"* offering preparation for community living, often in a facility on hospital grounds (APA, 1982).
- *"Halfway Houses"* with emphasis on the group milieu and on skills development (Glasscote, Gudeman & Elpers, 1971).
- *"Three-Quarterway Houses"* with less intensive staffing than "halfway houses" (Campbell, 1981).
- *"Family Foster Care"* in which alternative families are used as a transitional support as people leave the hospital, or as longer-term housing (Carling, 1984b).
- *"Crisis Alternative Models"* including family care, crisis residences, special apartment settings, or intensive on-site outreach to *any* setting in which a person in crisis resides (Polak, 1978; Stein & Test, 1980, 1985).
- *"Group Homes"* which are congregate living situations that range from custodial boarding-home settings to intensive treatment-oriented transitional residences (APA, 1982).
- *"Fairweather Lodges"* for a small group of patients who move out of the hospital to live and work together on a long-term basis (Fairweather, 1980).
- *"Apartment Programs"* which may involve live-in staff, staff living nearby, or visiting staff; models include "supervised apartments," "semisupervised apartments," "cluster apartments," "cooperative apartments," "semi-independent," and "independent living" (Carling, 1978; Goldmeier, Mannino & Shore, 1978).
- *"Boarding Homes"* settings in which ex-patients receive a room, including boarding homes, single-room occupancies (SROs), and rooming houses, or room plus meals, and/or services, personal care, or "supervision" in board and care, or residential care facilities (Kohen & Paul, 1976; Segal & Avirom, 1978).
- *"Nursing Homes"* to which large numbers of patients were inappropriately transferred and remain. Recent trends include increased mental health outreach to these facilities and training of nursing home staff to work with residents (Carling, 1981b).
- *"Shelters for Homeless Persons"* which provide overnight lodging for individuals and, in some cases, families (Bachrach, 1984).
- *"Services Related to Natural Families"* which assist families through education and training in coping with mentally ill relatives (Hatfield, 1984; Levine, 1984a).

Although there have been many positive developments in the field, there have been conceptual problems in the use of the continuum model and in the way the residential field has organized services. Some of these problems are described below, as well as in a series of critical issues raised in the final section of this chapter. One problem with the concept of a "residential continuum" is that it is often implemented in a rigid way with inflexible time limits. In many cases, the simplistic notion that people can be given "transitional" help through a series of time-limited stays in specialized residential settings, to achieve "independent living," has actually resulted in major difficulties for people with psychiatric disabilities. These problems include: (1) a need to adjust to predetermined programs rather than receive individualized services, (2) chronic dislocation through successive moves; (3) an ultimate return to family, boarding home, hospital, or homelessness due to the lack of assistance in securing permanent housing.

"Continua" usually emphasize separate residential facilities, rather than the services and supports people need to succeed in normal housing. Finally, the continuum concept often confuses the need for housing with the need for specific services and supports and, in effect, makes receiving housing dependent on participation in a service program (Carling, Daniels & Ridgway, 1985b). The case study by Mynks and Graham in this chapter highlights some of the real contrast between the continuum approach and the preferences of clients, as well as the difficulty staff have in determining when people are "ready" to move to another setting.

Another popular concept, that of "transition," reflects a positive recognition of the need for varying levels of support. The concept has also been problematic when, in many programs, the transition process has included unrealistic time limits, or when improvement in functioning is associated with a physical move from one setting to another. Finally, many "transitional" programs emphasize skills that apply either to a group living environment, and are therefore less relevant to living independently, or emphasize skills that cannot be easily transferred to another setting (Anthony, 1979b; Carling, Daniels & Ridgway, 1985b).

These concerns, and others, have contributed to a major rethinking, both within government and in local programs, about the most effective strategies to promote the successful functioning of people with psychiatric disabilities in stable housing settings. Concepts of normalization, the need for community support systems, and the importance of a rehabilitation approach are being introduced in many service systems and agencies. Thus, the field is a rapidly evolving one.

Case Studies

The remainder of this chapter is intended to present programs that have gone beyond the traditional approaches to residential services and have attempted to incorporate rehabilitation values and principles in their delivery. As such, they serve as a metaphor for the field as a whole, increasingly aware of some of the limitations of current program models and moving toward a rehabilitation approach.

Rice, Seibold, and Taylor describe the residential components of Alternatives Unlimited, Inc., which serves persons with severe psychiatric or developmental disabilities. The article stresses the importance of operating programs from a strong values base that emphasizes client involvement, self-determination, and growth. The agency offers four levels of intensity of residential support and services, in such settings as staffed apartments, congregate living sites, cooperative apartments, and follow-up in the community. Clients do not have to leave any of the programs within a specific period of time, nor do they have to move through a range of settings. The paper describes the matching process used to link clients with a specific living situation, based on each client's goals, needs, and skills. The authors describe the diagnosis, planning, and interventions used. The programs emphasize linking clients with existing community resources and activities, in addition to using agency resources. The authors stress the importance of creating an organizational culture that supports the rehabilitation approach, as well as developing external support for the agency's work. Client success and satisfaction have helped to engender support for this approach.

Mynks and Graham describe a psychosocial agency, Revisions, Inc., that was founded in 1983 to serve persons with long-term psychiatric disabilities. The agency has developed several residential alternatives, including clustered and satellite apartments, a respite apartment, and an eight-bed congregate living facility. Among the learnings presented in this article is the importance of fully integrating psychiatric rehabilitation into the agency's administrative functions, including its mission and goals and staff job descriptions, training, and supervision. The authors have learned that clients prefer a stable living situation but need intensive training and practice in real-life situations to develop the emotional and intellectual skills they need to be successful. The programs are struggling to balance rehabilitation-oriented programming with the normal activities of a person's home while flexibly supporting each client. The authors describe staff functions that aid such an effort, and identify problems that were found in implementing a rehabilitation approach.

Craig, Peer, and Ross describe a residential treatment program that is housed in several eight-person "cottages" at Greystone Park Psychiatric Hospital, a state hospital in New Jersey. The hospital serves persons with severe and chronic major mental illnesses, most of whom are admitted involuntarily. The cottages were developed to provide more humane and personalized settings that would improve patient participation. The psychiatric rehabilitation approach was selected as the clinical approach and implemented on a pilot basis in 1983. Functional professionals were taught to carry out the rehabilitation processes of diagnosis, planning, and intervention. The authors describe the formal evaluation measures that have been built into the program and the hospital procedures that have been adapted to mesh effectively with a rehabilitation approach. Staff focus on helping clients to acquire a few high-priority skills at one time and have integrated other clinical programming with the rehabilitation approach. Skill teaching is conducted in both formal and informal settings and is provided on both an individual and a group basis. The authors identify a variety of issues involved in implementing a rehabilitation approach in newly created environments that differed significantly from the previous ward environments. Staff had to develop new administrative strategies and participatory decision-making structures that involved families and emphasized client participation. Leadership and a clear philosophy and clinical culture were needed to create a rehabilitation orientation with the hospital cottage program. The authors describe changes that are underway in the broader system as it moves toward a rehabilitation orientation.

After describing these programs, the chapter then concludes with a detailed description of "Community Residential Rehabilitation." This approach to meeting the housing and support needs of people with psychiatric disabilities presents what we believe to be the next stage in the evolution of the field of residential services.

Psychiatric Rehabilitation in a Residential Setting: Alternatives Unlimited, Inc., Whitinsville, Massachusetts

DENNIS H. RICE, M.ED.; MICHAEL SEIBOLD, M.A.; AND JEAN TAYLOR, B.S.

Alternatives Unlimited, Inc., is a private, nonprofit Massachusetts corporation committed to offering community-based residential, vocational, and outreach services to severely psychiatrically or developmentally disabled individuals. The agency opened in 1976, at the beginning of the state deinstitutionalization process, with one voca-

tional and three residential programs. Most clients had spent a significant amount of time at state institutions with little input into the conduct of their own affairs. Alternatives was determined to develop an
approach other than the medical model, with a major emphasis on client input in all aspects of the program. "Self-determination," "mutual
growth and respect," and "cutting the distance between clients and
staff" became the agency's philosophy, focusing our efforts on making
available to disabled persons conditions as close as possible to the
norms and patterns of the mainstream of society.

In 1980, Alternatives had the opportunity to develop two additional, small residential programs for very low-functioning clients. To
serve this population effectively, the programs required more than the
usual role modeling and group processing that had previously been
the main treatment method. A new emphasis on skill development
with a high level of support to help clients progress at their own pace
was needed. Based on his study of various available methods, Alternatives' executive director chose the psychiatric rehabilitation approach. Psychiatric rehabilitation offered a comprehensive, skill-based
approach that embodied agency values of client involvement and provided measurable outcomes for both client and staff growth. It has
been implemented throughout the agency. Currently Alternatives'
mission for its thirty programs, in mental retardation as well as mental
health, is "to provide the necessary skills and supports to individuals
with disabilities so they may lead satisfying and successful lives in the
settings of their choice." Through a process in which individuals at all
levels of the agency participated, older agency values and principles
were combined with new rehabilitation ones, resulting in the following list:

1. The quality of an organization is reflected in the importance it
   places on its members.
2. Positive expectations (hope) are an essential ingredient in the rehabilitative process.
3. Helping is possible only in the context of a trusting relationship,
   which needs to be an established priority.
4. Realizing one's own potential takes courage, skills, and supports.
5. The direct involvement of the individual is necessary in all phases
   of the learning process.
6. Each learning environment needs to have its own unique qualities
   and structures that support individuals to make choices, encourage
   experimentation, and reward risk taking.
7. Programs that provide real benefits to individuals require a joint
   commitment to ongoing appraisal and evolutionary change.

8. People with disabilities have the right to live and work in the community under conditions similar to those of other members of society.

Program Description

ENVIRONMENTS

Alternatives has developed a range of mental health residential settings providing four levels or options for clients from which to choose depending on their skill level, needed level of support, and interest:

Level One: Three highly structured staffed apartments that provide intensive 24-hour support (staff ratio is 4:6) for low-functioning clients to stabilize in the community and learn very basic living skills.

Level Two: Two less-structured community residences that provide 24-hour support (staff ratio is 4:8) for stabilized clients to learn community and interpersonal skills along with decision making and sharing responsibility in running the house.

Level Three: Several cooperative apartments that provide four to ten hours of support (staff ratio is 2:10) to refine and utilize independent living skills and to develop the clients' own social networks.

Level Four: Follow-up is provided to monitor client skill utilization and resource linking for up to six months after graduation from any residential setting. This is achieved through a combination of active outreach staff and scheduled return visits to the residence by clients.

There are no set timelines for how long a client remains in a residential program, nor are they required to pass through the range of settings in any particular sequence. Whether clients stay or go is based very much on which setting provides the necessary challenge and support needed so that they may feel successful and satisfied in the program of their choice. To make an informed decision, clients are encouraged to visit several programs. The decision-making process has been strengthened by the identification of clear and realistic environmental demands for each program. This helps clients, with the aid of practitioners, to assess their skills and needed levels of support more accurately. At the staffed apartment level, for example, the client is not required to cook; he or she must be able to attend a half-hour house meeting, and medication is distributed by staff. The community residence, on the other hand, requires basic cooking skills, participation in a 1½-hour house meeting, and self-medication with assistance. The cooperative apartment level requires a client to plan and cook five different meals, self-medicate, and develop his or her own network of supports with assistance. In looking at these demands, the client is encouraged to view the entire range of services as options from which to choose.

The following section describes the basic rehabilitation components of diagnosis, planning, and interventions as defined and implemented at Alternatives.

Diagnosis

Alternatives' policy governing the diagnostic process states that "clients will actively participate in setting goals and assessing their skill strengths and deficits and needed levels of support in relation to achieving those goals." This assessment process begins immediately during program orientation. It is emphasized in the group interview when the client is accepted into the program and continues on an ongoing basis with the residential case manager.

What follows is a description of the procedures for referring new clients to Alternatives. Newly referred clients are oriented to the skill-based approach during initial program visits and are asked to begin assessing themselves based on the stated environmental requirements of the setting. Staff provide information and support during this transitional period which can take anywhere from one to four weeks depending on client need. Once a client begins to show interest in a specific residential setting, a group interview takes place. During the interview, referred clients have the opportunity to discuss with house members what they hope to accomplish by living there. At the same time, the current residents are encouraged to consider how they might support the new clients to be successful in the residence. Through this group process it is hoped that a tone of mutual support and an expectation of using feedback to encourage growth are created.

A case manager is assigned to work regularly with the new client in defining overall rehabilitation goals and assessing related skills and resources. Because of state requirements, a rehabilitation plan needs to be in place within thirty days. The case manager, however, continues to explore likes and dislikes, skill strengths and deficits, and needed resources with the resident on a weekly basis, so that more beneficial interventions can be developed. Diagnostic information is placed in the client record on functional assessment forms and is formally reviewed at least quarterly.

Planning

Alternatives' policy governing service planning states that client participation and service coordination will be maximized in the process of establishing the specific interventions to be implemented by all

AGENCY PROFILE (as of October, 1987)

A. AGENCY
Name: Alternatives Unlimited, Inc.
Location: Whitinsville, Mass. 01588   **Population:** 110,000
Type of Agency: Vocational/Nonprofit corporation   **Primary Sources of Agency Funding:** State contracts for services, Medicaid, individual fees
Agency Size: Total number of staff: 225   Total number of Clients: 500
    Direct care staff: 206   Administration staff: 8   Support Staff: 11

B. CASE STUDY PROGRAM/UNIT
Name: Mental Health Residential Component
Location: 54 Douglas Road, Whitinsville, Mass. 01588
Number of Programs in Unit: 6   **Type of Program:** Residential
Program Size:

Total number of staff: 30	Total number of clients: 46
Number of direct care only staff: 19	Male: 23 Female: 23
Number of supervisory/	Average age: 33
administrative only staff: 6	Age range: 21–65
Number of support staff: 5	Av. yrs. hosp.: N/A; Range: 1 year
Mixed Functions—direct care/super-	to 15 years
visory: N/A	Predominant diagnostic categories:
Administrative/supervisory: 2/6	60% schizophrenia
Number of	10% depressive
Ph.D./M.D.: N/A	30% bipolar depressive manics
M.S.W./.M.A./M.Ed.: 2	**Staff/client ratio:** 1:1 up to 2:1/2:10
B.S.W./B.A.: 29	
High school: 30	

Program Description:
Average length of stay in program: 14–15 months
Majority of clients are funded by: 100% Department of Mental Health
Majority of program activities are conducted: N/A
Program hours of service: 24 hours, 7 days a week

Average Length of Time to Conduct Program Activities:
DIAGNOSIS
Initial overall rehabilitation goal: 2 sessions a week
Functional assessment/resource assessment: 10 sessions over 30 days
OTHER TYPES OF DIAGNOSIS
Type: History, psych. test, verbal report   Number of sessions: 3
PLANNING
Developing the initial rehabilitation plan: 10 sessions over 30 days
Other plans if applicable: N/A
INTERVENTIONS
Conducting direct skills teaching of one skill: constant/2 sessions a week
Implementing a program for use of one skill: 2 sessions a week
Linking up with one resource: N/A
OTHER TYPES OF INTERVENTIONS
Individual therapy: through outside agencies
Group therapy: through outside agencies

service team members to help clients achieve their overall rehabilitation goals.

Once clients have prioritized skill and resource needs, they participate in three distinct stages of planning: (1) a preplanning meeting, (2) the overall rehabilitation planning meeting, and (3) the group feedback meeting. Preplanning meetings are designed to give all service providers and significant others an opportunity to communicate their perspectives, resolve disagreements, and prioritize interventions to meet client needs and wants. An effort is made to avoid surprises at the rehabilitation planning meeting. The overall rehabilitation planning meetings are designed to give clients an opportunity to present their progress to date in person and to target new skill and support goals. The service providers and significant others, in turn, coordinate the needed interventions to meet these goals and identify timelines and built-in monitoring steps. The group feedback meetings are designed to give the client an opportunity to share skill and support goals with other residents during house meetings. Other residents can offer encouragement and assistance in helping individuals to reach their goals. Planning information is placed in the client record on Rehabilitation Plan forms that include the signature of all participants. The plan is reviewed with the client every three months to ensure up-to-date assessments and relevant interventions.

INTERVENTIONS

Alternatives' policy governing rehabilitation interventions states that "service provision to clients will focus on maximizing client acquisition and use of relevant skills and resources critical to successful achievement of their overall rehabilitation goals."

The following procedures have been developed for rehabilitation interventions. Alternatives has implemented a full range of interventions in skill and resource development. Skill deficits, such as the inability to identify feelings, are prioritized and grouped across the range of programs. Individual sessions or group classes are scheduled based on need, with the learning styles of each client taken into account to maximize efficiency and effectiveness of staff time and client learning. Direct skill teaching has become the major emphasis in the staffed apartments, because lower-functioning clients are more likely not to know or have any experience with the required skills than higher-functioning clients. This is one example of how programs are specialized in specific interventions due to differences in client functioning. Programming skill use has become the major focus of the community residences and cooperative apartments where most of these clients are skilled but have difficulty in applying these skills in the needed environment. Case managers meet with clients weekly on a one-to-one basis to develop programs and to monitor their outcomes.

Resource development activities are accomplished through the relationships formed between staff and other service providers, through formal affiliation agreements with them, and, less directly, through formal and informal community education efforts aimed at community acceptance and integration. The staffed apartments' emphasis is on mobilizing basic community resources such as the mental health center, primary physicians, or transportation as the client comes out of the state hospital. Clients in community residences usually require linking of generic resources within the community such as going to the dentist or bowling at the local alley on their own. Clients in the co-operative apartments require even more sophisticated linking such as joining a local church group to develop an independent social network. Alternatives' management has been able to create additional resources through negotiation with our governmental funding sources and through fundraising.

Skill and resource development data are placed in the client record in the form of monthly progress notes and notes from quarterly reviews. Data are also recorded less formally in regular residential log notes.

Implementing the Psychiatric Rehabilitation Program: Strategies and Barriers

The implementation of a rehabilitation approach at Alternatives has been an exciting challenge to the very core of the agency's identity. Ultimately, it has been rewarding for both clients and staff. It required a rethinking and clarification of the agency's vision and values as well as persistent attention to the many details involved in designing and revising program structures to facilitate client growth.

THE CREATION OF A REHABILITATION CULTURE

A basic necessity for implementing the psychiatric rehabilitation approach is the creation of an organization-wide "rehabilitation culture." By this is meant a set of agreed-upon values and realizable expectations that give all members of the agency a shared identity, a sense of direction, and a commitment to the rehabilitation mission.

Ensuring Staff Commitment

The creation in a large, diverse agency of such a culture with broad values that are credible throughout the organization has been a difficult leadership challenge. As with any significant organizational change that is successful, it requires everyone's understanding, commitment, and personal involvement, especially on the part of managers. In Alternatives' experience, the chief executive had to become personally involved in promoting an ethic of persistent utilization and refinement of this approach by all other staff. Beyond that, he had to define the general policies and provide the necessary, specific interventions to highlight both the vision and the details needed to advance implementation of the agency's mission on a day-to-day basis. The roles of the other managers required redefinition. They were expected to be fully engaged in the implementation effort and were held accountable, through written work plans, for progress in their respective areas. All top managers eventually became trainers in their own right. Implementation became a fixed agenda item at weekly management team meetings. Managers were responsible for creating a real learning environment for staff growth. They were expected to practice rehabilitation skills themselves to have firsthand experience of what was being required of staff. Second, managers were expected to hold staff accountable for their work by monitoring progress on required work plans developed by each program team. Third, managers were expected to become directly involved in staff struggles to implement this new system by encouraging staff participation, praising and rewarding subordinates, and directly addressing practical obstacles encountered by staff in their day-to-day efforts. This required top managers to double the amount of time spent in the programs themselves in order to observe the operation directly and "catch people doing things right."

Clarifying Staff Roles

Beyond encouragement and inspiration by leaders, major change is not accomplished without clear direction. Alternatives spent considerable time developing and clarifying staff roles relative to the implementation effort, including attention to staff recruitment and orientation, job expectations, and performance appraisals.

The agency's hiring process was modified to include an orientation to the rehabilitation approach and an evaluation of candidates' interpersonal skills. Potential staff can now make an informed choice in considering employment with the agency. Furthermore, staff candidates are now required to participate in a short role play in which they demonstrate their helping skills and participate in a skill-based feedback session on their performance. This is done not only to assess a candidate's current level of interpersonal skills but also to evaluate the individual's willingness and ability to use feedback to learn new skills.

When Alternatives first introduced a rehabilitation approach, staff felt as though they had two jobs—their old duties, plus the new psychiatric rehabilitation tasks. The resulting drain prompted a redefinition and prioritization of job duties. This process was significant insofar as it enabled Alternatives to clarify the importance of certain aspects of rehabilitation work. It also underscored the need to perform other ongoing functions critical to the operation of a residential program, such as compliance with licensing requirements, which were occasionally neglected during bursts of enthusiasm for implementing the rehabilitation approach. Integrated job descriptions have proven to be a valuable tool in developing clear lines of authority and accountability within the agency. Clearer job descriptions also led to more objective performance appraisals. A new appraisal system was developed to evaluate specific rehabilitation and interpersonal skills. The use of this appraisal—specifically, the identification of staff skill strengths and deficits relative to job requirements—led to the innovation of individual staff development plans to which general personnel training plans were then tailored. Much of staff supervision time could subsequently be built around the utilization of newly acquired skills.

A Clarification of Values

Only when the rehabilitation mission becomes the essential, pervasive feature of clinical life in the organization do clients benefit fully from the innovation. Otherwise, this approach, like any other new technology, becomes another passing fad with no lasting impact. Consideration of questions of relevance, compatibility, and the basic desirability of a rehabilitation approach have brought Alternatives back to the fundamental question of what values and principles are most relevant to the agency's mission. Just recently the management team took an active role in redefining and clarifying the values listed above. What was needed, in some cases, was the identification of new meaning or the reinterpretation of previously held values and, in other cases, the inclusion of new rehabilitation principles and new managerial values to promote ongoing refinement of programs. For example, the egalitarianism inherent in striving for mutual growth and minimizing distinctions between staff and clients has always been an agency value. In the past, this was put into practice by having residential staff live in the residence. Further, staff were expected and willing to share with housemates their own positive life experiences as well as their struggles. This value has now taken on additional meaning to include stressing the importance of the client's individual choice in determining the direction of the rehabilitation plan. Before, staff controlled service plan development, with their perspective playing the predominant role in shaping the plan's content. Now, the client is assisted to assume as much control of the planning process as possible. Furthermore, the client's perspective significantly determines the content of the service plan.

Promoting relevant, living values and principles has been crucial in assisting staff to get back to the basics of helping clients and understanding the meaningfulness and necessity of Alternatives' work. A major part of management's leadership responsibility is to safeguard and promote these values.

OVERCOMING BARRIERS TO IMPLEMENTATION

Successful implementation of a rehabilitation approach over the past six years involved overcoming many practical problems, obstacles, and agency mistakes through the development of creative strategies as well as modification of many program structures. Among the issues encountered were:

The Problem of Too Much to Do

Revised job descriptions made clear what staff had to do. But initially, practitioners became overwhelmed with the amount of time and work involved in the psychiatric rehabilitation approach. Functional assessments needed to be completed so that initial rehabilitation planning meetings could be held within the short timelines dictated by licensing requirements. Success, in turn, was contingent upon the time-consuming, but all-important, trusting relationship between client and practitioner. Staff balked at the number of forms and worksheets required. Other program demands seemed to compete with the many steps required for quality rehabilitation. In short, it seemed impossible to actually *do* rehabilitation. It was as if there were two separate entities: daily operation of the residential programs *and* doing rehabilitation. A breakthrough for Alternatives came with the realization that our overall goal was to operate residences that rehabilitated people, that rehabilitation was not a "nice extra feature" to existing programs, but the *heart* of them.

Given that sober yet liberating realization, efforts began to focus on integrating rehabilitation within already existing program structures and procedures. Part of the staff meeting became a study group for providing feedback to staff as they practiced rehabilitation skills. Supervision was used to provide individual skill teaching and monitoring. House meetings were adapted to include group direct skill teaching of clients. The existing internal case-management system, which matched two or three clients with one staff member in each residence, became a natural structure for developing functional assessments.

The in-service training plan was condensed. Initially, six hour-long trainings over ten weeks were offered to cover all aspects in a certain skill area—for example, all skills involved in setting an overall rehabilitation goal. Staff were thus taken away from their programs for up to one day per week. They often felt overwhelmed by the comprehensive dimensions of the trainings. Since then, content areas have been shortened so that a staff person can attend a training every three months in one of several graduated six-hour sessions. There, staff hear, see, *and practice* the essential ingredients of a basic skill. The finer points are added in subsequent trainings. Staff also receive feedback on their efforts, as well as further information and assistance at regularly scheduled study groups between trainings. This approach enables them to begin immediately to use the skills they learn.

Requiring staff to learn all aspects of the rehabilitation approach (i.e., all of the diagnosis, planning, and intervention strategies) did not work well, nor was it practical. Besides exhausting everyone, the program became impossible to monitor, and it was difficult to support the application of all aspects, in every program, at the same time. Currently, staff are asked to specialize in a certain aspect of the approach based on personal interest and program need. This approach enables them to become more motivated and more competent in areas of their choice. Monitoring is also rendered more coherent. By simplifying the presentation of the approach and having staff choose what they want to work on, divisional integrity and ownership are developed. Programs then focus on the creative implementation of a particular aspect of the rehabilitation technology.

To meet state time constraints, the elaborate values-clarification piece contained in the process of establishing an overall rehabilitation goal was eliminated in the first round of working with the client. The process is simplified to a more informal exploration of the client's wants so that an initial directional goal can be set. Further work in the area of values clarification is then done in ongoing rehabilitation counseling sessions in which the consumer gradually learns how to identify his or her values and make choices based upon them.

Finally, other changes helped alleviate frustration. The number of forms required was reduced from eleven to five, and other forms were simplified. Perhaps the best criterion to judge a form is a test for utility: "Does this form, in its present design, best serve to communicate the required information that is pertinent to the client, the agency, and the state?" Several years of struggling to integrate the various aspects of the psychiatric rehabilitation approach into the life of the agency through a process of values clarification, modification of existing program structures, and simplification of operating procedures have made it possible to pursue meaningful rehabilitation work throughout Alternatives' programs.

The Problem of Ongoing Maintenance

Maintenance of a sufficient number of trained trainers in this rehabilitation approach is indispensable for implementation. Over time, most of the agency's original trainers moved on to other positions. In response to this dilemma, one trainer instituted an apprenticeship program to train new trainers. Using this approach, interested individuals paired up with an experienced trainer and, under supervision, assisted in training groups of staff. The combination of support, consultation, and the right amount of risk taking enabled individuals using this trainer apprenticeship method to progress rapidly. By late 1985, and continuously since then, the agency has had a dozen or more individuals at any one time offering trainings in selected aspects of the model in which they had expertise and supervised experience.

Alternatives' most effective strategy to ensure the ongoing and improved practice of rehabilitation skills was probably the institution of a resource staff position entitled "Director of Program Development." The cost of this position was spread over all of the residential budgets. It was established primarily to consult on-site with each residential team on a weekly basis in order to facilitate study groups and offer feedback on staff skill development and technical assistance on program development issues. Rapidly increasing staff expertise, program consistency, and the development of more useful program structures resulted from this investment. Smaller agencies could create such a position by modifying an existing position or by creating an affordable part-time one. Alternatives has found that its resources are well spent on having someone provide consistent attention to implementation issues. This focusing of resources has also led to increased efficiency since, aside from the added expense of the Director of Program Development position, the cost per client day, the basic unit of service, has not increased as a result of implementation of this rehabilitation approach. Staff roles have been modified to reflect new responsibilities. However, much has been accomplished with the same staff-to-client ratios as those that were present before adoption of a rehabilitation approach.

The Problem of External Support

Support from government and the public is critical for any agency. Unfortunately, Alternatives erred in initially coming across to government funding sources and other mental health agencies with a certain amount of arrogance about the rehabilitation approach. Convinced that it had discovered *the* Way, Alternatives spent considerable time attempting to convert brother/sister agencies and to impress government officials. Needless to say, feelings of resentment and hostility arose, which led to defensiveness, criticism, counterattack, and the never-ending challenge to "put up" or abandon this so-called new approach to treatment. The agency learned that discontinuing the flag waving resulted in less confrontation. Efforts were made to clarify the agency's position and practice of rehabilitation technology in a more matter-of-fact way. As a result, more reasonable expectations of the agency's performance have arisen. For public support the agency now relies more upon the messages sent by parents and consumers themselves concerning their level of satisfaction with the project. This, at times, has also generated legislative and other official interest and support in the agency's programs. For example, the mental health commissioner visited one residence and described it as a model program as a result of a parent's urging him to make an on-site visit. Collecting meaningful statistics about the progress made by the residents toward achieving their rehabilitation goals has proven very beneficial. Alternatives learned that statistics that *demonstrate* success are certainly more compelling than flowery talk that promises success. Striving for mutual understanding and acceptability of agency goals and producing desirable results have gone far to correct older, more negative images of the agency. Along with more sophistication in publicizing successes and needs, a definite amount of public support has been achieved and maintained.

Program Evaluation

Questions focusing upon the overall effectiveness of programs are sometimes difficult to answer objectively and accurately. In 1983, two Alternatives' community residences participated in a research project with the Boston University Center for Psychiatric Rehabilitation in order to measure the impact of the use of direct skill-teaching and skill-programming interventions. Eleven residents were randomly placed into an experimental group to receive the interventions. Eleven other residents were randomly assigned to a control group to monitor their level of skill goal attainment without the interventions. Each client was individually assessed to identify the skills critical to his or her personal overall rehabilitation goal. Four of eight staff were trained as skill teachers. Their selection was based primarily upon the likelihood of their remaining in the programs for the duration of the research project. The outcome was that clients in the experimental group learned and put into use significantly more skills than did the clients in the control group.

Participation in the research project contributed greatly to the clients' learning about themselves and about psychiatric rehabilitation. Some problems arose concerning time management and concerns about the potentially intrusive nature of research "in people's homes." These could have been alleviated with advance orientation of programs, better planning, and greater facilitation by agency managers. In general, however, the careful measuring of skill goal outcomes enabled all staff and managers to appreciate the efficacy of teaching and programming interventions in the rehabilitation of psychiatrically disabled individuals. Program goals relating to rehabilitation became better defined. Skill-based program criteria and expectations for movement within program levels could also be redefined as a result of the process of identifying critical skills to be researched.

In fiscal 1986, Alternatives collected data to measure two distinct outcomes: (1) the level of client progress in terms of stability or movement to more independent settings, and (2) the level of client satisfaction in terms of positive expressions by clients about programs and their degree of participation.

CLIENT PROGRESS

Of the 47 clients served, 22 (47 percent) moved to more independent settings. These moves were client-initiated and were targeted in their rehabilitation plans. Three clients (6 percent) moved to more highly structured living arrangements in order to receive more staff support and training. The remaining 22 clients (47 percent) were stable in their existing settings. The total of possible service delivery days was 12,023 with 903 days of vacancy (7½ percent). All clients spent only 277 days (2 percent), total, in the hospital.

CLIENT SATISFACTION

When surveyed, 85 percent of all clients reported that they were satisfied in their current living situation; 15 percent stated that they wanted to move to their own apartments; and 0 percent stated that they wanted to return to the hospital. Perhaps more telling is the fact that 80 percent of all clients surveyed could name their current skill goals and the benefits of achieving those goals as targeted in their rehabilitation plans. In 1987, Alternatives served 66 individuals in six residential settings. Of these, 15 (23 percent) moved to more independent settings; 43 (65 percent) additional clients remained stable in their current programs, with only 6 (9 percent) needing to move to more highly structured living arrangements.

In conclusion, Alternatives attributes its success in stabilizing and graduating severely psychiatrically disabled clients with histories of long-term hospitalization to the comprehensive rehabilitation approach that it employs. Staff perform more skillfully and confidently, and managers have measurable criteria with which to evaluate services and make effective change to ensure program success in benefiting clients.

Starting a New Psychiatric Rehabilitation Residential Program: ReVisions, Inc., Catonsville, Maryland

DEAN A. MYNKS, M.A., AND R. SCOTT GRAHAM, M.A.

This chapter describes a program that chose to implement psychiatric rehabilitation in its residential unit. The implementation was greatly influenced by the experiences of another residential setting that had previously incorporated psychiatric rehabilitation into its program. In 1981, Boley Manor Inc., St. Petersburg, Florida, had an opportunity to become one of the first programs to be involved in a project to train a core group of Boley staff to train other staff as psychiatric rehabilitation practitioners. The experiences gained through the implementation process at Boley Manor were utilized by the executive director, who went on to develop a new program, ReVisions, Inc., in Catonsville, Maryland.

ReVisions, Inc., was founded in 1983. When its residential program opened, the typical consumer for the services averaged forty-five years of age, had been in a state institution for four to five years, and had experienced five to six hospitalizations in the time preceding the most recent hospitalization. ReVisions has developed an array of residential services to meet this population's needs.

Program Description

ReVisions has two separate apartment programs. One residential program has six apartments scattered throughout a complex with three clients per apartment. There is also an apartment rented for the staff office where individual and group skill classes are taught and administrative issues are addressed. A satellite program is located in another complex consisting of six apartments with three people each. Those apartments have drop-in supervision and are for those individuals who need a less restrictive environment. There is also a one-bedroom apartment in this complex that is used for respite care. The two apartment complexes are within one-half mile of each other, offering easy access for both clients and staff. The newest program is an eight-bed congregate-living facility for those individuals not having the skills necessary to live in a less supervised apartment situation.

ReVisions also operates a psychosocial program, approximately two miles from the apartment complexes, offering vocational and social rehabilitation for the residential population. ReVisions' case management system is distinct from the residential and vocational programming and offers a coordinating role between the two environments.

The implementation of residential programming at ReVisions was built on learnings from Boley Manor. The following learnings form the conceptual foundation on which the ReVisions program was built:

STAFF DEVELOPMENT LEARNINGS

1. Staff practitioners trained early in their careers in the residences are easier to motivate because they aren't set in their ways.
2. Incorporation of the psychiatric rehabilitation model into agency mission, program objectives, and activities provides for consistent integration of staff learnings.
3. Training program supervisors in the initial training effort provides encouragement and promotes leadership for implementation of the models.
4. Job descriptions should include activities specifically intended to provide diagnosis-planning-intervention functions.
5. When practitioners' roles are specialized in one component of D-P-I, it is easier for staff to develop competence and confidence in these roles.

CLIENT DEVELOPMENT LEARNINGS

1. A graduated system of service such as the continuum model of residences did not seem to match clients' wishes for a place to live. Clients made it clear by the type of goals they set that they wanted just one place to live and wanted to adjust to that one place.
2. Clients were able to learn physical skills more easily than other types of skills. Less teaching but more practice in a real environment was necessary.
3. Clients need structured, detailed teaching in more complicated emotional and intellectual skills, and this teaching is best done in a simulated environment that provides supervised practice in real-life situations.
4. Residential programs heavily laden with rehabilitation activities,

AGENCY PROFILE (as of October, 1987)

A. AGENCY
Name: ReVisions, Inc.
Location: Catonsville, Md.   **Population:** 50,000
Type of Agency: Psychosocial
Primary Sources of Agency Funding: state of Maryland
Agency Size: Total number of staff: 47   Total number of clients: 85
   Direct care staff: 38   Administration staff: 7   Support staff: 2

B. CASE STUDY PROGRAM/UNIT
Name: Residential Program   **Location:** Catonsville
Number of Programs in Unit: 2   **Type of Program:** Residential
Program Size:

Total number of staff: 28	Total number of clients: 44
Number of direct care only staff: 26	Male: 22 Female: 22
Number of supervisory/admin-	Average age: 45
istrative only staff: 2	Age range: 22–67
Number of support staff: 0	Av. yrs. hosp.: 4½ yrs.; Range: 6
Mixed functions—Direct care/super-	months–10 yrs.
visory: 0	Predominant diagnostic categories:
Administrative/supervisory: 0	75% schizophrenia
Number of	25% manic/depressive illness
Ph.D./M.D.: 0	**Staff/Client ratio:** 7:11
B.S.W./B.A.: 25	
M.S.W./M.A./M.Ed.: 3	
High school:	

Program Description:
Average length of stay in program: 18 months
Majority of clients are funded by: 86% state funded   14% private pay
Majority of program activities are conducted: on a one-to-one basis
Program hours of service: 24 hours a day, 7 days a week

Average Length of Time to Conduct Program Activities:
DIAGNOSIS
Initial overall rehabilitation goal: 6 weeks—1 session per week
Functional assessment/resource assessment: 2 weeks
OTHER TYPES OF DIAGNOSIS
Type: N/A   Number of sessions: N/A
PLANNING
Developing the initial rehabilitation plan: 1 session
Other plans if applicable: N/A
INTERVENTIONS
Conducting direct skills teaching of one skill: 6 sessions over 6 weeks
Implementing a program for use of one skill: 6 sessions over 6 weeks
Linking up with one resource: 1–2 sessions over 2 weeks
OTHER TYPES OF INTERVENTIONS
Individual therapy: N/A   Group therapy: N/A

such as skills teaching, every afternoon, night, and weekend, are burdensome for clients already heavily involved in daily rehabilitation activities.

5. Residential environments should provide a balance of rehabilitation and homelike activities, such as watching TV, talking with roommates, and attending to household chores.

6. The skills required to succeed in particular residential environments are not always clear to staff. Nor is it clear when a resident is ready to make the next stay-or-go decision.

As the Boley experience indicated, any organization wishing to provide quality residential rehabilitation services to the psychiatrically disabled population must have a stated rehabilitation mission or philosophy. One of the elements of that mission is that an organization must involve itself in "providing residential services of an indefinite duration which emphasize improving deficits and supporting strengths" for clients to reach their expressed living goal in a community (Mynks, 1982). This mission has set the tone for the development of programming at ReVisions. The implementation of rehabilitation began with the development of the diagnosis process in residential programming.

REHABILITATION DIAGNOSIS

Rehabilitation diagnosis begins prior to the individual entering ReVisions. When someone is referred by the State Hospital, a ReVisions worker goes to the hospital to conduct an interview with the client at that setting. The procedures for conducting a diagnosis include exploring the client's desire for moving into a community residence and his or her values (important considerations) in choosing a residence. The residential program, including the concepts of psychiatric rehabilitation, is described in detail, so that the individual understands the expectations of the environment. If, in the staff person's opinion, there seems to be a match between the desires and values of the individual and the environment available, the worker will make a recommendation to the hospital that the individual enter ReVisions' residential program. This matching process is very important because the client's choice of entering a rehabilitation program that meets important values provides the motivation to pursue the rehabilitation process. Essentially, an overall rehabilitation goal of community residential tenure is developed while the individual is in the hospital.

The individual is assigned to a "primary" counselor whose responsibility is to conduct the rehabilitation process. This staff person, who usually works full time during the evening, is responsible for acclimating the individual to the residential environment. The "primary" conducts a functional assessment in the first two to three weeks of the individual's stay. This functional assessment presents a comprehensive picture of the specific critical skill and/or resource strengths and deficits the individual needs to be successful in the residential program he or she has chosen (Cohen & Anthony, 1984). ReVisions stresses to its staff that rehabilitation assessment is not a finite process. Despite the fact that the initial diagnostic phase will lead to a rehabilitation plan, ReVisions insists that the "primaries" continue to do assessment after the initial plan is developed, so that new skill and resource deficits can be added to the plan over time.

In developing its residential program, the management of Boley decided to deal with the issue of lack of clarity in determining when a stay-or-go decision was appropriate by developing a "level system." The system was developed and refined at Boley (Mynks, 1982) and then implemented at ReVisions. The level system is a graduated delineation of the critical environmental skills necessary to maintain oneself in an environment or move on to another environment. It helps objectify the stay-or-go decision for the resident and staff, which removes the ambiguity of determining client success.

The "primary" uses the level system interactively with the resident and collects observable data regarding the resident's ability to perform the critical skills identified as necessary for success in the particular residential environment. It is during this time of rapport building and observation that the resident is oriented to the program's philosophy, objectives, expectations, process, level system, and opportunities within the particular environment. The "primary" and the resident then resume the rehabilitation diagnosis process using the level system as a guide to help clarify the skills required of the current environment or the skills required to move on to another environment. This process is completed within four weeks of the end of the initial adjustment period.

With an understanding of the resident's performance of the critical skills identified in the level system, the staff and resident can determine specifically when the skills necessary for success in the current environment are in place. Resident success in their current environment at ReVisions provides confidence and prepares clients to begin setting overall rehabilitation goals to move to another environment.

At this juncture, the overall rehabilitation goal is recycled to determine whether the resident wishes to maintain the achieved level of functioning or set a goal to move into a less restrictive environment (e.g., a community residential setting). If the goal that is established is to move on, the rehabilitation diagnostic process would be repeated to determine whether preparation (skills development) or additional support is needed.

It should be mentioned that the level system can determine if the resident is in need of more support than is offered in the residential environment. For example, if the level of functioning for the current environment indicates a skill that an individual must have to succeed in that environment and the resident, through continual level system evaluations, indicates an inability to learn or perform that skill, then the "primary" needs to address the issue of increasing supports or, if that is not practical, helping the resident move to an environment where the indicated skill is not required. The most likely resource that might be prompted by the level system would be the increase of staff's presence in the client's environment. The level system might also prompt the withdrawal of staff time as skills increase. The level system, then, is an important way to objectify behavior, determine skills needed for a particular environment, and those behaviors and skills needed to help a resident attain his or her own residential goal.

REHABILITATION PLANNING

Planning based on the information collected during the assessment phase is also done by the "primary." The "primary" begins working on a plan to meet the overall rehabilitation goal for the particular individual in the residential environment. For the most part, the primary deals with plans to develop skills. The client either does not have or has not practiced the skills necessary to make it in the residential environment. The plan specifies over what time period the person is likely to develop the assessed skills to be at the level required in the chosen environment. This organized strategy of skill development is reviewed with the staff from other programs in the organization. The case review occurs after the individual has been in the program for six weeks. The process brings together staff from the residential, vocational, social, and case-management programs to discuss the progress and rehabilitation plans of the individual at that point.

REHABILITATION INTERVENTIONS

The "primary" who does the planning for the resident also becomes the person providing interventions. The interventions are, in most cases, skill teaching and programming skill use.

ReVisions' management had learned from its Boley experience that clients do not improve their performance of critical skill deficits merely by practicing them. Programs had to be developed that required staff to teach or program skills (Cohen, Ridley & Cohen, 1983).

"Primaries" usually do skill teaching or programming on a one-to-one basis with individuals on their caseload. There are times, however, when a group of individuals needs the same type of skills, such as cooking or budgeting. The "primary" might then conduct a skill class with a small group of residents. It is the responsibility of the "primary" to monitor the acquisition and practice of the needed skill and to make monthly progress reports on the person's movement toward the needed level of functioning. This needed level of functioning is determined by the critical skills defined in the level system.

Since most resource development is done by the agency's case manager, the only time the "primary" might become involved in resource development would be if the individual seeks a new residential environment. At that point, the residential primary would be involved in making arrangements for the individual to access a new environment within the ReVisions system or to contact the case manager to help the client link to a resource outside the ReVisions system. An emerging role of ReVisions' case managers is that of housing developers who help clients find housing that matches their overall rehabilitation goal.

An aspect of Boley's program which was not able to be implemented at ReVisions was the Social Network Program. The Social Network Program (Kinder, Thompson & Edmundson, 1982) was devised in Boley's Satellite Apartment Program to facilitate social interaction among residents and teach them to develop their own social support networks instead of relying only on professionals. The network was facilitated by paid residents and monitored by a professional staff person. In lieu of a social network, ReVisions promotes client-driven and client-funded programs. ReVisions has promoted the formation of a self-help group in the community for the purpose of providing informal networking.

Implementing the Psychiatric Rehabilitation Program Strategies and Barriers

The implementation of psychiatric rehabilitation was facilitated by facets of the approach that fostered a significant amount of consistency in new and existing programs.

The following major aspects of psychiatric rehabilitation helped facilitate implementation:

1. Articulation of a clear rehabilitation philosophy and program helped program managers hire staff who had the skills and desire to use the technology. ReVisions recruited key personnel for the program

director and residential program manager positions who were trained in psychiatric rehabilitation so that they could hire appropriate direct service staff.

2. Administration and supervisors developed consistent expectations about role performance which included the delivery of psychiatric rehabilitation. ReVisions expresses its expectations in interviewing, orientation, and staff evaluation processes.

3. Implementation of an innovative technology is facilitated by a technology that is understandable to all parties involved. Staff and residents learn to use common language about skill expectations, levels of performance, resources, deficits, and assets. Psychiatric rehabilitation is a technology that has been developed to be understandable at all levels: by administrators, program managers, direct service staff, and residents.

When implementing the psychiatric rehabilitation technology into new or existing programs, problems also exist. The major barriers to implementation are:

1. The initial training takes a great deal of time and energy by staff which conflicts with the time and energy required to start a new program. ReVisions management began to understand that training required long-term commitment and was more feasible when it was done in small increments. ReVisions is still struggling with the prolonged period of time required to make a significant impact on programming because technologies have not been taught.

2. Boley Manor's experience indicated that high staff turnover can seriously impede the implementation of psychiatric rehabilitation. High turnover required many repetitions of staff training in order to make psychiatric rehabilitation the method used for treatment delivery. By doing training in small increments, however, fewer resources were invested in staff who left the organization.

3. ReVisions has not been able to offer as many environmental choices as Boley Manor. The lack of options has restricted the ability of the program to provide clients with opportunities to establish an overall rehabilitation goal. This has been a resource issue for the organization. The organization has sought to press for additional resources to provide more choices for people coming into the system. One result of this has been the recent development of one-bedroom apartments for individuals who choose not to have roommates.

What has become clear in ReVisions' implementation of psychiatric rehabilitation is that growth and the addition of resources have helped the organization overcome the barriers. As more resources become available it is expected that the pace of rehabilitation training for staff will quicken and that the level of expertise in implementing the model will increase.

A final important aspect of the implementation of psychiatric rehabilitation is the administrative support required to implement the technology. Boley Manor's psychiatric rehabilitation efforts rose and fell on the support of its administration and board of directors for the concept. ReVisions' board of directors has heartily endorsed the concept, and the executive director has been involved in and supportive of the concept since its early years. In the process of implementing psychiatric rehabilitation, ReVisions has lost a certified trainer who was its first program director and a trained practitioner who was its first residential program manager. If it had not been for the support of the board and the investment of the executive director, these losses could have eliminated the process.

The administration and board of directors of an organization need to have vision regarding the implementation of the psychiatric rehabilitation approach in order for it to be successful. Major innovative developments usually take three to five years to stabilize before significant impacts are realized. ReVisions has been in existence for four years. It took several years before staff were able to implement pieces of the technology successfully.

A major learning from the implementation of psychiatric rehabilitation technology at Boley Manor and ReVisions seems to be that the process is an evolutionary one. When consumers, as well as practitioners, are involved in learning the psychiatric rehabilitation process, they keep it going and evolving. Their involvement points out directions the agency might take to provide more effective service. The program becomes client driven rather than practitioner driven, which causes new issues to emerge. For instance, it was learned at Boley that when clients specify their own goals as to where they really want to live, they ask for stable housing with flexible support rather than a continuum that requires frequent disruptive movement. ReVisions has found that two levels of residential programming may be sufficient to meet the needs of its particular residents. The first level would be a congregate living residence for those individuals who simply do not have the skills to live in an apartment setting. This environment offers more staff support and an opportunity to let residents learn skills that are necessary in a less restrictive environment. The second environment is an apartment environment where staff support is added or withdrawn according to the ongoing needs of residents.

In this client-driven system, which developed programs based on clients' goals, the need for having one-bedroom apartments for individuals who chose not to live with others became apparent. ReVisions has also had to look at the practical issues regarding individual choices to stay in ReVisions apartments, rather than to move to places outside the ReVisions system. ReVisions has been forced to address the fact that new resources will be required to open up additional apartments because a significant percentage of its current population will not move from their current environment.

A client-driven system has led ReVisions to deal with these crucial issues. If the agency is indeed to provide effective services the organization must advocate for the resources to resolve these problems.

Program Evaluation

The implementation of psychiatric rehabilitation at ReVisions has produced several important outcomes. Over the past three years ReVisions has gone through its initial implementation phase in its residential program, and the program has grown significantly. Despite this significant growth ReVisions has maintained relative stability in its staffing and in its residential population. Fifty-eight individuals have entered the residential program over the three years of its existence. Four of those have moved into less restrictive settings within ReVisions' residential program. Six have moved into less restrictive settings in the community, and four have had to be rehospitalized. The remaining forty-four are currently in ReVisions programs. According to written psychiatric histories, 100 percent of the individuals who have entered the residential program have had their longest community stay since the onset of their disability. Based on the use of a skills development approach, and evaluated by the use of the level system, there has been a consistent upward movement in the skill levels of the individuals since their entrance to the programs.

Although it is difficult to attribute all of these achievements to the introduction of psychiatric rehabilitation in ReVisions' residential program, ReVisions has done better than most new programs throughout the state in terms of maintaining a low level of recidivism as well as a relatively stable staff to deal with consumers in the system. Statewide statistics show that recidivism in programs throughout the state averages about 15 pecent per year. ReVisions' recidivism rate has been at about 7 percent for the entire three years of its existence as a residential provider. Since psychiatric rehabilitation is one of the few factors that differentiates ReVisions' program from others in the state, it would

seem that the development in implementation of the psychiatric rehabilitation approach has been a significant factor in its success.

Psychiatric Rehabilitation in a State Hospital Transitional Residence: The Cottage Program at Greystone Park Psychiatric Hospital, Greystone Park, New Jersey

THOMAS J. H. CRAIG, M.D., M.P.H.; SHIRLEE M. PEER, R.N., B.S.N., M.A.;
AND MICHAEL D. ROSS, A.B., PH.D.

Greystone is a New Jersey state psychiatric hospital, 110 years old,
with a current census of 800 patients. It serves six counties, as the
backup hospital to a large public mental health system. The community agencies and other hospitals send patients who are severely ill,
"dangerous to self and/or others," and unable to be treated at that moment in any other (less intensive and less restrictive) facility. Patients
are usually admitted involuntarily and generally suffer from severe
and chronic major mental illness, often complicated by violent behaviors, alcohol (and other substance) problems, legal or criminal issues,
and resistance to treatment. Their families are often overwhelmed,
and struggling to help both the patient and themselves.

In the late 1970s, it was apparent that some of Greystone's old
buildings would have to be replaced. The environment in them had
been undermining patient dignity and incentives for growth. Rather
than construct another traditional building, it was decided (in the midst
of controversy) to create twenty cottages, each to house eight patients.
Part of the decision was based on the hospital's experiment for the preceding six years of using two staff houses as patient cottages.

The overall purpose of that experiment had been to see if a more
humane setting would lead to greater participation by patients in their
treatment. The patients did respond well to the more intimate and personalized surroundings. Most patients, for example, began to participate actively in the maintenance of the house, in trips for shopping,
and in the hospital workshops.

A clinical program, adapted to the special architecture of the cottages, was needed. The psychiatric rehabilitation approach, based on
establishment of clients' goals, assessments of skill behaviors needed,
and treatment adapted to achieving needed skills and resources,
seemed ideal.

Greystone had previously come to focus on patient behaviors,
rather than just on "insight." Boston University's approach to psychi-

atric rehabilitation (Anthony, 1980; Anthony, Cohen & Cohen, 1983) was seen as a method of advancing this direction. The approach was well structured. It had a clear and simple language, relevant to both the professional and paraprofessional staff. Staff responses to introductory training were positive. Some community mental health centers were showing interest in the approach, opening possibilities for a more coordinated mental health system.

Selected staff were trained to train other staff in psychiatric rehabilitation. In June 1983 the cottages were opened, and rehabilitation program implementation was begun in a pilot group of cottages.

Program Description

DIAGNOSIS

Every patient is assigned a clinician known as the "one-to-one." Although this can be any member of the team, in the cottages it typically is a resident living specialist (RLS). The RLS is a "functional professional," who in the old hospital buildings would have been mainly a custodial care person. In implementing the psychiatric rehabilitation approach, it became clear that a major task for the one-to-one would be to work with the patient to develop his or her overall rehabilitation goal (ORG).

The patient and the one-to-one, who has previously received psychiatric rehabilitation training, begin meeting, and are expected to start to work toward the ORG by the tenth day and complete it within a month. The staff member works with the patient, family, other clinicians, and the "significant others" to help the patient formulate and negotiate his or her goals. Another clinician, frequently the head cottage training supervisor (HCTS), is assigned to overview and supervise.

There has been an evolution in the people that patients name as the "significant others." At first, they were making traditional choices almost exclusively of the doctor and social worker. Now, they have added a broader range (i.e., the one-to-ones and the community liaisons), reflecting more accurate perceptions of helpers and less passive compliance to former hospital practices.

Greystone has a strong commitment to family support (Craig et al., 1985). This has been an asset in the development of the ORG. Patients often have a strong desire to return to live with their families, even after violent episodes and decisions that they cannot return. The exploration of the patient's situation, areas of satisfaction, and possible alternatives has been helpful as a process to assist the patient, family, and team in clarifying these complex issues.

AGENCY PROFILE (as of October, 1987)

A. Agency

Name: Greystone Park Psychiatric Hospital
Location: Greystone Park, N.J.   **Population:** 65,000
Type of Agency: State psychiatric hospital   **Primary Sources of Agency Funding:** New Jersey State Treasury (through governmental budget and appropriations processes)
Agency Size: Total number of staff: 1,450   Total number of clients: 830
   Direct care staff: 986   Administration staff: 122   Support staff: 342

B. Case Study Program/Unit

Name: Cottage Program (20 cottages)
Location: Greystone Park, New Jersey
Number of Programs in Unit: 1
Type of Program: Psychiatric rehabilitation, in transitional residence
Program Size:

Total number of staff: 134
Number of direct care only staff: 118
Number of supervisory/administrative only staff: 1
Number of support staff: 13
Mixed functions—direct care/supervisory: 0
Administrative/supervisory: 2
Number of
   Ph.D./M.D.: 5
   B.S.W./B.A.: 2
   M.S.W./M.A./M.Ed.: 4
   High school: 123

Total number of clients: 160
Male: 84   Female: 76
Average age: 30
Age range: 20–55
Av. yrs. hosp.: 6 months 3 weeks.;
   Range: 1 day–48 yrs.
Predominant diagnostic categories:
   80% schizophrenic disorders
   10% major affective disorders
   10% various organic disorders
   (over 50% have problems with substance abuse)
Staff/client ratio: 3:4

Program Description:
Average length of stay in program: 28 months (with a wide range)
Majority of clients are funded by: 100% state & county funds
Majority of program activities are conducted: in groups, but with significant one-to-one work also
Program hours of service: 24 hour, 7-day-per-week services. (staff on all 3 shifts are trained in psychiatric rehabilitation approaches)

Average Length of Time to Conduct Program Activities:
DIAGNOSIS
Initial overall rehabilitation goal: 8 sessions over 4 weeks
Functional assessment/resource assessment: 8 sessions over 4 weeks
OTHER TYPES OF DIAGNOSIS
Type: psychiatric, social, psychological
Number of sessions: 1 or 2 for each assessment
PLANNING
Developing the initial rehabilitation plan: 1 or 2 sessions (review)
Other plans if applicable: Hospital Treatment Plan*** (quarterly)

INTERVENTIONS

Conducting direct skills teaching of one skill: at least 1 per week per skill

Implementing a program for use of one skill: same as above

Linking up with one resource: one group per week

OTHER TYPES OF INTERVENTIONS

Individual therapy: the one-to-one (both day and evening shift), at least twice per week

Group therapy: at least once per week (evening shift)

***The Psychiatric Rehabilitation Plan is incorporated in the Hospital Treatment Plan (the D.O.S.P.)

Patient goals in the pilot cottages have become clearer and more specific. They are being used more effectively to drive the rest of the diagnosis, planning, and interventions. In other parts of the hospital, although staff attempts to develop and utilize patient goals, they remain less clear, not connected to the planning and interventions, and they generally receive less emphasis.

The functional assessment (FA) is begun by the patient and the one-to-one upon development of the ORGs. The state of New Jersey ten years ago developed a level of function (LOF) tool, used to specify patients' skill behaviors. Boston University modified the LOF form, making it more concrete and requiring less subjective judgments. This has been distributed to our community residences, treatment agencies, and families, asking them to specify (on a numerical scale) the level of each skill behavior required for success in their setting. The patient and the one-to-one, assisted by their significant others, delineate the current level of patient skills and match them with those required in the chosen settings. The process is facilitated and supervised by other team members. The functional assessment should be completed within a month after the ORGs. We have found that a great deal of work is required to translate the global skill areas to specific behaviors required for specific patients in specific settings.

The resource assessment (RA) is addressed by the patient and the one-to-one. Traditionally, the social worker unilaterally searched for resources required, often without much input by the patient or family. Now, the social worker assists the patient and the one-to-one, in conjunction with the family, other teammates, and the community liaisons. He or she also assists the patient in practicing the skills necessary to use and keep the required resources effectively.

Boston University also devised a Psychiatric Rehabilitation Form, which includes sections for the ORG, the FA, and the RA. This document is completed and placed in the assessment section of the patient's medical record.

PLANNING

All members of the team and the patient meet at the end of the first month to review progress with the rehabilitation diagnosis, to review the psychiatric and other assessments, and to incorporate these into a psychiatric rehabilitation plan (Anthony & Farkas, 1982). The state has standardized hospital treatment planning in a discharge-oriented service plan (DOSP). In the psychiatric rehabilitation approach, the one-to-one and the patient meet with other team members, family, and the community liaison, to review the goals and specify the skills needed and the resources required. A contract is made, specifying who will do what within which time frames. This process is incorporated into the DOSP. It has required time and repeated effort, however, for the clinicians to integrate the two. After the initial plan, a review is held every three months.

INTERVENTIONS

We have learned to focus on only a few top priority skills at a time, so as not to overstimulate or confuse the patient. Communication, emotional, and general social skills are taught and practiced. In addition, we have added some specific skill areas that specifically relate to a high percentage of the patients admitted to the hospital. These include skills of taking prescribed medications, avoiding alcohol, preventing violence, utilizing family support, and managing one's physical health. The psychiatric rehabilitation approach has provided the incentive for us to integrate our clinical programs. For example, violence programming had been a separate entity. Now it is acknowledged to be an important skill area for a number of the patients, essential to the achievement of goals, and has become a part of the rehabilitative program.

Skill teaching and practicing are done both in formal settings and in informal ones. The formal sessions are usually based on lesson plans and are held in groups. The informal ones utilize natural daily events (for example, making lunch) and provide opportunity for working with individual patients. Some of the groups are held in the cottages, some in the hospital's workshops. The teaching is done by a mix of staff, often a combination of professionals and paraprofessionals. For example, the teaching and practicing of skills of taking prescribed medications may be done and led by a team of the one-to-one, the registered nurse, and the physician. To date, we have not differentiated sharply between skill learning (teaching) and skill practicing. In groups, those patients more advanced in a skill-learning sense can practice by assisting in the teaching of less advanced patients.

The skill teaching and learning done in groups get individualized mainly by the work of the one-to-ones, in the practicing and informal teaching done in the cottages. Assignments are given patients between formal sessions, using the one-to-ones for individual instruction and feedback. The cottage environment has proven excellent for learning and practicing a broad range of personal care, social, and community living skills.

The decentralized nature of the cottage setting has proven to be a challenge in regard to the need for a high level of communication among all staff. It has been difficult to coordinate scheduling for skill teaching sessions, to know which patients in which cottages require which specific skill teaching courses when they are scheduled. We are working for better feedback from the group sessions to each individual's cottage and team.

ENVIRONMENTS

There is a wide range of environments available to the patients. In the hospital, they vary from locked wards to the open cottages, with a number of in-between areas. Some patients enjoy full privileges to attend hospital activities, community agencies, work, and visits to family. Others are restricted to closed areas, unable to leave without staff escort. Some choose their setting; others are forced to adhere to staff, community, or judicial decisions. As an example, a high percentage of the hospital's patients initially come on involuntary commitments. Somewhat unexpectedly, not all of the hospitals' patients prefer the cottages. A number seem to choose the older, traditional areas, stating that not as much work is expected of them in those settings.

The work settings available in the hospital are undergoing an exciting expansion. As we learn to adapt our programs for our clientele, and as they develop better confidence and self-esteem, their abilities and success in work settings have far exceeded our earlier predictions.

In the community, there are also a wide variety of environments available to the patients. But there are still inadequate numbers and types of housing, workshops, and work opportunities. Mental health services vary from agency to agency, but still tend toward "insight" techniques or a nonspecific "therapeutic process." The specific behaviors required in a number of the community settings still have not been clarified.

From a psychiatric rehabilitative perspective, the public mental health system in northern New Jersey is not consistent. Patients leaving the hospital go to a wide range of settings, some adhering to psychiatric rehabilitation principles, and many not. Patients going to settings using rehabilitation approaches seem to fare better, with a smoother transition. Data are being collected to analyze this.

Implementing the Psychiatric Rehabilitation Program: Barriers and Strategies

EARLY ISSUES AND EXPERIENCES

The opening of the cottages (June 1983), and the implementation of the program, required a number of steps. Planning was complicated by the fact that we knew of no other state hospital that had opened a large number of small cottages. An entire patient group had to be selected. An entire staff needed to be chosen, and the clinicians in the first cluster of eight cottages had to be trained. Psychiatric rehabilitation trainers had to be designated and trained.

Job descriptions were prepared for cottage staff that accentuated skills teaching. Increased pay was obtained. We had anticipated that staff assignments would be difficult. Previous experience had shown that any staff change produced concerns and resistance. In this case, however, many staff volunteered to work in the cottages, eliminating the need to make involuntary assignments. The new group had previously worked in all parts of the hospital, with all types of patients. Their length of employment ranged from one to thirty years.

There were many enthusiastic applicants for the positions of psychiatric rehabilitation trainers. A number came from the two experimental houses. An almost even mix of professional and paraprofessional clinicians was selected.

The training of trainers, and the initial training of clusters of staff, required a time commitment and an intensity of effort greater than any in our past experience. Each Greystone trainer received 300 hours of training. The process required an open sharing and a self-exposure with which not all of the staff were familiar.

In selecting a group of 160 patients to occupy the cottages we were forced to choose some whom we previously had considered too dysfunctional for the open setting. We did not predict the degree of positive effect the improved environment and program would have on many patients. Most adapted better than we had expected.

There were concerns also that the new team members and patients did not know each other well. Rules and routines for safe and efficient daily living were not established. Some of the basic provisions for delivery of food, medicine, mail, and other items, were not clearly set.

The uplifting environment of the cottages, however, gave a positive "family" feeling that facilitated rapid formation of good staff and patient relationships. The focus on practical skills and tasks needed for daily living enhanced active participation by most patients, better than any in the hospital's previous experiences.

Now, for example, patients shop at local supermarkets for food.

They supply and maintain their own clothing, with help as needed from staff. Most work within the hospital, and a growing number go out to work in the community.

At this point, the principles of psychiatric rehabilitation have been put into place. We still struggle with the weight of state hospital history. The hospital is emerging from a self-contained system. The skill-teaching activities still require better integration with the requirements of community environments. There is a clear plan, however, to keep the initiatives moving to this end.

ADMINISTRATIVE STRATEGIES

The experience at Greystone makes us emphasize the importance of the following: (1) A focus on client-staff negotiation in developing, dynamically revising, and achieving the goals of a plan of care; (2) a focus on the teaching and learning of skills by both staff and patients to achieve growth and change; and (3) a focus on nonelitist patterns of interaction among staff and between patients and staff.

Although these features have not historically characterized public psychiatric hospitals, they are appearing increasingly and can certainly be developed. Greystone's organization seems to combine successfully the usual array of administrative structures, a supervision that is hierarchic, an emphasis on broad participation by all, and decision making at the most appropriate local level.

A most basic consideration for any hospital considering the implementation of a psychiatric rehabilitation approach is that of determining the scope of the program. We began by setting up one cluster of five cottages. Our experience has been so positive that we not only have progressed through all of the cottages but also are adapting and extending the approach to the entire hospital. We hope that its concepts and practices, adapted for each locality, will eventually form the underpinning of the six-county mental health system.

In looking back at the successful experience at Greystone, it appears there were prerequisites that facilitated the development of the approach. While these factors would probably vary in different settings, the ones we found helpful were:

1. Participatory Decision-making Structures—Hospital staff had become accustomed to act as decision makers. Patient/staff participation in program development at local levels has been essential. The emphasis on patient and staff participation provided the impetus for the development of community meetings, small groups, family work, and the one-to-one program. The tradition of patient involvement in these approaches facilitated the implementation of

psychiatric rehabilitation by providing a supportive organizational culture. Psychiatric rehabilitation, in turn, helped to define the content of these participatory meetings. It has given the process a goal, namely, that of helping patients succeed in a chosen setting.

2. Cohesive and Consistent Clinical Leadership—The clinical leadership had maintained a commitment to the multidisciplinary team and to the clinical approach of helping patients build relevant skills. This helped prevent clinical splintering and bureaucratic inertia.

   In the cottages, for example, planning was complicated by the presence of two different groups—the "cottage team" (the paraprofessionals stationed in one house) and the "roving team" (the professional backups for ten cottages). Initially, the professionals would tend not to focus consistently on the approach, using a smattering of other concepts from their specific disciplines. With the ongoing commitment of the clinical leadership to the rehabilitative approach, the focus and consistency have improved.

3. Clear, Strong, but Flexible Clinical Culture—Greystone had developed a set of values, roles, and expectations that responded well to change. It was open to the incorporation of new roles and did not have rigid patterns of status differentiation. It was driven by client need, an emphasis on every person's participation, a focus on patient outcomes, and a pragmatic readiness to change to incorporate new and promising ideas.

4. A Skill-oriented Clinical Philosophy—Greystone's clinical philosophy had come to focus on the importance of patient skill behaviors, and on an optimism that people suffering from major mental illness could still learn and improve their skills. It did not emphasize exclusive medical or somatic approaches, or "insight therapy" types of interventions. Direct skill teaching approaches, therefore, were congruent with the philosophy.

5. Active Treatment—The expectation had been developed that all clinical staff members, regardless of credentials, would make active and positive contributions to patient care and would discuss the treatment with their teammates. We had affirmed that our task was to help patients build their skills, rather than to do "caretaking" of them.

6. Multidisciplinary Clinical Organization—Nonelitist patterns of interaction had been developed among all members of the team. Staff had positive experiences working together in "democratic" structures, so as to promote coherent, orderly, and focused work with clients. They were prepared to do the conjoint assessments, planning, and skills teaching required.

Families have shown great interest in the program. Some have received psychiatric rehabilitation awareness training and now serve as clinical volunteers.

7. Clinical Supervision—We had developed a model of clinical supervision that emphasized the importance of clinical experience as well as formal training and of open sharing and discussion with teammates. This allowed staff to be clinically supervised by other staff without due reliance on the possession of degrees and/or formal status in the organization. It promoted the culture that all staff could function as teachers of each other and of clients.

8. A Training System—We had previously established our commitments to training, to be done in a multidisciplinary setting. This set the scene for the intensive training needed to be done in psychiatric rehabilitation, for the availability of a cadre of trainable trainers, and for a training organization capable of a sustained effort over a multiyear period.

9. Administrative Support—A stable, long-term administrative commitment to the approach proved essential. The commitment of training funds, support for clinical reorganization, and commitments to utilize support staff in new ways were all needed. We needed at least three years to implement the approach in the cottages and five years to extend it throughout the hospital. Evidence is not yet available regarding the durability of the approach, even after successful implementation, if the leadership were to change.

An incentive for administrators to make this type of commitment may be found in the fiscal considerations. We found it considerably less expensive to build cottage beds than to build traditional hospital beds. Also, the costs of maintaining the cottages are significantly lower.

10. Favorable Environments—Clearly, the environment of the cottages was highly congenial to the emphasis and technology of psychiatric rehabilitation. We also found, however, that the approach can be implemented in more traditional (though not bleak) ward settings. Whatever the physical environment, it can be adapted for cooking, shopping, washing, and other activities of daily living. Also, a culture can be built that expects all members to participate in daily chores, work tasks, and treatment procedures.

The Greystone experience does not dictate a single strategy applicable to all hospitals. Administrators would certainly have to take into consideration the budgetary, political, administrative, organizational, and clinical forces unique to their own setting. It appears the approach is flexible enough for this to be done.

THE PLACE OF PSYCHIATRIC REHABILITATION
IN A STATE OR REGIONAL HOSPITAL

One barrier to the implementation of this approach was the public perception that a state hospital could not "do rehabilitation." Our experience suggests that the regional hospital can play a major role in the development and implementation of system-wide programs. It is a natural centering place, where clients come at the most troubled times, and a place where clients with the weakest skills and support systems appear. There is a core of experienced clinicians who can be trained in the approach, and who in turn can train others. Programs in the hospital should serve as a major backup, and reinforcer, of the community programs.

The focus at Greystone is more and more toward community integration. Opportunities are provided for patients to interact and perform daily activities in the community, while still receiving the intensive support of a hospital setting. We work with community agencies to clarify the range of housing and vocational options that patients say they would like to have. Finally, we provide backup when community options seem to have failed to support the person in that area.

Program Evaluation

Greystone has now been involved with psychiatric rehabilitation for four years. In the broadest sense, it has come to dominate the clinical thinking and practices of the hospital, and to increasingly influence the six-county mental health system. It has shown itself to be compatible with the previous clinical efforts of the hospital, but also has offered a significant advance in clarity and relevancy. It has proven to be flexible and adaptable to a wide range of clinical settings. It is received with enthusiasm and positive involvement by clients, families, and staff.

SPECIFIC ITEMS ACHIEVED

The original group of eight Greystone trainers has been thoroughly trained. In addition, a second group of five trainers has been prepared. This pyramidal system now gives the hospital the capacity to generate and maintain its own corps of trainers. The hospital, therefore, now has the ability to train all of the clinical staff thoroughly. This will be a powerful factor in developing and maintaining an organized and consistent system of treatment.

All members of the cottage clinical staff have now been thoroughly trained in the psychiatric rehabilitation approach. Staff throughout the remainder of the hospital are being trained as well. The experience has been a positive one. The combination of the environment and the approach has elevated former custodial workers to the role of functional professionals. Staff morale has increased. The majority of staff involved believe this constitutes an effective approach to patient care (Craig & Ross, 1987).

The psychiatric rehabilitation program has been implemented in the cottages. The program is now operating at various stages and to varying degrees, mostly affected by the dates of training of the staff in the different clusters. The implementation started slowly, and somewhat haltingly, but it has steadily picked up speed. The culture of psychiatric rehabilitation at the hospital is growing.

Research data are being collected. Results obtained in the first year and a half of operation showed that 145 patients were discharged from the cottages, with a recidivism rate of 20 percent, significantly lower than the general readmission rate of 45 percent. This needs study over a longer period of time. Our intent is to do long-term tracking, and to gain clearer and more detailed outcome data.

A staff opinion poll (Craig & Ross, 1987) showed positive correlations between psychiatric rehabilitation training and optimism regarding patients' abilities to learn needed skills. It also indicated generally positive attitudes about team membership, and about the future directions of the hospital.

ITEMS STILL TO BE ACHIEVED

The program implementation will continue to be deepened, refined, and better standardized among the different units of the hospital. We strive to utilize the ORGs more strongly to drive the rest of the treatment planning and interventions. We will improve the specifications of the behaviors needed in each community setting, in order to improve the quality of the functional assessments. We plan to strengthen our skills-teaching approaches, especially in the development of the topics and curricula for the formal sessions.

Expansion of the psychiatric rehabilitation approach in the community mental health centers is under way. A growing number of centers, at different stages of development, are now involved. This has benefits in coordinating clinical approaches throughout our multicounty region. Concerned Families and the New Jersey Alliance for the Mentally Ill are now asking for training and involvement.

Long-range evaluative research regarding the outcomes of this extensive program is needed. We are tracking patients, making more accurate assessments of readmissions, lengths of stay in the community, numbers and types of functional roles played in the community, and the quality of life that the clientele experience.

Conclusion

Our experience has been that successful implementation has required a strong commitment "at the top," and hard work by all. The benefits have outweighed the challenges and difficulties. The program is providing us with the basis for a system of care that is highly relevant and well accepted by the chronically mentally ill.

The ultimate factors that either facilitate or retard the development of any system of health care relate to the accuracy with which it connects with the problems of the afflicted population and the relevancy of the helping practices it generates. From our experience, the psychiatric rehabilitation approach is remarkably "on target."

• • •

Emerging Directions

As noted, the field of community residential services is undergoing a critical transformation as it moves toward a rehabilitation approach. The case studies illustrate the field's struggle with some important issues that programs and practitioners must confront if they are to begin achieving more rehabilitative outcomes. At the same time, there are not yet clear answers to some of these dilemmas that the field faces, and very little systematic sharing of relevant information across programs has occurred.

The most critical issues facing the field, as reflected in the case studies, are described below. These critical issues include:

1. The extent to which housing needs should be met in "residential facilities," that is, discrete residential programs, or in normal housing linked to services;
2. whether "transitions" should necessarily, or even typically, involve changing one's housing arrangement;
3. the content of a rehabilitation "mission" related to housing;
4. the role of consumer choice, preference, and involvement in housing and support arrangement; and the role of families of consumers;
5. the extent to which services and supports should be made available flexibly to *all* housing arrangements where people with psychiatric disabilities live, as contrasted with having these services available in only a small number of "residential programs";
6. the extent to which supports should be "transitional" or are required on an indefinite basis.

This final section of the chapter presents a rehabilitative approach to these issues, and describes the emerging perspective on what an ideal rehabilitation program model might be in some detail.

HOUSING AS AN INTEGRAL PART OF A COMMUNITY SUPPORT SYSTEM AND THE EMERGENCE OF "NON-FACILITY-BASED" APPROACHES

Those working in the field of residential rehabilitation have begun to rethink the concepts of residential continuum and transition and the reliance on relatively costly "facility-based" approaches serving small numbers of persons. Several alternative strategies have emerged from this process that emphasize the need to balance facility-based approaches with assistance to psychiatrically disabled persons in choosing, acquiring, and maintaining stable, decent, and affordable housing (Carling, Daniels & Ridgway, 1985b).

Rice et al. described an attempt to introduce a rehabilitation approach into the traditional program structure of a "residential continuum." Such a model involves a high level of physical movement among settings which can be dislocating and can jeopardize client functioning. Further, such a model tends to offer particular types of skills training in only one setting (e.g., Rice et al. give an example of a client needing to move physically into a group residence to learn a specific skill). There is some evidence that clients react negatively to such programmed movement. Mynks and Graham mention this dilemma in their article and add that clients prefer more choices than the limited options available in most "continua." Finally, according to both of these articles, clients seem to prefer normal housing and indefinite term supports. It can be assumed that agencies like the ones described above, which have adopted a rehabilitation mission, will tend to change in the direction of increased responsiveness to client preferences over time.

Developing housing options based on consumers' actual preferences, however, is a difficult shift for most programs in that it challenges many traditional clinical and programmatic practices. It requires new methods of data collection and needs assessment, and a fundamentally different set of beliefs about the ability of consumers to express preferences and to set goals. Finally, movement toward meeting clients' stated needs involves a willingness to prioritize long-term support to consumers in a range of housing settings, as opposed to the "transitional" models that now predominate in the field.

New approaches that will grow from a client-centered, rather than a program-centered, approach must be based on an understanding that "transitions" occur within the person, and that success can be gauged by the "fit" between a person's skills and resources, on the one hand, and the demands of his or her specific living environment, on the other. This suggests that skills should be taught in the actual location where they will be used. Mynks and Graham, as well as Craig et al., point out the difficulty of trying to identify the specific skills required for specific program environments. This problem is greatly compounded when the skills used in one setting must be transferred to the housing situation the consumer has chosen to live in on a long-term basis. A rehabilitation approach assumes that the key to successful transition is not in movement from one facility to another, but in flexibly lessening or, where needed, increasing the level of support provided across a range of living situations. Finally, these approaches emphasize providing housing as a basic support, as distinct from the service programs an individual may wish to access. Mynks and Graham stress the importance of a home being a place of rest and not a place for "programming." As a result, a greater emphasis is placed on differentiating between peoples' need for housing and their need for services. Thus, these strategies emphasize the need for a stable "home," in which the individual has access to a stable but flexible support system.

These emerging programmatic trends have drawn heavily from several significant conceptual developments in the mental health field in the last two decades: normalization (Wolfensberger, 1979); the community support systems model (Turner & TenHoor, 1978; Carling, 1984a); the growing self-help and advocacy movements among consumers and their families (Chamberlin, 1978; Hatfield, 1984; Levine, 1984a); and the psychiatric rehabilitation approach (Anthony, 1979a; Anthony, Cohen & Farkas, 1982).

COMMUNITY RESIDENTIAL REHABILITATION: MISSION AND PRINCIPLES

Community residential rehabilitation (CRR) is a complex set of interventions that is intended to change systems, programs, and people in order to assure that individuals with psychiatric disabilities have access to decent living situations that match their particular skills and resources, which aid them in realizing their own goals and promote access to the range of formal and informal supports they need to be successful.

Several characteristics set the CRR approach apart from other residential services orientations. First, rather than simply developing a series of "residential alternatives" for a set of "prototypical" clients, the community residential rehabilitation approach is individualized. It should be noted, as Rice et al. point out, that the more severely disabled the client, the more critical the need for an individualized approach. This is in stark contrast to the prevailing practice in the field to "congregate" severely disabled persons in group living programs. In the CRR approach, the articulated needs of consumers play a primary role in the selection and development of housing options. Mynks and Graham and Rice et al. both emphasize the need to base programming decisions on consumer goals. Also, meeting the needs of these consumers for stable, affordable, and decent housing is seen as an important goal in itself. As a result, specialized housing or group facilities are developed only when it can be demonstrated that provision of normal community housing, even with extensive supports to that housing, is clearly inappropriate. Finally, all services are provided in a rehabilitation approach.

CRR Mission

The psychiatric rehabilitation mission (Anthony, 1979), when applied to residential environments, becomes "to assist people with psychiatric disabilities to *succeed* in *housing* of their *choice* with the *least amount of help* from formal helping systems."

As in all rehabilitation efforts, positive expectations and hope are primary ingredients of a residential rehabilitation approach. In such programs, staff function typically as facilitators, mediators, advocates, consultants, and "helpers" rather than in traditional residential treatment roles. Staff work as a team on the basis of a rehabilitation plan that includes the individual's specific housing goal and an assessment of his or her current and needed skills and resources. Finally, in a residential rehabilitation approach, the problem of providing housing and supports for people with psychiatric disabilities is seen as a community responsibility that requires the resources of multiple agencies and groups, not just those of the mental health system or agency.

CRR Principles

Several rehabilitation principles illustrate the altered focus that the CRR mission provides.

Access and Choice: Each person has a right to choose where and with whom he or she will live. The rehabilitation approach avoids the notion of "placement" in favor of "choice." People should be able to terminate certain services if they wish to, without losing access to their housing. Finally, choice is a function of the options available—increased options must be developed to ensure meaningful choices in housing and related supports.

Consumer Involvement and Control: Closely related to consumer choice is consumer participation and influence in program goals and content. In a rehabilitation approach it is through the exercise of control over manageable environments that one learns greater self-sufficiency. Service systems that seek to expand consumer control minimize rules, external (e.g., staff) structuring, while maximizing active consumer responsibility for day-to-day problem solving and promoting mutual support, self-help, and client-operated services. The perspective of consumers is a valuable resource to mental health systems in understanding housing needs. Consumers also are potential helpers of other consumers with housing needs.

Involvement of Family Members: Family members have legitimate roles at all levels of mental health service systems. They should not be forced into the status of primary caregiver, but should be given support, information, and the resources they need. They also have a vital role in planning, program development, and evaluation. Like that of consumers, as Craig et al. noted, families' perspectives are a critical resource for service providers in planning and operating programs.

Use of Normal Environments and Roles: A key principle is the importance of natural daily rhythms, and the availability of bona fide social roles such as tenant and neighbor. Normal community housing is preferable to environments organized only for people with psychiatric disabilities. Natural support systems are most easily fostered in normal housing. In fact, many programs, including those described by Mynks and Graham, are using apartment settings for the most severely disabled clients. Agencies are now finding that they can accomplish rehabilitation outcomes in those settings rather than in traditional group-home settings. The option of living alone, with a family, or with a peer group should be primarily decided by the individual.

Skills that Are Related to Specific Housing Settings: Each housing setting demands a unique set of skills. To the extent possible, people should learn skills in the specific environments in which they will be used. This approach avoids the problem of skills transfer from "preparatory" settings, noted by Mynks and Graham and Rice et al. Similarly, people should learn the skills they need for independent or semi-independent living rather than those they need for institutional or large-group living. If environmental demands exceed abilities, flexible supports and resources should be brought to bear until the necessary skills are learned or relearned. This is preferable to moving the individual as his or her service needs change, which often promotes continued dislocation.

Availability and Responsiveness of Supports: Many people with disabilities require the availability of a well-coordinated set of supports and services, both informal and formal. Informal supports consist of peers, roommates, neighbors, families, volunteers, and other community members. Mynks and Graham stress the need for long-term peer support. Formal services that provide practical concrete support for developing and maintaining a decent living situation must also be available. Other community support services, and particularly case management, should be routinely available. Many individuals with psychiatric disabilities experience periodic crises. One of the primary goals of crisis services, and of respite care, must be to assist individuals to secure and maintain stable housing. Similarly, when a crisis or even hospitalization does occur, the person's living environment should be protected until discharge.

Flexibility and the Need for Indefinite-term Support: One hallmark of a rehabilitation approach is a commitment to flexibility at each level of intervention. Individual needs must be met flexibly, and supports are developed for specific individuals, rather than expecting people to be molded to present program goals or standardized services. Services and supports should not be time-limited but should be available indefinitely. Many programs, while acknowledging the need for longer support, in fact invest most of their staff resources into "transitional" living programs, and significantly decrease support at precisely the time when an individual's needs may be greatest (i.e., at the time of a move). Such transitions should be based on changing goals and should avoid dislocating the person. The most effective way to preserve the continuity of supportive relationships, and yet to meet a person's changing need for support, is to vary the amount of support or service provided while continuing to provide a stable living environment.

The Need for Advocacy: Efforts to assist individuals to achieve stable living situations may meet with only limited success unless they are accompanied by comparable efforts to overcome housing discrimination and community resistance, and to expand the availability of affordable housing. While both stigma and the lack of affordable housing are broad community problems, people at all levels of the service system must take leadership roles in planning and developing housing for people with psychiatric disabilities, and in advocating for change.

One emerging controversy in the field centers on the use of "preparatory" environments, and particularly psychiatric hospitals, to help consumers become "ready" for integrated community housing. It is the view of the authors that hospital settings, as can be seen from the principles described above, typically contain extraordinary barriers to a rehabilitation approach. Craig et al. discuss one program that worked to modify many hospital attitudes and practices to implement a rehabilitation approach. Typically, these barriers are found in terms of the hierarchical organizational structure of the hospital, conflict between a traditional treatment mission and a rehabilitation mission, and the primacy of the patient role, in the consciousness of both staff and patients. It is also exceedingly difficult and, in the view of many, inappropriate, to create "normal" housing on hospital grounds. Preparatory housing also falls prey to the problems of transition and dislocation described above. Finally, major skills-transfer problems may occur. According to one prominent psychiatrist, "It's like trying to teach a person to swim on a badminton court!" (Stein, 1986). Thus, although there has been no systematic research comparing residential programs in hospital and community settings, the authors believe that the long-term disadvantages to clients in trying to meet housing needs in such settings far outweigh such short-term "advantages" as accessible land, lack of community opposition, and so forth.

IMPLEMENTING A REHABILITATION APPROACH TO HOUSING

The key to implementing a rehabilitation approach to housing builds on the processes of rehabilitation assessment, planning, and intervention, (Anthony, 1980). This section reviews these processes in housing and residential services, and discusses the implications for change in current practices.

The Diagnostic or Assessment Phase

The primary goal of community residential rehabilitation is to enable persons with psychiatric disabilities to be successful in the housing they prefer. This mission calls for an approach that begins with developing an adequate understanding of the individual's values and aspirations with regard to a living situation.

The rehabilitation approach dictates (Anthony et al., 1980) that the primary consideration in the assessment process is an exploration and understanding of each individual's desires in relation to his or her living situation. Mynks and Graham and Rice et al. described two different applications of this model. The rehabilitation process begins with an exploration of the person's current living situation, for example, hospital, family home, boarding home, rooming house. The steps of the process have been systematically detailed (Farkas, Cohen & Nemec, 1988). Beginning with the client and his or her current environment, the aspects of the current living situation that the person values and does not value are discussed. Further exploration around past living situations is also undertaken. Through this process an understanding is developed about the person's individual living situation with regard to a variety of dimensions. Some factors considered in this exploration may entail choosing an urban or a rural setting, living alone or with others, and if with others, living with disabled peers, nondisabled peers, living with family or in familylike situations, or living with a small group of other persons. Another consideration may be the choice of living in a situation that provides a good deal of support, or living in a situation that provides more independence or autonomy but which may be linked to needed supports.

A variety of additional perspectives may also be brought to bear on the process of developing an understanding of the individual's goal for his or her living environment. For example, family members' perspectives may be needed, and clinical concerns may require exploration.

The first phase of the assessment process results in an understanding of whether or not the individual desires to stay in his or her current living situation for a significant period of time, or whether he or she wishes to move. Once a goal is established for the living environment the remainder of the rehabilitation process is geared toward ensuring the person's success in his or her chosen living situation.

The second step in the assessment or diagnostic phase of the rehabilitation approach is a functional assessment in relation to the person's preferred living situation (Anthony, 1980; Anthony, Cohen & Nemec, 1986; Cohen, Farkas & Cohen, 1986). An individualized functional assessment is conducted rather than simply using a standardized checklist of symptoms, negative behavior, and skills. This assessment is undertaken in relationship to either the current living situation (if the person intends to stay in that environment) or the environment that the person wants to achieve within a specific period of time.

The final aspect of the assessment process relates to the resources or supports that the individual needs in order to be successful in the chosen living situation. These can range from the support of a specific person, such as a case manager, through specific resources, such as furniture or rental subsidies. Supports also include activities that will help the person be successful, such as transportation. In a rehabilitation approach, natural supports are explored and seen as bona fide resources. Often the individual's own resources need to be augmented by formal supports.

In summary, the client and the practitioner begin the assessment process where the client *is* and develop an agreement as to the type of living situation he or she wants to attain in the future. Once the client's goal for a living situation is set, the mix of client skills and environmental supports that will help the client to be successful must be explored and specified. This part of the rehabilitation process requires the practitioner to have skills in aiding clients to identify goals, as well as skills in assessing clients' skill strengths and deficits in relation to particular environments and their demands (Anthony, Cohen &

Farkas, 1987). Finally, this assessment process requires practitioners and local systems to move beyond a few limited housing options and to begin to support consumers in all of the various housing situations in which they live. It also implies that the service delivery system be organized in a more flexible manner to meet a wide variety of needs.

Rehabilitation Planning

Rehabilitation planning flows from a comprehensive assessment and is intended to specify clear, systematic interventions (Anthony & Nemec, 1984). This process involves developing a rehabilitation plan for the living environment and implementing that plan. Mynks and Graham and Rice et al. both describe approaches to developing a rehabilitation plan.

Necessary skills are prioritized, with particular emphasis on those that will "make or break" success in the living environment. Resource needs are also prioritized. The plan specifies interventions to overcome skill deficits and support needs. The plan specifies the people and activities involved in each step of the rehabilitation process.

Rehabilitation Interventions

Rehabilitation interventions are geared toward the specific skills and supports needed to ensure success in selecting, acquiring, and maintaining the living environment. Specific strategies for skill development are outlined in Rice et al. and in Mynks and Graham. Rehabilitation interventions are the activities that help the client acquire the skills and supports he or she needs. Rehabilitation interventions are used to facilitate or enable the client's success in his or her living environment. This facilitation or enablement approach differs significantly from more common treatment roles and demands a new set of skills from the practitioner (Anthony, Cohen & Farkas, 1987).

In a rehabilitation approach clients are aided to learn new skills and to practice the skills they have that need improvement. While strengths and deficits are always individualized, they entail all of the physical, emotional, and intellectual skills that help the person to be successful in his or her living situation. Skills deficits often include problems in self-care, interpersonal problems, and daily living and consumer abilities. Persons with psychiatric disabilities also often have very low incomes, which makes acquiring decent housing difficult, and they often lack the essential materials necessary to set up housekeeping as well.

Rehabilitation interventions involve directly teaching clients, either in groups or on an individual basis, the skills they need, or giving them specific opportunities to "polish up" the skills they already have (Cohen, Danley & Nemec, 1985b). Equally important efforts must go into resource development so that clients can be assured the supports and resources they need in the residential rehabilitation process (Cohen, Anthony, Pierce & Vitalo, 1980; Goering, Farkas, Wasylenki, Lancee & Ballantyne, 1988).

Skill development is often most successful when conducted in vivo or in the actual community setting. Mynks and Graham's, as well as Craig et al.'s, program descriptions point up the limitations of being able to teach a specific set of skills only in one particular environment, thus forcing clients to move physically to learn a particular set of skills, or of teaching skills when the actual skills required in longer-term housing are not clearly known. Unfortunately, many psychosocial programs offer standardized classes that do not take into account the client's own skills deficits or his or her particular living environment. Skills learned in a "model kitchen" when cooking for ten persons in a cooking class may not be transferred to cooking for one on a hot plate, or to a less well-equipped efficiency kitchen. Similarly, other self-care or daily living skills must be learned in relation to the particular tools available in the living situation. Because of these problems, outreach services and in-home training and monitoring must become key components in residential rehabilitation.

Resource development is a critical aspect of the rehabilitation process. Residential rehabilitation occurs in a variety of living situations, and knowing the available living situations is itself a critical resource in the rehabilitation process. People may need many other resources to achieve an adequate living situation—for example, help in moving, utility deposits, household goods, subsidized housing, linkage in support services, transportation, help in finding roommates, and so forth. Many of these resources and activities have not been offered in traditional mental health programs. Mynks and Graham, for example, focused on the critical need to develop peer support. New alliances must be formed and new services developed to address these resource needs adequately.

Resource development in the area of housing often requires a reorientation of the activities of staff and a major shift in program and system resources. Many local systems have moved from simply providing one or two specialized facilities to working with clients on a broad range of housing issues, while other local programs have resisted taking on such roles. A number of successful models for resource coordination and resource development do exist and are becoming more prevalent (Anthony, Cohen, Farkas & Cohen, 1988; Farkas, 1981; Goering, Farkas, Lancee, Wasylenki & Ballantyne, 1988).

Community service coordination and resource development efforts in residential rehabilitation often entail working with non–mental health resources, for example landlords, foster families, housing authorities, and utility companies, as well as accessing non–mental health resources such as furniture. Often agencies find it initially difficult to make the transition from traditional clinical services and "residential treatment" to working on resource coordination and housing development. Many local programs have made this transition either through extensive development of apartment living options, creating a housing assistance program, or routinely dealing with housing as a part of the case management function.

Interventions in residential rehabilitation may involve teaching someone to cook, moving furniture, working with roommates to increase their success at specifying and carrying out household tasks smoothly, crisis intervention during periods of stress, getting utility companies to forgo deposits, and hundreds of other tasks large and small. For mental health or psychosocial programs to address adequately the needs of their clients they must see residential rehabilitation as one aspect of their overall mission, and must redesign their programs in light of this new approach (Anthony & Nemec, 1985). The importance and the difficulty of achieving this clarity of mission are described well by Rice et al., Mynks, and Graham, and Craig et al. This process entails developing clear policies and dealing with issues of flexibility, risk, and decentralization. This often requires changing staff's attitudes and increasing their knowledge and skills in relation to housing and community-based rehabilitation, as well as developing assessment practices, planning processes, and interventions that deal with the housing needs of all clients who wish to have assistance with improving their living situation.

The lack of true community integration of many psychiatrically disabled persons and the prevalent stigma associated with mental illness typically require agencies to have a commitment to improving the quality of life of psychiatrically disabled persons, and to a long-term-change process within the local community. Agencies must deal directly with issues of discrimination, the lack of entitlement to adequate housing, and strong community opposition. Those agencies and communities that make a strong commitment to overcoming the barriers to community integration will serve as models as residential rehabilitation matures.

CONCLUSIONS AND IMPLICATIONS FOR
MENTAL HEALTH SYSTEMS CHANGE

Implementing a rehabilitation approach to meeting housing needs has significant implications for mental health service systems, since the resources and priorities of mental health and other relevant service systems will largely determine the housing opportunities available to disabled individuals. Thus, local community and state systems need to engage in a process of diagnosis and assessment that is analogous to the rehabilitation process used with individuals. They must strive to: (1) examine their current mission in relation to people's rehabilitation needs; (2) identify consumer needs through a coordinated planning process; and (3) identify major barriers at state and local levels to meeting those needs.

Local and state systems should undertake such planning efforts in close coordination with the full range of relevant constituent groups, including consumers, their families, public housing agencies, private sector groups such as lenders, realtors, and developers, and advocacy organizations. With the strong involvement of these constituency groups, local and state systems can begin establishing a clear mission that promotes the meeting of housing needs, and can organize and target their limited resources most effectively to promote successful rehabilitation outcomes.

3
A Psychiatric Rehabilitation
Approach to Vocational Rehabilitation

KAREN S. DANLEY, PH.D.; E. SALLY ROGERS, SC.D.;
AND DEBRA B. NEVAS, B.S.

Historical and Current Perspectives

Work plays a central role in the rehabilitation of individuals with psychiatric disability, yet a person discharged from a psychiatric hospital "has a better chance of returning to the hospital than of returning to work" (Anthony, Cohen & Danley, 1988, p. 59). Early studies of rehabilitation outcomes concluded that one year after hospital discharge, no more than 30 percent of psychiatrically disabled persons were working competitively (Walker & McCourt, 1965; Anthony, 1979a). More recent studies suggest even lower rates of competitive employment (Farkas, Rogers & Thurer, 1987; Unger & Anthony, 1984). For example, Goldstrum and Manderscheid (1982) examined data on 1,471 community support program clients nationwide and reported that only 11 percent were competitively employed. Anthony and Dion (1986), in their extensive review of rehabilitation research, found a fairly consistent full-time competitive employment rate of 20–25 percent for *all* persons discharged from psychiatric hospitals. If just severely psychiatrically disabled persons are considered, the full-time competitive employment figure drops below 15 percent.

Research strongly suggests that we are not succeeding in the provision of vocational rehabilitation services to individuals with severe psychiatric disabilities. In 1979 the National Institute of Handicapped Research drew the same conclusion, stating that psychiatrically disabled clients have the least probability of success both before and after rehabilitation services. Such dismal prospects for rehabilitation engender hopelessness in both clients and providers of vocational rehabilitation services.

Harding, Brooks, Ashikaga, Strauss & Breler (1987) described one of the few studies in which more encouraging vocational outcomes were found. A 20–25-year follow-up of severely disabled, once institutionalized clients revealed that 26 percent of the cohort were competitively employed; 27 percent were elderly or retired; 33 percent were unemployed, and the remaining 14 percent were not working for other reasons.

CLIENT-RELATED PREDICTORS OF SUCCESSFUL
VOCATIONAL REHABILITATION OUTCOMES

Research suggests that variables once thought to correlate with successful vocational outcome, such as diagnosis, severity of impairment, and other demographic characteristics, are not helpful in predicting outcome for psychiatric clients (Anthony & Jansen, 1984; Cummings & Markson, 1975; Freeman & Simmons, 1963; Lorei & Gurel, 1973). Research also suggests that we cannot predict an individual's ability to perform vocationally simply on the basis of performance in nonvocational settings (Ellsworth, Foster, Childers, Arthur & Kroeker, 1968; Forsythe & Fairweather, 1961; Summers, 1981; Tessler & Manderscheid, 1982). Strauss and Carpenter (1972, 1974) concluded from their research on rehabilitation outcomes that dimensions such as work, psychiatric symptoms, social relationships, and recidivism are largely independent factors. Thus, it seems we cannot accurately predict a client's present or future vocational potential from his or her psychiatric history or present symptomatology.

PROGRAM-RELATED PREDICTORS OF SUCCESSFUL
VOCATIONAL REHABILITATION

Several authors have examined the program variables that affect vocational rehabilitation outcome. Anthony and his colleagues, for example (Anthony, Buell et al., 1972; Anthony, Cohen & Vitalo, 1978), concluded that the majority of traditional interventions such as outpatient therapy and drug maintenance did not differentially affect later hospital recidivism or employment. The authors concluded that an inpatient program must have an "extremely comprehensive and multifaceted design if it is to have an impact on community functioning" (p. 368). Erickson (1975), following a thorough review of outcome studies, concluded that an approach which emphasizes the teaching of skills and comprehensive community support services was the most likely to be effective.

Just as the relationship between traditional treatment interventions and therapeutic outcome is not well understood, there is little adequate research that examines the relation between specific rehabilitation services and vocational success (Bond & Boyer, 1988). However, there is growing evidence to suggest that various components of the psychiatric rehabilitation approach can significantly effect vocational outcome for the psychiatrically disabled (Anthony & Dion, 1986; Anthony, Danley & Howell, 1984).

The major components of an ideal vocational rehabilitation program, based upon the psychiatric rehabilitation approach, have been described and defined elsewhere (Anthony, Cohen & Danley, 1988). Critical among those components is a program mission that integrates effective vocational rehabilitation practice with core principles of the psychiatric rehabilitation approach.

THE PROGRAM MISSION

The mission of a vocational rehabilitation program establishes the direction for program development and operation. Without a stated rehabilitation mission, vocational rehabilitation programs often lose their focus and become variations of therapeutic programs, whose missions are to cure, or of custodial programs, whose missions are to help clients maintain their functioning by insulating them from stress. In contrast, the mission of a psychiatric rehabilitation program focuses on development of the skills and supports needed to function successfully in an environment of choice (Anthony, 1979a; Farkas & Anthony, chapter 1, this volume).

Effective vocational rehabilitation practice focuses on identifying and providing services that help clients attain realistic vocational goals. Vocational outcome is considered successful when the client is employed in a job that fits his or her values, abilities, and aptitudes and that is related to his or her *preferred* occupation. Clients need vocational services that help augment their strengths and develop the competencies required to perform specific occupational tasks.

Persons with severe psychiatric disabilities often require numerous and protracted vocational services because of their vocational immaturity which is a result of limited vocational experience (Ciardiello & Bingham, 1982). Vocational maturity refers to the ability of an individual to make and implement constructive vocational decisions (Super, 1964; Crites, 1969). These decisions result in an individual's success as a worker, occupation member, and employee. Vocational maturation is a developmental process that begins in childhood and continues throughout one's life. Key vocational issues must be continually addressed (see Table 3–1).

These issues first appear during adolescence, but the need to address them again may reappear throughout life, particularly if the vocational development process is delayed or disrupted by disability.

TABLE 3-1   Vocational Maturation Issues

Dimensions of Vocational Identity

	Choose	Get	Keep
Worker	Can I/Do I want to work?	How can I obtain work?	How can I continue working?
Occupation Member	Do I want to/Can I become a _____?	How can I become a _____?	How can I continue working as a _____?
Employee	Where do I want to/can I be a _____?	How can I obtain employment as a _____ at _____?	How can I continue to work as a _____ at _____?

Persons who experience the onset of psychiatric illness during childhood or adolescence may miss the opportunity to undertake important vocational development tasks. As a result, they may perceive themselves, or may be perceived by others, as vocationally immature (Ciardiello & Bingham, 1982). Evidence suggests that they may have low or vacillating vocational aspirations (Plata, 1981). Persons who become disabled later in life must often come to terms with new limitations that require a redefinition of their previous vocational identities.

Vocational rehabilitation programs for persons with psychiatric disabilities must offer the opportunity to resolve vocational maturation issues. Thus, one client may need assistance with deciding whether or not the role of worker is one he or she wants to play, while another may be certain about wanting to work but may have no information about or possess any of the marketable skills required by a specific occupation. Still another person with skills and vocational identity intact may need assistance in learning and applying coping skills or in selecting an employment environment that permits some accommodation to his or her disability.

To be effective with persons who have a psychiatric disability, traditional services of planning, placement, and follow-along must be modified to incorporate psychiatric rehabilitation research. That research indicates that the major variables impacting vocational success are skills and supports (Anthony & Jansen, 1984). There is also evidence to suggest that vocational maturity is an important factor (Ciardiello & Bingham, 1982). A mission statement for an effective psychiatric vocational rehabilitation program might be stated as follows: To improve the skills, supports, and vocational maturity for persons with psychiatric disabilities by providing planning, placement, and follow-along services so that the client can choose, get, and keep a work environment in which he or she can be satisfied and successful.

Thus, effective psychiatric vocational rehabilitation programs identify the vocational maturation needs unique to each individual and provide opportunities and interventions that develop the skills and supports each client needs to succeed in vocational environments of his or her choice.

Case Studies

The following case studies describe existing vocational rehabilitation programs that incorporate the psychiatric rehabilitation approach (Farkas & Anthony, 1989). While no program is ideal, each reflects the ingredients found in a vocational rehabilitation mission and all attempt to operationalize psychiatric rehabilitation values and principles.

The New York Hospital-Cornell Medical Center program provides exploratory vocational experiences in the community through its volunteer placement programs. This type of activity allows the client the firsthand experience in a variety of occupations needed to define occupational values. This program, through hospital-based classes, also offers the chance to develop and improve the "getting" and "keeping" skills needed for success in the worker role.

The program at the Social Center for Psychiatric Rehabilitation offers clients a variety of developmental activities in a range of vocational environments. Clients can use experience in the work units to clarify basic work values and to develop basic worker skills. The vocational counseling group offers clients the chance to gather occupational information and to improve decision-making skills. Vocational training offered in the various skill-training programs improves marketability by developing specific occupational competencies. Services are also provided to help clients choose, get, and keep specific jobs.

Laurel Hill Center places heavy emphasis on technical skill development using a wide range of occupational skill-training options provided within the agency. In addition, emphasis is placed on the need to develop and improve basic work behavior. All of this is done within the context of a psychiatric rehabilitation approach which focuses its program resources on successful vocational outcome.

The TEE program, with its emphasis on supported employment, uses methods specifically designed to help clients choose, get, and keep paid employment. Although some time is allotted for occupational exploration and the development of occupational skills and generic work competencies, the primary focus is on helping clients to succeed in a competitive job, in a work environment of their choice.

The vocational programs described operate in a variety of service agencies, including a psychiatric hospital, a psychosocial agency, a vocational rehabilitation agency, and a private, nonprofit supported work agency. All serve persons with severe psychiatric disabilities. In each program service delivery is focused on the final desired outcome of successful vocational placement.

A Psychiatric Rehabilitation Vocational Program in a Private Psychiatric Hospital: The New York Hospital-Cornell Medical Center, Westchester Division, White Plains, New York

ELISSA LANG, M.ED., C.R.C., AND JOHN RIO, M.A., C.R.C.

The New York Hospital–Cornell Medical Center, Westchester Division, is a voluntary, nonprofit, private psychiatric teaching hospital located on a large suburban campus in White Plains, N.Y. It serves 285 inpatients, 55 day-hospital patients, and several hundred outpatients of all ages.

The Therapeutic Activities Department is composed of 43 staff members from the six major activity disciplines of occupational, recreational, art, dance, and music therapies and vocational rehabilitation counseling. The department operates from a skill-based health model that focuses on what is "right" with patients rather than from a disease model that focuses on what is "wrong."

The vocational services team is administratively attached to the Therapeutic Activities Department and the Community Services Division. The ten-member hospital-wide vocational services team has "liaison" responsibilities to specific units or specialty groups and provides rehabilitation services to an average of 150 patients daily from all hospital areas.

Vocational services are conducted in one of three activity buildings as well as in central hospital buildings where a restaurant, patient library, and other facilities are housed. Volunteer placements are located in various hospital departments as well as in community settings (Lang, Richman & Trout, 1984). The development of vocational services began in 1977 in the adult day hospital (Lang, 1980). Vocational services were gradually made available to patients in other areas of the hospital through additional staff in renovated buildings. Two long-term patient units have reorganized treatment to include a rehabilitation focus, and vocational services have been available to outpatients since 1984.

AGENCY PROFILE (as of October, 1987)

A. AGENCY
Name: New York Hospital—Cornell Medical Center, Westchester Division
Location: 21 Bloomingdale Road, White Plains, N.Y. 10605
Population: 60,000
Type of Agency: Private psychiatric teaching hospital   **Primary Sources
of Agency Funding:** Private insurance; Medicare; Medicaid; private pay
Agency Size: Total number of staff: 1,100   Total number of clients: 500
Direct care staff: 900   Administration staff: 100   Support staff: 100

B. CASE STUDY PROGRAM/UNIT
Name: Vocational Services Program   **Location:** Same
Number of Programs in Unit: 1   **Type of Program:** Vocational rehab
Program Size:
Total number of staff: 10   Total number of clients: 150–200
Number of direct care only staff: 9   Male: 75   Female: 75
Number of supervisory/admin-   Average age: 25
   istrative only staff: 1   Age range: 18–80
Number of support staff: 0   Predominant diagnostic categories:
Mixed functions—direct care/super-   65% schizophrenia
   visory: (1)   20% personality disorder
Administrative/supervisory: (1)   15% bipolar disorders
Number of   **Staff/client ratio:** 1 : 15
   Ph.D./M.D.: 0
   B.S.W./B.A.: 2
   M.S.W./M.A./M.Ed.: 8
   High school: 0

Program Description:
Average length of stay in program: 6 months
Majority of clients are funded by: 49% Medicare, Medicaid   45% group
   insurance   6% private pay
Majority of program activities are conducted: 1 : 1 and groups
Program hours of service: 8:30 A.M.–8:00 P.M., Monday through Friday; 9:00
   A.M.–5:00 P.M., Saturday
Average Length of Time to Conduct Program Activities:
DIAGNOSIS
Initial overall rehabilitation goal: 2 sessions over 1 week (acute); 12 sessions
   over 4 weeks (long-term)
Functional assessment/resource assessment: 1 session (acute), 3 sessions
   (long-term)
OTHER TYPES OF DIAGNOSIS
Type: none   Number of sessions: 0
PLANNING
Developing the initial rehabilitation plan: 2 sessions
Other plans if applicable: N/A

Conducting direct skills teaching of one skill: 6 sessions over 3 weeks
Implementing a program for use of one skill: 4 sessions over 6 weeks
Linking up with one resource: 3 sessions over 2 weeks
OTHER TYPES OF INTERVENTIONS
Individual therapy: N/A   Group therapy: N/A

The Psychiatric Rehabilitation Program

The overall mission of the Vocational Services Program (VSP) is to provide persons recovering from major mental illness with *an opportunity to identify, develop, or practice the skills they will need to succeed in hospital and community environments where they learn or work and to coordinate resources to support people in these environments* (Anthony, 1980). The hospital program includes service components in Assessment and Evaluation, Job/School Skills Training, Work Adjustment and School Readiness, Career Skills Training, and Career Counseling.

Patients referred to VSP are introduced to the program by unit activity staff. They come with an understanding of the basic behavioral expectations for program participation, for example, completing a structured application form, transporting oneself to VSP, and following written, oral, or visual two-step instructions. Patients receive help in meeting the requirements by treatment in prevocational and therapeutic activities available in each hospital division program.

REHABILITATION DIAGNOSIS

The procedures for conducting a rehabilitation diagnosis begin before the initial intake interview. Each patient completes a VSP application designed to gather pertinent information from the patient's viewpoint about the direction he or she wants to take in the program. The patient, with the assistance of staff, answers questions about such topics as previous educational and work experiences, factors that influenced vocational decisions, and goal-related assets and deficits. The patient's unit activity coordinator completes a similar form that describes how he or she and unit staff view the patient's situation and needs based on functioning in division activity programs. Generally, VSP staff do not have direct contact with family members or with persons significant to the patient outside the hospital system. Information from these sources is gathered by other personnel.

The use of structured application and interview has helped to support early patient involvement in the rehabilitation process and to encourage the patient to assume as much responsibility as possible in determining his or her own successful restoration (Quinn & Richman,

1980). Patients' first exposure to VSP is designed to encourage them to make active choices about their future situations. Some patients apply to VSP with specific overall rehabilitation goals (ORG) and time frames. Patients who stay for brief periods may expect to return to work, school, or other settings immediately after discharge. For these people, the assessment process is guided by that choice.

More frequently, patients will not return to the job or school they held before admission, and the assessment process involves exploring alternative work or school environments. The written intake summary, completed within seven days of the patient's acceptance into VSP and recorded in the patient's chart, includes a functional assessment of the patient's behavioral strengths and deficits in relation to the goals.

REHABILITATION PLANNING

Although procedures call for each VSP case manager to be ultimately responsible for the rehabilitation plan of each patient, many other VSP staff contribute to the overall effectiveness of discrete rehabilitation plan components (Lang & Mattson, 1985).

A "Book of Goals" is available to all staff and is used as a reference during biweekly feedback meetings. This book records individual patient overall rehabilitation goals, skill development goals, and the progress toward each goal as evidenced by performance in groups in any area of the program. Individual group leaders monitor specific performance behaviors, and this information is shared with case managers. This information is, in turn, passed on to unit staff or unit activity coordinators who use results to help develop or evaluate discharge treatment plans.

Weekly performance review forms from each VSP group are discussed with patients to involve them in the continuing revision of overall treatment goals and discharge plans. In all cases, these results are shared with unit staff and help to implement these plans.

REHABILITATION INTERVENTIONS

Based on initial assessments, patients may be involved in one or more of the VSP intervention components. There are four major components in which a variety of interventions are grouped: CHOOSE; GET; KEEP; and ADVANCE. Each of these phases has a specific set of anticipated patient needs, typical goals, and methods used to increase skill performance.

The CHOOSE phase aims to increase patient abilities to make decisions about their educational and/or vocational futures. This phase is most helpful for people seeking to select, change, or explore careers, initial rehabilitation goals, school locations and majors, and overall plans. Patients in this phase may have been unable to identify the type of work they want to do and the scope of preparation for a job, or may have unrealistic expectations about the tasks of a job in which they express interest. The particular interventions selected are based upon the individual patient. Vocational testing may be suggested for a patient without the personal knowledge needed to choose a career. In other instances, patients may gather information through direct observation or may gain firsthand knowledge in volunteer jobs or work adjustment groups. They may also participate in groups working on vocational goals, career exploration, or vocational planning. The information patients gain about their interests, aptitudes, and values is used to make a decision about vocational direction. Throughout the process of assessing, exploring, and choosing, patients receive individual counseling from their VSP case manager.

The GET phase or second component of VSP interventions helps patients develop skills or secure the supports needed to get the job or school identified in their overall goal. It answers the question "how to get work." Patients learn how to present themselves in person or in writing in a job/school seeking skills class, locate work or school placements, as well as practice those skills with peers through videotape or hospital and community volunteer job interviews.

"Getting" skills essential in vocational goal selection are needed for patients who are planning to go to work or school or to participate in training or other treatment programs. Patients receive assistance in seeking financial aid, preparing application forms or résumés, and developing interview skills. They are expected to learn and practice the interpersonal skills they will need to use to be successful in their chosen learning or working environment.

The patient who has skill or behavioral deficits in holding on to a job or staying in school may benefit from the KEEP phase. This phase requires that people increase their awareness and ability to perform the work, school, and social behaviors they will need to succeed at their overall goal. KEEP activities include work adjustment training and school readiness interventions.

Work adjustment activities include putting out the monthly VSP newsletter; maintaining an in-hospital volunteer job at the gift shop; working as a waiter, short-order cook, or manager in the Friends Place, the patient-run restaurant; supervising Boutique operations; working in the horticulture garden; or inspecting the quality of products made in the production woodshop or jewelry shop. All patients in the KEEP phase monitor and evaluate their progress in applying needed skills.

Weekly performance reviews in each work adjustment group are conducted to give feedback in sixteen essential skill areas and other personally important skills patients have identified. The reviewer (patient and/or staff) monitors the patient's performance in the setting and rates the skill on a five-point scale that reflects the presence or absence of the specific component behavior in identified skill areas. The ratings of performance and amount of time in the activity are the bases for an incentive system that offers financial encouragement to patients in their skill practice. Revenue from the Friends Place and the sale of products from the VSP Boutique program support this incentive system.

The ADVANCE phase is a career-skills training track where actual job-related skills may be learned. This includes training in the areas of word processing, food service occupations, office management and bookkeeping, and clerical skills. A grant program with the Volunteer Department provides word-processing skills training, and plans exist for transitional employment and a community business.

REHABILITATION ENVIRONMENTS

An extensive network of hospital and community volunteer placements has been developed which provides patients with the opportunity to gather information about specific jobs, general work roles, and practice work behaviors. Since 1981, over 475 patients have been placed in hospital and 150 in community settings, and many have secured competitive employment at their volunteer sites. Within the hospital, the patient-operated restaurant offers a setting in which patients can work in various positions to increase awareness of work habits, practice them, or learn specific food service jobs. The self-supporting Friends Place is a 35-seat restaurant serving visitors, patients, families, and staff a daily lunch and dinner service. The Boutique program designs and implements a variety of products for sale. Simpler tasks involved in making boutique items are completed by prevocational and unit-based patients with the aim of early exposure to work experiences.

The overall aim of all program phases is to help patients acquire the highest level of skill possible to ensure community success. For short-term patients, this may mean an accurate diagnosis of skills and deficits as related to overall rehabilitation goals and the ability to communicate this to subsequent community rehabilitation staff. For longer-term patients, the assessment process may be followed by the practice of skills sufficient to implement goals upon discharge. The important factor is that treatment plans are initially based upon length of stay and location of intervention resources.

Implementing the Rehabilitation Program: Strategies and Barriers

Hospital psychiatric rehabilitation programs fail often because too much time is spent trying to decide *whether* rehabilitation can take place in a hospital instead of *how* it is going to take place. We agree with Dellario and Anthony (1981), who suggested that the *where* of service delivery is less important than the *what* and *how* of service delivery. Like rehabilitation for patients, program development in any setting takes time, energy, optimism, and the absolute refusal of the program leader to give up. We found that it requires unflinching belief in the significance and value of the rehabilitation process and the ongoing desire, ability, and willingness to acquire skills needed to communicate this to others.

Program development is best begun with services that are easiest and most familiar within the environment. One of the first "high profile" services developed in the adult day hospital was a complete vocational test battery. While not considered a high priority in overall program development, testing was familiar to all hospital staff and offered an opportunity to put written results in the patient chart.

Many programs begin with a few program components that they offer to a larger number of patients rather than with a full range of rehabilitation services that are offered to fewer patients. At the New York Hospital, we chose to begin by referring many inpatients to the adult day hospital for a full range of rehabilitation services. Since the day hospital served only thirty-five patients, the number of consumers who received services was small but the services received were comprehensive. When other rehabilitation counselors were hired later on to provide services to inpatients, careful attention was paid to providing the full range of service for a few patients. It appeared as though this created a demand for more services. It is our opinion that the need already existed and was more clearly identified because this greater range of services addressed the needs of all patients and not just a few. The Vocational Services Program as it exists today is a replica of the initial program which was developed in the adult day hospital in 1979 and now serves 150–200 patients. It has expanded in size but not in scope. This attention to comprehensiveness created an essential image early on which did not radically change over time. It proved to be an advantage because it helped patients and other hospital staff to learn *what* rehabilitation is.

Patients have, from the very beginning, been significantly involved in all phases and aspects of planning and decision making. Patient planning committees consisted of representatives elected and selected to represent peer concerns to staff developers. Their voice was and is real. Patient consumers are a highly valued resource to us in that they regularly share information with peers and other staff about what treatment is helpful and what is not. In the process, they also practice valuable communication, planning, and systems-negotiating skills, while participating in program development. Initially, patients helped select specific program groups, locations, and content. Today, program contribution and evaluation are a matter of course. Patient committee members, for instance, regularly assess various groups, write work performance evaluations, conduct surveys on feedback effectiveness, plan special events, share complaints, teach technical skills, manage enterprises, and attend staff meetings. We found that it was important never to ignore our consumers. Their support and understanding were the *most important factors* in making the program successful.

Rehabilitation administrators often feel alone and either insulate themselves or are insulated in the planning stages of each phase of developing a rehabilitation program. Historically, in psychiatric hospitals, proposals are often developed by rehabilitation staff only and then presented to physicians and others for approval. Chances for education and understanding at this late stage are slim as attention turns more to "practical" issues such as money and staff. Many good ideas are thus lost because those in charge do not understand what they are being asked to approve or how it fits into the total hospital picture. We found that it is essential to gather multidisciplinary support early in the development of any major program. For example, early program innovations in the day hospital involved input from all staff as well as from the unit director. The 1980 Rehabilitation Task Force, sponsored by the associate medical director, included several physicians, as well as social work, nursing, and psychology staff. The final, 100-page report was presented by the entire committee for administrative approval, and although it took one year to complete, there were no real surprises since it had already been discussed on many levels.

A colleague at a neighboring hospital began to develop rehabilitation programming at around the same time as it was developed at the New York Hospital. A particularly heated battle arose when he attempted to get approval to call consumers "clients" instead of "patients." While this change has clear symbolic importance to consumers and rehabilitation personnel alike, the battle brought intense, negative feedback from important administrative and medical staff. In our opinion, credibility and support are enhanced by negotiating about important things like staff, space, money, and program additions. The symbolic changes do take care of themselves once the program is working.

Most people spent a good deal of time trying to avoid or ignore hospital bureaucracy as much as possible. This can be a mistake since important decisions get made in established committees. Joining committees such as Medical Records, Utilization Review, and Quality Assurance served the twofold purpose of informing the administrator of what and how things were moving within the hospital and of offering opportunities for important input into system decisions. Vocational testing, evaluation, and intake reports became a required part of the patient record, in part because rehabilitation was regularly represented on the Medical Records Committee. An important article by Lang and Mattson (1985) was written with the assistant medical director of quality assurance, who became interested and involved in the program. Making time for hospital-wide involvement on existing committees provided some degree of certainty that decisions, once approved, would be systematized. Enlisting the support and expertise of other hospital departments was also helpful. Since volunteers are located throughout the hospital, volunteer administrators have valuable information about hospital and community workings and the capacity to offer patients valuable volunteer work experiences. Since they have already developed job sites and job analyses, time is saved and duplication of efforts is avoided.

Many rehabilitation administrators have viewed the development of rehabilitation in a hospital as "medicine versus rehabilitation" as though it were a battle that only one team could win. Time and energy have been spent expecting nonrehabilitation staff to know what rehabilitation was and to accept it without question. We had to be comfortable with the parallel systems of rehabilitation and medicine and to be willing to act as educators and learners at all times. Rather than being angry at physicians or others because they did not know what psychiatric rehabilitation is, energy was spent in teaching at every opportunity. Rehabilitation administrators are still "ambassadors" for the field and need to be comfortable with this role. Consistency in language and concept was critical in this area. In 1979, all third-year psychiatric residents rotated through the adult day hospital for a ten-week period with the dual goal of learning about partial treatment care and rehabilitation. This group of ten residents then returned to inpatient and outpatient areas, then without rehabilitation, for their fourth year of training. They carried their increased awareness and attitudes regarding rehabilitation with them to team meetings and treatment rounds, and helped highlight the need for these services hospital-wide. In 1985, the first fourth-year resident elected to specialize in psychiatric rehabilitation and spent six months involved in various aspects of the program.

It was important for rehabilitation personnel to learn and understand the role of the physician, who has "bottom line" responsibility for a patient's care and a need to know what is going on as well as what is the best form of care. The educational process we used for physicians was *not* aimed at preparing them to *do* rehabilitation. Rather, we sought to inform them about goals, objectives, and the operation of a psychiatric rehabilitation program to the extent that they could monitor the service, assist with timely referrals, and help patients integrate this aspect of care with their psychotherapy, family, and milieu therapies. It was also critical for physicians and others to have a complete understanding of patients' rehabilitation goals and skill assets and deficits so that they could effect relevant discharge planning (Shapiro, 1985).

During the course of our efforts from 1981 to 1987, there was a temptation to give up during "dry spells" in the development process. Program proposals may have been temporarily defeated. Recognition and support from inside the institution may have been in short supply. It did feel lonely at times, with the job too hard, too thankless, too long. Implementation did take five years of work and may take five more to be complete.

At this point, it was important to do something that revitalized interest and provided support and recognition *outside* the institution. We wrote papers, spoke at conferences, had lunch with colleagues, started an organization for rehabilitation administrators in our area, organized a conference at our hospital, went back to school, and when all else failed, went on vacation. Several articles have been published, numerous presentations given nationwide, a major conference on Volunteerism and the Psychiatrically Disabled sponsored in 1981, the program accepted by the Research and Training Center for Training in 1982, and a donation secured from a foundation to start the patient-run restaurant in 1984.

Our line staff needed education and support in all phases of their work. The psychiatric rehabilitation project in which we developed three supervisory staff as trainers began the process. When any program was developed, administrators needed to "model" on front lines not only to negotiate problems but also to represent the technology accurately. This support helped line staff learn their jobs well and provided a high standard profile for nonrehabilitation staff. Formal education within the rehabilitation department was also essential to introduce and reinforce needed learning. When the patient-run restaurant opened, the rehabilitation administrator assumed line-level responsibilities in order to model for staff and patients the way in which rehabilitation technology needed to be applied. Some line staff were uncomfortable with this role flexibility and went so far as to suggest that they (and she) would not be seen as "professionals" in the institution if someone from their unit saw them "waiting on tables."

Herein lay the greatest deterrent to rehabilitation development in an analytic setting. Psychotherapy is held as a primary value, while functioning is apparently not. Staff members seek to model the behavior of psychotherapy and they do this poorly. Meanwhile, they do not learn and practice their own profession. Most nonrehabilitation staff members are grateful for a functional focus and are willing to listen precisely *because* psychiatric rehabilitation is different from everything else that is going on. Line staff needed help to be comfortable and proud of their ability to assist patients with functional recovery so that they could represent what *they* did do well and not mimic someone else's profession. It was more difficult to organize the hospital rehabilitation department effectively with frequent staff turnover and rotation from year to year. The need for consistency required constant training, repetition, and strong reliance on the staff who remained. Lack of understanding and respect was probably the most difficult problem to solve. Tackling some hospital staff's negative views of rehabilitation was often harder than educating staff who had no previous exposure at all. In 1977, when rehabilitation first began at the New York Hospital, patients had knitting and basketball available as activities. Patients and staff alike saw these events merely as ways to keep patients busy and off the unit so nursing staff could complete paperwork. It was therefore important to encourage hospital staff not to make judgments about rehabilitation until they really knew what it was.

Implementing a rehabilitation program requires particular talents on the part of its leaders. Verbal and written communication skills are critical on many levels. Social and interpersonal skills are essential because rehabilitation is often initially judged by evaluating the person "selling" it rather than the practice itself. Extreme flexibility and the ability to move from high-level administrative negotiating, to staff supervision and education, to direct clinical care are crucial, as is a strong willingness to learn other perspectives. There should be nothing unusual about rehabilitation and psychoanalysis working side by side to help individuals recover or develop mental health. Simply because that has not been done often does not mean it presents inherent problems that are insurmountable.

Program Evaluation

Several variables have been used to measure the effect of services. In 1978, fewer than 50 percent of inpatients participated in an organized rehabilitation activity program. By 1986, nearly 100 percent received one or many rehabilitation services and began this use on admission. Daily use of vocational services alone has risen from 30 patients per day in 1980 to 150 in 1987. A significant related factor is that these patients are also all on "self-transport" which was a rarity in this locked facility prior to 1981. (Many patients used to remain on restricted status until the day of discharge.)

By 1986, 12 percent of the 150 patients in the community volunteer placement group had been hired competitively by placement site agencies. Evidence suggests that the greater number of hours in the volunteer placement, the wider range of rehabilitation services received, and a high level of practitioner skills yield the most positive results. More patients now go to work or school or continue rehabilitation part-time in the outpatient department.

On a day-to-day basis, vocational services are now routinely included in mainstream treatment and discharge planning and feedback. "Getting into vocational services" is seen by patients and staff alike as a symbol of increased health, responsibility, and involvement in recovery. Patients and nonrehabilitation staff are more verbal, more knowledgeable, more helpful, and more vigilant about evaluating program relevance and effectiveness and referring patients to vocational services. Rehabilitation staff have a greater sense of pride and purpose in their work and are not easily discouraged by minor obstacles. People complain when vocational reports are overdue in the chart.

Suggestions for program expansion and grant applications now come from senior medical staff as well as from rehabilitation administrators. Currently, the demand to expand services far exceeds the current staff capacity to fill the needs.

A formal research study is being conducted on two long-term units to "study the impact upon patients and staff of a series of planned rehabilitation changes in the milieu" (Shapiro, 1985; Munich, 1986). Since October 1984, 22 patients (14–30 years old) have participated in the study. All patients are considered to be chronically impaired and have failed to benefit from outpatient or brief inpatient care. The focus of all unit activity groups is to assist patients in acquiring skills needed for posthospital discharge and "here and now" living issues. Global assessment and ward atmosphere scales were used to evaluate outcome. Global assessment scores decreased insignificantly from November 1984 to February 1985, indicating little effect on global assessment of functioning. The comparison of scores on all ten ward atmosphere subscales revealed consistent significant improvement in all areas, meaning that patient perception of their social environment was more favorable. Patient and staff scores became more similar as time went on, suggesting a mutually agreed-upon perception of the social environment. No relationship was found between patient GAS and WAS scores, but a significant and positive relationship was found between patient GAS scores and staff WAS scores in subscales of personal problem orientation, program clarity, order and organization, and staff control. It is not yet clear whether these preliminary data suggest that higher patient functioning leads staff to see a more positive social environment or whether a more favorable environment promotes better patient functioning.

Vocational Programs in a Psychosocial Rehabilitation Setting: Social Rehab Center, Fairfax, Virginia

VERA MELLEN, M.A.

The Social Center for Psychiatric Rehabilitation (Social Rehab Center) was founded in 1963 as a free-standing, private, nonprofit corporation. Its mission is to provide comprehensive psychosocial rehabilitation services to adults with a severe and persistent psychiatric disability, helping them attain the highest possible quality of life by acquiring the skills and resources needed to live, learn, and work in the community. The agency is governed by an active volunteer board of directors that is representative of our community.

The Social Rehab Center serves a suburban area of Washington, D.C., consisting of two cities and two counties covering 414 square miles. There is a lack of low-cost housing in this area. Board and care homes do not exist. Only 17 percent of the members live in some form of supported housing, while 62 percent are living with their families at the time of referral. A majority are served by a short-term state hospital located in the community, and many are able to start attending the program while still on the inpatient service. The Social Rehab Center serves 350 to 400 different people each year; 240 at any one time. Almost half of the "members," as clients are called, are in the 18- to 30-year age range, and of these, a majority are young men.

Program Description

ENVIRONMENTS

Two programs of equal size at opposite ends of the county (Merrifield and Engleside) service between 100 and 140 members each at any one time. The buildings are large, office-type buildings in industrial or commercial areas of the county. In addition to the usual kitchen,

A. AGENCY

Name: The Social Center for Psychiatric Rehabilitation
Location: Fairfax, Va.   **Population:** 780,000
Type of Agency: Comprehensive psychosocial rehabilitation service; private, nonprofit corporation   **Primary Sources of Agency Funding:** 2 counties, state Mental Health, Dept. of Rehabilitative Services
Agency Size: Total number of staff: 35 day; 18 evening
    Total number of clients: 450   Direct care staff: 26 day; 17 evening
    Administration staff: 8   Support staff: 1 day; 1 evening

B. CASE STUDY PROGRAM/UNIT

Name: Comprehensive Psychosocial Rehabilitation
Location: 2 locations—opposite ends of Fairfax County
Number of Programs in Unit: All
Type of Program: Day support, vocational, evening & weekend recreation
Program Size:

Total number of staff: 35	Total number of clients: 350
Number of direct care only staff: 19	Male: 193 Female: 157
Number of supervisory/admin-	Average age: 33
istrative only staff: 5	Age range: 18–70
Number of support staff: 1	Av. yrs. hosp.: N/A;
Mixed functions—direct care/super-	Range: 0–27 years
visory: 7	Predominant diagnostic categories:
Administrative/supervisory: 3	70% schizophrenic disorders
Number of	28% affective disorders
Ph.D./M.D.: 1	2% other
B.S.W./B.A.: 23	**Staff/client ratio:** 1 : 15
M.S.W./M.Ed.: 6	
High school: 6	

Program Description:
Average length of stay in program: 6–9 months
Majority of clients are funded by: 95%—state & county
    mental health   5%—Dept. of Rehabilitative Services
Majority of program activities are conducted: in groups
Program hours of service: Mon., Tues., & Thurs.: 9:00 A.M. to 9:00 P.M.
    Wed.: 9:00 A.M.–5:00 P.M.   Fri.: 9:00 A.M.–11:00 P.M.
    Sat. & Sun. 1:00 P.M.–5:00 P.M.

Average Length of Time to Conduct Program Activities:
DIAGNOSIS
Initial overall rehabilitation goal: 2 sessions
Functional assessment/resource assessment: 4–5 sessions
OTHER TYPES OF DIAGNOSIS
Type: DSM III R, medical, social, vocational   Number of sessions: 1–2
PLANNING
Developing the initial rehabilitation plan: 2 sessions
Other plans if applicable: N/A

INTERVENTIONS
Conducting direct skills teaching of one skill: 4–6 weeks
Implementing a program for use of one skill: 5 weeks
Linking up with one resource: 3–6 weeks
OTHER TYPES OF INTERVENTIONS
Individual therapy: No   Job preparation group: 4–8 weeks
Group therapy: No   Job choosing group: 6 weeks

dining room, and meeting rooms, there is a vocational workshop with state-of-the-art screen printing as well as packaging and mailing equipment. The Merrifield Center also houses a Thrift Shop which trains and employs members as well as serving as a source of low-cost clothing and household goods to members and customers from the general community.

The vocational workshops at each Social Rehab Center provide a work environment within which clients can learn and practice vocational skills. Each workshop is certified by the Department of Labor as a sheltered workshop. This allows the center to pay trainees based on the amount of work they produce and also has implications for the kind of supervision provided.

The agency's comprehensive psychosocial rehabilitation program has its base in the experiential clubhouse environment (Beard, Propst & Malamud, 1982). People who have been seen as "isolated" and "different" become the members whose needs and interests drive the program, members without whom the meals would not be prepared and the newsletter would not be written. All clients start as members of a unit of the clubhouse.

In the first month, agency policy is to describe clients as in "socialization-maintenance" status in the psychosocial rehabilitation program. The purpose is for members to develop a sense of trust and membership in the program and to assess with staff whether or not they currently have the skills needed to succeed in the learning environment of the Social Rehab Center.

DIAGNOSIS

Members' initial overall rehabilitation goals are usually "to stay at the Merrifield Center for the next six months" or longer. This is a positive goal, a first step in preventing rehospitalization. Membership criteria do not include vocational feasibility, and only about 40 percent of our members are receiving vocational services at any one time.

The procedure for developing a rehabilitation diagnosis has several steps. The new member and the center director begin the diagnosis phase of the psychiatric rehabilitation approach during an intake inter-

view. Clinical, social, and vocational histories are reviewed. Exploration of interests, skills, and values is begun. Members take part in the
activities of the particular unit where they feel most comfortable and,
therefore, are most likely to experience immediate success.

A member with a vocational goal moves to a vocational setting as
soon as possible after demonstrating the skills required for success in a
chosen unit. The workshop environment serves a variety of purposes.
Two or three clients are usually in evaluation status. They are trying
out the workshop to see if they can tolerate the structure and demands
which are considerably higher than those in the general psychosocial
program. Eight to ten clients in each shop have extended sheltered
employment (ESE) status. These slots are supported by funds from the
Virginia Department of Rehabilitative Services. The ESE clients can
meet workshop requirements but are not likely to move beyond this
setting with less than a year or two of training. Almost all stay a minimum of six months. The remaining clients are receiving work adjustment training (WAT). Those funded on a purchase-of-service basis
by the Virginia Department of Rehabilitative Services usually stay
three months and can move to vocational skill training, school, transitional employment (TEP), supported employment (SE), or competitive
employment. For most clients, work adjustment training is a six- to
eight-month experience geared toward a movement to competitive
placement.

Agency policies require that clients in WAT complete a functional
assessment with their case manager. Functional assessments might list
such critical work behavior skills as arriving on time, asking questions,
getting along with co-workers, accepting supervision, accepting feedback, completing assigned tasks, initiating tasks independently, and
improving grooming. The current level of functioning in each critical
skill is based on the member's perspective and observations of the case
manager and the workshop supervisor. Each skill is defined by the
member and the case manager based on the demands of that environment. In this way they each know whether or not the member is per-
forming the skill and at what level. A description of the skill behavior
of "arriving on time" might be "number of times per week client
is seated at workbench in vocational workshop at 10:00 A.M." The
present level is three times per week and the needed level is five times
per week.

PLANNING

The planning procedures are designed to help the member identify
appropriate interventions for his or her deficits. The member and case
manager also rank defined skill deficits in terms of urgency, motiva-

tion, capability, and availability of support. It is important that the member not try to overcome all deficits at once since this task would be overwhelming. Using a priority-setting matrix also gives the member an important decision-making tool that can be used in other situations.

Agency procedure is for members in the planning phase of psychiatric rehabilitation to also attend career counseling (job choosing) classes taught by a vocational counselor. In these classes, which meet weekly for 1-1/2 hours, students learn how to explore the world of work and to identify personal values and interests. This instruction is done in a group setting with each participant developing individualized and personalized plans to move from the general role of worker to occupational member.

Vocational settings serve the planning and intervention phase of rehabilitation and are designed to provide practice, training, and support to clients at all levels of vocational maturity. In-house sheltered work, simulated work environments, classes and group discussions, placement services, transitional employment programs, supported employment, and postemployment services are provided. While a network of environments is available, each client's plan is individualized.

INTERVENTIONS

Direct skill teaching of specific work behaviors is also performed regularly by the vocational counselor in each shop. This is, of course, supplemented by supervision and teaching by workshop supervisors during production hours as the need arises. The rehabilitation staff teaches such work behaviors as asking questions or getting along with co-workers; the production staff teaches workers the job tasks, that is, to line up the cards so the printing is straight and the colors properly aligned in the screen printing process.

"Job getting" classes teach such skills as writing a résumé, identifying job sources, filling out job applications, and interviewing.

Most clients move from WAT in the workshop to a transitional employment placement. In the career counseling groups, they have explored their skills and values in relation to various vocational goals and have chosen a TEP that matches these goals. At the end of four to six months, the clients, with a reference from the employer and the assistance of the job placement specialist, will move into another TEP or into competitive employment. New federal emphasis on supported employment will change what is defined as employment. TEP will be only one of several possible vocational opportunities in community-based settings. Group or enclave placements meet the needs of some clients who perform better with the support of peers as co-workers.

Agency policy ensures that clients who demonstrate required skills in prevocational units may bypass the workshop and move directly to a TEP placement or to competitive employment. The job placement specialist at each location works individually with a client to help look for and obtain competitive employment. He or she shares information about job opportunities and, usually, goes on an interview with the clients and then provides feedback and additional training and practice as indicated. Some clients have strong feelings that they do not want to be identified to employers as taking part in a rehabilitation program. These clients also receive a high level of support but without involving the employer.

All members in vocational placements outside the building are encouraged to attend follow-along groups offered by the vocational counselor. These groups meet outside of work hours and often include a social aspect such as preparing and eating a meal together. Discussions are focused on solving problems, learning or practicing job-related skills, and sharing experiences and feelings about work. The clients' goals are either to stay on the job or to advance to a better one.

The level of postemployment support is mutually determined by the client and the counselor and can range from intensive (on-site support for the client) to occasional, on-call interventions. Evening and weekend recreation programs are also seen as an important resource for vocational clients.

CASE STUDY: AN EXAMPLE OF THE PSYCHIATRIC REHABILITATION APPROACH

The following case history illustrates the psychiatric rehabilitation approach as implemented with one typical client. Agency policy allows this client flexible access to activities based on his individual needs and at his own pace. The importance of coordinating the resources available to this client across a network of environments is emphasized and is perhaps the key to the successful outcome.

John, a 24-year-old white male, most recently diagnosed as having chronic, undifferentiated schizophrenia, has just been discharged from the state-hospital. This was his third admission, his first having occurred during his last year of high school.

A low dosage of psychotropic medication has been prescribed, but he resists taking it and frequently uses alcohol instead or in addition. He has a poor history of compliance with day treatment, group, or individual therapy. He is likely to show up without an appointment and demand service. He is articulate and his intelligence is well within the normal range.

John admits to hearing voices when feeling stressed. He has few independent living skills, feels angry and frustrated as he sees his peers finishing college, marrying, and launching careers. He fits Sheets' and others' (Pepper & Ryglewicz, 1982) description of the high-energy, high-demand young chronic adult. In terms of vocational maturity, he sees himself in the worker role, asking the question, "Can I work?" (see Table 3–1, Danley et al., chapter 3, this volume).

John starts attending the Social Rehab Center in January while still a patient at the nearby state mental hospital. He chooses to join the maintenance unit and agrees to attend five days per week. In the afternoons he will attend a medication group, adult basic education classes, and recreation activities.

His course is difficult. He has several brushes with the law precipitated by his excessive use of alcohol. He has joined an A.A. group that meets at the center, and has received support and encouragement from his friends at the center and from his parents, who are active in the local Alliance for the Mentally Ill (AMI) group.

When John demonstrates the needed level of performance of maintenance unit skill behaviors, he transfers to the vocational unit, working three hours a day, three times a week. As he succeeds in the worker role, he increases to six hours per day, five days per week. He is now in work adjustment training status. With other members of the vocational unit, he works to define the skill behaviors necessary for successful performance in the shop. A new functional assessment of John's skill strengths and deficits is developed with his case manager. He attends career counseling classes.

John quickly learns the tasks of screen printing. He enjoys the structure of the shop. He knows whether the printing is up to standards or not. If it is not, he knows why it is not and what has to be done to correct it. John enjoys seeing a weekly increase in the quantity and quality of work he performs as well as an increase in his paycheck.

When John has trouble getting to the center, he and his case manager work out a skill program that includes the major steps of setting his alarm clock across the room so he does not turn it off and go back to sleep; and showering, dressing, and having breakfast at times that allow him to be ready when the center van arrives. His reinforcement for succeeding with this program is the extra money he earns from the additional hours of work as well as the praise of his supervisors and co-workers.

After four months in work adjustment training, John turns his skill deficits into strengths. He completes the job choosing group. He understands his own interests and abilities and knows which occupations relate to them. His career plan calls for him to finish his adult basic education (GED) within the next month and to train as a word processor. His counselor knows that there are many job opportunities for reliable, skilled word processors in this community. They are well paid, and this is also important to John.

John decides he is not ready to train for a full-time job and elects to go into a transitional employment program. Because his vocational goal is to work in a clerical setting, John applies for and is hired for a mail-room job. He will work the morning shift, which allows him to ride in on the van, work until one o'clock, then walk to the center for afternoon activities such as adult basic education, money management, budgeting, and meetings with his case manager. Most important is the opportunity to visit with his friends at the center and to report to them on his progress.

John's placement in the mail room starts when the job-site supervisor meets him and goes with him on the job. The mail-room supervisor provides a standard orientation to the job. Both John and our staff member perform required tasks. Both are given employee I.D. badges, and John wears his proudly to the afternoon and weekend recreation programs as well as to work. Using a task analysis performed by the job development Specialist, the staff member is able to facilitate John's learning the new job. She helps him deal with his anxieties about being able to learn the job and getting along with his co-workers. After the third day, John and the staff member agree that he can make it on his own. The staff member agrees to be on call and to pay a site visit each week. On Monday evenings, John stays at the center to have dinner with other members who have jobs and to attend a job follow-along group afterward.

After six months, John has a sense of competency, a stable supportive living environment, and a greatly expanded community support system. On the basis of his success in WAT and TEP, the Virginia Department of Rehabilitative Services agrees to subsidize training in word processing. At different times the vocational counselor and vocational placement specialist will meet with John. He also has the support of the apartment counselor, the psychiatrist who monitors his medication every six weeks, the vocational rehabilitation counselor, his A.A. group, his family, and friends.

John completes the training and finds an entry-level job as a word processor. He has confidence in himself and in his support system. He is feeling independent because there are many people and agencies in his community support system on whom he can depend. He has progressed from patient to member of the center. He has matured vocationally as he has experienced the roles of worker, occupational member, and, finally, employee (Danley, et al., chapter 3, this volume).

Implementing the Psychiatric Rehabilitation Program: Strategies and Barriers

The preexisting culture of our agency greatly facilitated the introduction of psychiatric rehabilitation. The agency, like all psychosocial rehabilitation programs, was based on the concepts of the client as member, of member needs driving the program, and of a sense of hope. These values are highly congruent with the basic values of the psychiatric rehabilitation approach.

Striving for excellence is inherent in the policies of the agency. In-service training opportunities and active participation in professional organizations such as the International Association of Psychosocial Rehabilitation Services give staff current, relevant information. Management's ethos of constant growth and learning allows staff training in the skills of psychiatric rehabilitation to be easily introduced.

Program activities are regularly monitored and adapted to meet client needs effectively. An example of this is the Transitional Employment Program which was modeled after that developed by Fountain House (Beard, Propst & Malamud, 1982). Originally, entry-level jobs were identified as "belonging" to the agency. Suitable applicants were promised training on the job for the first several days, regular and on-call support, and a substitute worker as needed.

As with most models, this program has changed in several ways over the years. For example, when the jobs "belonged" to the agency, sometimes the client pool was simply not large enough to fill every job that became vacant. Also, as the amount of psychiatric rehabilitation goal setting, assessment, and training provided by the agency increased, it seemed more logical to match the TEP setting to the client's skills and vocational goal rather than just filling a job because it was "ours" and was vacant. Staff now maintains regular contact with a large group of possible employers but does not always replace a client who leaves. No two clients share one job; all slots, however, are part-time.

Introduction of the psychiatric rehabilitation approach was also facilitated by its relevancy to one of the special concerns of the Social Rehab Center. Several years ago the center recognized that a significant number of clients were not better off as a result of being in the program. What had emerged was what staff called a "smokers' unit," made up of people who had been in the program for several years and who had tried out activities without success. They spent their time sitting in the lounge, often chain smoking (hence the name), and rarely interacting with anyone.

It was concluded that these were people who do not learn from role models. Even when motivated, they simply do not have the skills necessary for independent living and vocational placement. Finally, it seemed that symptom reduction did not always lead to improved client skills. It was at this point that the center decided to maintain the experiential and environmental support already being provided, while supplementing it with the psychiatric rehabilitation approach.

The greatest change has occurred in direct skill teaching. In the past, the expectation was that if a supportive, clubhouse environment was provided, members would be able to assume resonsibility for functioning in that environment. Once center staff were able to identify needed skills, they realized that members in the smoker's unit simply did not have or could not use necessary skills. The "smoker's unit" was developed into the "skills unit," where members learned the basic skills needed to participate successfully in the other prevocational units.

The center was now able to assess its programs in terms of the skills clients would need to function effectively. Psychiatric rehabilitation was especially helpful in clarifying reasons for selecting or continuing multiple activities that could be pursued concurrently. Using the psychiatric rehabilitation approach, the program is now driven not by past patterns of doing things but by what the members need in order to meet specific goals in specific environments.

This new approach also provided a methodology with which to assess staff counseling skills. The ability of senior staff members to upgrade their staff's interpersonal and rehabilitation skills has led to a cohesiveness of approach that greatly strengthens the program.

Such a change required major adjustments in staff roles and took over two years to accomplish. Psychosocial rehabilitation programs are deliberately understaffed so that members are truly needed. The staff role is primarily that of facilitator and/or role model. The psychiatric rehabilitation approach puts the staff in the additional role of counselor and skill teacher and requires a unique sensitivity to the appropriateness of different roles in different activities.

Finding the time and ways of accomplishing diagnosis, planning, and interventions in a program that is understaffed, as well as group and activity oriented, has been a challenge. The psychiatric rehabilitation approach, however, has complemented the basic psychosocial rehabilitation philosophy of the agency. The clubhouse model provides the foundation of work units and environments needed to practice the skills of psychiatric rehabilitation. Clients and staff report they have a sense of direction, a "road map in their heads" which is, for both groups, empowering.

Program Evaluation

Case managers carefully document each portion of the rehabilitation process on individual client rehabilitation records. Client demographics and status changes such as rehospitalization or employment are compiled from these records and computerized. Once a year all clients who are employed are surveyed by mail or phone as part of an ongoing follow-up study. An attempt is made to survey all clients six months after discharge to determine their status.

Rehospitalization rates for clients in the program are significantly below those presented in the literature for this population. In the course of a year, fewer than 20 percent of all clients seen are rehospitalized. Those who are, are rehospitalized for shorter periods of time, partly because they have a program to return to and partly because hospital policies require a rapid return to the community.

Wages earned by clients in the sheltered workshop, either in extended sheltered employment or work adjustment training, have tripled in the past year. While the number of people placed in TEP and competitive employment has remained constant, agency records indicate that the number of successful outcomes has increased; more people are staying on jobs for longer periods of time.

A Five-Stage Vocational Rehabilitation Program: Laurel Hill Center, Eugene, Oregon

MARY ALICE BROWN, PH.D. CANDIDATE, AND DAVE BASEL, M.S.

Laurel Hill Center, a nonprofit agency located in Eugene, Oregon, assists individuals with psychiatric disabilities to function as independently as possible in the community and to lead full lives that include jobs and friends. While Laurel Hill Center operates a variety of programs, this chapter is concerned with the vocational division: the Supervised Work Experience and Employment Program (SWEEP).

Laurel Hill Center is located in a former elementary school. The previous library has been converted to a social center called Harmony House where people participate in a variety of social-recreational activities. To help individuals develop specific social skills, Harmony House also offers group discussions and social skill training groups.

In addition to social and vocational programs, Laurel Hill Center offers outreach assistance to individuals who want to live in their own apartments. Staff in the Independent Living Program help individuals assess their skills and resources, evaluate different housing options, and move in and get settled. Individuals learn basic living skills such as cooking, budgeting, shopping, or getting along with neighbors.

Program Description

ENVIRONMENTS

The vocational rehabilitation program is the primary focus of the agency. The number of spacious rooms in the building helps to create work environments that replicate those of business and industry. SWEEP offers trainees five different work environments in which to develop useful job skills. All five environments correspond to high demand areas in the labor market:

1. Electronic/Mechanical Assembly
2. Retail/Inventory
3. Word Processing/Data Entry
4. Food Service
5. Custodial

The vocational program has five progress levels; work exploration, work evaluation, work adjustment training, job search, and job placement. The rehabilitation process of diagnosis, planning, and intervention is designed to take clients through each of the five progress levels.

DIAGNOSIS, PLANNING, AND INTERVENTION AND SWEEP'S
FIVE-STEP VOCATIONAL REHABILITATION PROCESS

Counselors and other human service specialists know that goals not truly "owned" by the people who are working on them are doomed to failure. Consequently, at Laurel Hill Center, diagnosis and planning involve the participants. It's a partnership process.

Diagnosis—which involves establishing an overall rehabilitation goal in one or more areas (social, living, or working) and evaluating skills and resources in relationship to that goal—is ongoing throughout the program but emphasized primarily during intake and evaluation. At intake, which takes place prior to entrance into the vocational rehabilitation program, individuals learn about agency services and make key decisions about their future by answering two questions:

1. Are the agency's services appropriate for me?
2. What is my overall rehabilitation goal?

The intake counselor assists individuals in this early, decision-making process by helping them to identify what they like and dislike in their current situations. The result of this exploration is the establishment of overall rehabilitation goals and the identification of resources that will be needed to reach this goal. Listed and described on a Resource Assessment Chart are the people, places, and things that can assist the person in reaching his or her goal, as well as the present and needed levels of those resources.

Individuals whose overall rehabilitation goal includes "getting a job" begin the five-step vocational rehabilitation process. Diagnosis continues in level one: Work Exploration. At this stage, counselors focus on assisting trainees to articulate their reactions to their experiences as they work in the different work areas. By careful questioning, clarifying concerns, responding to comments, and answering questions, staff help trainees to identify differences among the kinds of work tasks and to express their personal preferences. For example, working in the retail store requires standing and moving around all day and involves many different gross motor tasks as well as people contact. On the other hand, working in the electronics area requires sitting for long periods and involves repetitive, small motor tasks and independent work. Identifying each person's interests, values, and aptitudes is an important outcome of work exploration. Staff have learned that the meaning of work for each person is an important factor in the rehabilitation process and varies just as people do. Making the connection between preferences, values, training area demands, and a job goal provides a clearer focus.

Diagnosis is a major component of level two: Work Evaluation. Midway through this stage, after individuals have worked in one area for approximately one month, they begin to assess their skill strengths and deficits that relate to their vocational goals.

A significant amount of time is spent defining those skills that are critical for vocational success. To further clarify these skills the counselor and trainee work together to develop a "Functional Assessment Chart." The Functional Assessment Chart lists and describes critical skills and indicates the present and needed level of those skills. For example, a functional assessment for a person desiring a data entry job might note that the job requires working at the computer for ninety minutes without taking a break, whereas the trainee is currently able to work on task for only twenty minutes.

Once the diagnosis is relatively complete, the emphasis can shift to developing a plan that outlines necessary interventions. Planning and intervention are critical aspects of level three: Work Adjustment Training. Working together, the trainee and counselor redefine the vocational goal (i.e., "getting a job by ⟨month/year⟩" to "completing training. Working together, the trainee and counselor redefine the voca-

AGENCY PROFILE (as of October, 1987)

A. AGENCY

Name: Laurel Hill Center

Location: Eugene, Oreg.　　**Population:** 106,500

Type of Agency: Psychosocial Center　　**Primary Sources of Agency Funding:** State contract for services from Vocational Rehabilitation Division; business contracts; services contract from Lane County Mental Health Division; Medicaid funding

Agency Size: Total number of staff: 27　　Total number of clients: 225
　Direct care staff: 20　　Administration staff: 4　　Support staff: 3

B. CASE STUDY PROGRAM/UNIT

Name: SWEEP　　**Location:** Same

Number of Programs in Unit: 5　　**Type of Program:** Vocational

Program Size:

Total number of staff: 17	Total number of clients: 94
Number of direct care only staff: 12	Male: 54　　Female: 40
Number of supervisory/admin- 　istrative only staff: 2	Average age: 30 Age range: 19–58
Number of support staff: 2	Av. num. hosp.: 3; Range: 0–8
Mixed functions—direct 　care/supervisory: 1	Predominant diagnostic categories: 　50% schizophrenias
Administrative/supervisory: 0	35% affective disorders*
Number of	15% other
Ph.D./M.D.: 0	**Staff/client ratio:** 1:4.5
B.S.W./B.A.: 5	*Breakdown of affective disorders
M.S.W./M.A./M.Ed.: 6	15%—bipolar
High school: 6	10%—major depression
	10%—dysthymic

Program Description:

Average length of stay in program: 8 months

Majority of clients are funded by: 90% Vocational Rehabilitation
　5% Veterans Administration　　5% Private rehabilitation organizations

Majority of program activities are conducted: Both 1:1 and groups

Program hours of service: 8:30 A.M.–10:00 P.M., Monday through Friday

Average Length of Time to Conduct Program Activities

DIAGNOSIS

Initial overall rehabilitation goal: 2–3 sessions over 2 weeks

Functional assessment/resource assessment: 3–4 sessions over 2 months

OTHER TYPES OF DIAGNOSIS

Type: N/A　　Number of sessions: N/A

PLANNING

Developing the initial rehabilitation plan: 1 session

Other plans if applicable: N/A

INTERVENTIONS
Conducting direct skills teaching of one skill: 10 sessions over 8 weeks
Implementing a program for use of one skill: 4 sessions over 8 weeks
Linking up with one resource: 2 sessions over 2 weeks
OTHER TYPES OF INTERVENTIONS
Individual therapy: N/A   Group therapy: N/A

---

tional goal (for example, "getting a job by ⟨month/year⟩" to "completing training in data entry by ⟨month/year⟩") and develop a plan for learning high-priority skills. In addition to a start date and a completion date, these plans usually call for two kinds of remediation: "skill development" and "programming." Skill development involves a structured learning situation (for example, "learning computer commands for data entry"). Programming occurs when a trainee knows how to perform a skill but, for some reason, doesn't perform it as needed. With counselor assistance, the trainee identifies the barriers that are keeping him or her from carrying out the needed skill and maps out steps for overcoming those barriers.

At Laurel Hill Center, staff work with participants on interventions both individually and in groups. Because of a 1:5 ratio of staff to participants there are frequent opportunities for training and coaching. Since individuals are rarely in the same phase of training at the same time, individualized instruction is important. For example, as a trainee is shown how to solder a joint on a specific circuit board, the trainer can break the task into smaller steps as needed. The trainee also learns how to apply the standards so that self-evaluation and correction can occur.

Group discussions are also an important part of the program. Daily group discussions focus on specific work issues: ways to improve the product, ways to improve the work environment, and individual problems on the job. Other discussion groups and workshops cover topics of common concern: communicating with supervisors and co-workers, asking for help, using community resources, identifying and participating in satisfying leisure activities.

A CASE STUDY OF THE PSYCHIATRIC REHABILITATION APPROACH

Richard, a 42-year-old white male, was diagnosed at age 34 as having paranoid schizophrenia. His illness was marked by disorganization in thinking, anxiety, fear of people, and inability to concentrate. When he was referred to SWEEP he had not worked regularly for eight years and, during this time, had experienced multiple hospitalizations.

During the intake interview Richard explained that the longest he had held a job—one of his few jobs as a laborer—was thirty days. He was receiving $188.00 a month in welfare assistance and lived with a friend. Through exploration with the intake counselor, Richard identified his overall rehabilitation goal as working in Lane County, doing physical labor, by August 1986.

During his two weeks in work exploration, Richard worked in each of the five training environments where he compared his interests and aptitudes to the demands of the particular environment. After completing all the "work samples," Richard and his counselor discussed his reactions: his likes and dislikes as well as his interests and aptitudes. From this discussion, they identified the custodial unit as Richard's preferred work environment.

During the two months of work evaluation, Richard worked four hours each day in the custodial unit. With his counselor, he identified his skill strengths and deficits and chose one priority skill deficit to work on during the evaluation period.

In work adjustment training, Richard started working longer hours and attended daily group discussions. Richard and the vocational counselor also met regularly to update and revise his functional assessment. While in work adjustment training, Richard revised his overall rehabilitation goal to "getting a job as custodian at the University of Oregon by August 1986."

Upon completion of work adjustment training, Richard was ready to begin level 4, Job Search. He met with SWEEP's job placement coordinator, who arranged for him to attend the local Private Industry Council's workshops. Each day she talked with Richard and helped him work out any problem areas. Within three weeks, Richard was interviewed and hired at a local hospital. Richard has held this job for over a year. Regular follow-up contacts with SWEEP's job placement coordinator and vocational counselor during level 5 (Placement) provide an opportunity for support and problem solving as well as time for sharing accomplishments.

Implementing Psychiatric Rehabilitation: Strategies and Barriers

In January 1978, Laurel Hill Center applied for and received a grant from the Comprehensive Employment and Training Act to develop a work program. From the beginning, the program emphasized work experiences that paralleled the "real world" so that people could prepare for and obtain competitive employment in the community. SWEEP began by accepting contracts for landscaping, car washing, and janitorial services—all jobs that allowed staff to work side-by-side with participants.

Throughout the two years when the program was funded by CETA, staff also focused their efforts on understanding the Vocational Rehabilitation Division (VRD) system—how it worked and how it could serve Laurel Hill's members. Consequently, SWEEP has been partially funded by the state of Oregon's Vocational Rehabilitation Division since 1980.

But more legislation was needed to ensure the success of individuals in the program. People who were earning money by working in SWEEP were threatened with the loss of their welfare assistance. New legislation was enacted in 1981, and the director assisted in writing the administrative rules providing an "income disregard" while individuals participated in qualified vocational rehabilitation programs.

Laurel Hill has created an organizational tradition that places a high priority on "real work" with "real pay", staff involvement in work tasks rather than just therapy, and agency activism or advocacy to support clients' ability to work. This tradition made the practical, outcome-oriented approach of psychiatric rehabilitation highly congruent with the ongoing direction of the agency.

In 1981, Laurel Hill Center was selected to participate in a "train-the-trainers" project at Boston University's Center for Psychiatric Rehabilitation. The project offered staff an opportunity to learn state-of-the-art skills and to develop skills in training other staff. Although Laurel Hill Center had always emphasized the building of skills rather then the treating of symptoms, staff expanded its own skills in functional assessment, resource assessment, programming, and the linking and modifying of resources. In addition, they learned effective ways to develop overall rehabilitation goals, plans, and curricula for skill training.

Learning about the entire psychiatric rehabilitation approach (diagnosis, planning, and intervention) helped staff understand the process but was difficult to apply. Consequently, the management team analyzed the responsibilities of all Laurel Hill's staff and compared them to the major phases of the psychiatric rehabilitation approach. As a result, all the important steps of the process were assimilated without overwhelming the staff. For example, the intake counselor focused on learning and practicing the skills related to the overall rehabilitation goal and resource assessments; the vocational counselor focused on the skills of conducting functional assessments and developing rehabilitation plans; and the vocational trainers focused on skill training and programming. This approach to teaching the skills of psychiatric rehabilitation has also helped to solve the problem of in-service training for new staff. New staff are provided with an overview of the entire psychiatric rehabilitation approach and in-depth training that relates to their specific job responsibilities.

To increase trainee involvement in decision making, SWEEP has continually expanded the range of its work options, developing work environments that reflect current demands in the labor force. SWEEP added the electronics component in 1980, the store in 1983, the word processing classroom in 1984, and the food service area in 1985. However, as the psychiatric rehabilitation approach was implemented more fully, staff realized that offering a range of options doesn't guarantee better decisions. Individuals need encouragement to try out these options, and they need a process for sorting out their experiences. The result was the development of work exploration program, the first level in SWEEP, which encourages trainees to explore many possibilities and offers a structured process for evaluating the options and making a decision.

The psychiatric rehabilitation approach also offered staff additional skills in linking individuals to existing quality resources in the community and modifying those resources if necessary. Coordinating services with other community resources has always been a high priority at Laurel Hill Center, and staff were eager to improve their skills. Staff know that these linkages create a continuum of high quality, cost-effective services within the community.

One example of improved community-service coordination is the liaison between SWEEP and the Southern Willamette Private Industry Council (PIC). While Laurel Hill Center has been developing a reputation for its ability to train dependable workers with good job skills, the Southern Willamette Private Industry Council (PIC) has been developing a reputation for the excellence of its job search program. However, in the past, SWEEP's graduates have had difficulty using the PIC's job search workshops because their staff were not trained to meet the special needs of individuals with psychiatric disabilities. With a Vocational Rehabilitation Division grant, a job placement coordinator was hired who is stationed at the PIC part-time. The counselor works with SWEEP's graduates as they participate in job search workshops, providing additional support to the individuals during a transition that can be stressful. Not only does the SWEEP job placement counselor offer a necessary link between two effective services, but he or she can also modify the workshop demands if needed.

Program Evaluation

By working closely with local businesses, Laurel Hill Center has integrated into its program many businesslike practices that foster an accountable, results-oriented system. Since SWEEP is a subcontractor with businesses, "paying jobs" must be completed on schedule. This requires the setting of tasks and timelines that are met by working in partnership with SWEEP trainees.

But trainees have other tasks and timelines as well: an overall rehabilitation goal, specific skill goals, and timelines for meeting these goals. With this dual role, the system seems to work. Research covering a three-year period (Coiner, 1987, 1986) noted that 69 percent of those individuals who completed SWEEP obtained employment. Coiner also found that many SWEEP graduates continued to progress in their employment and often moved to jobs earning significantly higher wages. As a result of SWEEP's performance in these and other areas, SWEEP received an award in the 1986 Search for Excellence in Vocational Programs competition. The national competition, sponsored by the J. M. Foundation, recognized SWEEP as one of two finalists in the work adjustment category. SWEEP was proud to accept the award as an indicator of an effective partnership—with the program participants, referral sources, families, businesses, and the community. Through SWEEP's development, it is clear that committed, enthusiastic staff applying the skills of the psychiatric rehabilitation approach can enable individuals with psychiatric disabilities to work in the community.

A Supported Work Program: Transitional Employment Enterprises, Inc., Boston, Massachusetts

KATHERINE HARRISON, LICSW, AND VIRGINIA PERELSON, M.ED.

ACCESS, now in its third year of operation, is the newest supported work program operated by Transitional Employment Enterprises, Inc. (TEE), in downtown Boston. For over twelve years, TEE, Inc., has successfully operated supported work programs for people with labor market disadvantages, that is, people labeled mentally retarded, single parents receiving public assistance, and people over the age of 54. The particular mission of the ACCESS program is to provide employment opportunities for people with psychiatric disabilities by developing the needed skills and supports in order for them to function in competitive employment with minimal yet consistently available mental health supports.

Two corporate representatives, from the ACCESS program, develop private-sector job placements and then provide support and supervision to the supported workers at the host companies. By June 30, 1987, the close of its second full year of operation, the ACCESS program serviced 157 people. At the end of the second contract year, 36 percent of the people serviced by the program entered unsubsidized, permanent employment in Boston-area companies. Some participants decided to enter a specific skills-training program, and others left the program and will return when their functioning stabilizes. The ACCESS program at TEE, Inc., is currently funded by the Massachusetts Department of Public Welfare's Employment and Training CHOICES Program. ACCESS is one of the state's three supported work programs for the psychiatrically disabled.

Program Description

In the course of developing this new program, the ACCESS staff has begun to evaluate how the principles of psychiatric rehabilitation and the elements of supported work complement each other. Although the program has not yet formally integrated the process of diagnosis, planning, and intervention, elements of the process exist in the supported work model and in the adaptations made to service people with psychiatric disabilities effectively. A decision to operationalize the principles and process of psychiatric rehabilitation formally will be made as the staff continues to receive further training and the program results continue to be evaluated.

Throughout the supported work process of intake, preemployment training, job placement, and a company's decision to hire, the ACCESS staff and participants identify, plan, and act on each participant's strengths, supports, and barriers to employment.

The ACCESS program serves people who meet the following criteria:

- a diagnosis of schizophrenia or a major affective or paranoid disorder or a persistent history of psychotic symptoms;
- an age of 21 years or older;
- unemployment or underemployment for three of the last four years;
- engagement in some form of mental health treatment;
- a major impairment in a social role.

DIAGNOSIS

Eligible applicants, referred by the local offices of the Massachusetts Rehabilitation Commission (MRC), day treatment programs, therapists, and a variety of other sources, meet for an hour-long interview with the ACCESS resource developer. The resource developer coordinates and mobilizes the support system for each of the participants from the point of initial referral and throughout job placement. Assessment, or diagnosis, begins as the applicant's work, educational, social, and psychiatric histories are explored. Applicants are asked to describe their level of functioning in past and current settings, and the resource developer pays close attention to the applicants' likes and dislikes and to their past successes and barriers to success. The levels of support and the quality of each applicant's environment are also reviewed. When describing future and current goals, the applicant's level of vocational maturity is often revealed (Danley & Rogers, in press). For example, an applicant at the "worker level" stated that although his future goal was to return to drafting, he currently wanted to learn if he could do work in a maintenance position without becoming ill. Another applicant with recent word processing training appeared to be at the "occupational level" when she stated that her current goal was to become employed as a word processor.

Applicants who orally express an interest in the program and demonstrate some needed critical skills, such as being on time for their interview, having an ability to maintain some eye contact or to describe, after explanation, expectations of the ACCESS program, are asked for written authorization to contact their treatment team. The resource developer then discusses with the therapist the applicant's current level of functioning and available supports.

The process of diagnosis continues throughout the participant's involvement in the ACCESS program. ACCESS staff members and participants regularly meet to diagnose what skills and supports are needed to pursue the individual participant's job goal. For example, if "selecting interview clothing" is a deficit, plans are made for a participant to accumulate the proper interview attire. When the ability to "interact with others" is the identified deficit, the established plan includes identifying the nature of the needed interaction and the frequency with which it needs to occur. These assessments are designed to identify what is needed to overcome the participant's barriers to employment. In the psychiatric rehabilitation model, this same process, with some refinement, is known as functional assessment.

PLANNING

Participants in the ACCESS program go through four distinct phases: Preemployment I; Readiness-to-Work Modules; Job Placement; and Roll-over—moving from TEE's payroll to the host company's payroll. During each phase of the program, participants and staff are involved in planning the necessary interventions that will enable the participants to reach their vocational goals. Planning occurs on a number of different levels. For the first eight weeks of their in-

AGENCY PROFILE (as of October, 1987)

A. AGENCY

Name: Transitional Employment Enterprises, Inc.

Location: Boston, Mass.   **Population:** 2,000,000

Type of Agency: Supported work   **Primary Sources of Agency Funding:** Department of Public Welfare; revenues generated from private sector; MRC; and RSA

Agency Size: Total number of staff: 47   Total number of clients: 140
Direct care staff: 25   Administration staff: 11   Support staff: 11

B. CASE STUDY PROGRAM/UNIT

Name: The ACCESS Program   **Location:** Boston

Number of Programs in Unit: 1

Type of Program: Supported work for the psychiatrically disabled

Average length of illness: 11 years; range of years: 1–20+

Program Size:

Total number of staff: 6½

Number of direct care only staff: 4

Number of supervisory/admin-
istrative only staff: 1

Number of support staff: ½

Mixed functions—direct
care/supervisory: 1

Administrative/supervisory: 0

Number of
Ph.D./M.D.: 1 (consultant)
M.S.W./M.A./M.Ed.: 5
B.S.W./B.A.: 1
High school: 1

Total number of clients: 42

Male: 25   Female: 17

Average age: 35

Age range: 22–52

Av. yrs. hosp.: 4; Range: 0–10+

43% schizophrenia

16% bipolar illness

10% depression

Staff/client ratio: 1:8

Program Description:

Average length of stay in program: 8 months

Majority of clients are funded by: 41% SSI   17% SSDI
17% Public Welfare

Majority of program activities are conducted: in groups for 2–5 months; and individually for 4–6 months

Program hours of service: 9:00 A.M.–5:00 P.M., Monday–Friday

Average Length of Time to Conduct Program Activities:

DIAGNOSIS

Initial overall rehabilitation goal: 1 one-hour interview; (consultation with treatment staff, 1 hour)

Functional assessment/resource assessment: Ongoing

OTHER TYPES OF DIAGNOSIS

Type: N/A   Number of sessions: N/A

PLANNING

Developing the initial rehabilitation plan: 7 weeks of 4 days/week, 3 hours/day of vocational planning

Other plans if applicable: N/A

Conducting direct skills teaching of one skill: Open-ended period during 8
  weeks of classroom work on developing "world of work" skills
Implementing a program for use of one skill: N/A
Linking up with one resource: As needed
OTHER TYPES OF INTERVENTIONS
Individual therapy: Developing "world of work" skills while on the job; par-
  ticipant meets with staff, 2 times each week to discuss adjustment to work
  world. Twice a week supervision continues for 4–6 months. Weekly meet-
  ings then occur for 4–6 weeks: duration is 15–45 minutes.
Group therapy: N/A

---

volvement in the program, participants and their supervisor meet for
weekly individual evaluations. Evaluations then occur on a biweekly
basis throughout the remainder of the program. On average, participants are in the program for eight months. During each evaluation,
the participant's progress is reviewed and plans are made to address
specific skill or resource needs. For example, a participant may be
having difficulty with punctuality. In reviewing the reasons for this
problem, the participant and staff member may decide that purchase
of an alarm clock would help to resolve this problem. Plans are then
made regarding where and when the clock can be purchased and who
will provide the resources.

On another level, planning goes on in weekly and monthly staff
meetings and in monthly meetings with staff and the program's consulting psychiatrist. During each of these meetings, staff discuss the
barriers that are affecting the individual participant's achievement of
the identified vocational goals. Plans are made for interventions that
will address and, it is hoped, resolve these barriers. Staff members are
assigned to meet with participants to review the proposed interventions and report back about the results of their meetings with the participants and the interventions that have been put into practice. For
example, one participant, with excellent secretarial skills, had several
unsuccessful interviews for potential job placements. Based on the
feedback from the participant and the company interviewers, the identified barrier was the participant's very heavy breathing and the occasional distortions of her mouth during an interview. The participant
was able to identify that both behaviors occur when she is under
stress. The plan then created and successfully put into effect was the
direct skills teaching of relaxation techniques that the participant could
use before and during an interview.

INTERVENTIONS

Preemployment classes are scheduled in eight-week cycles. The classes meet four days a week for three hours a day. The classes vary in size from seven to twelve participants. The curriculum for the preemployment training is organized around "Choosing a Job" and "Getting a Job." The ACCESS trainer has the primary responsibility for the skill development of the participants in this eight-week cycle. Participants who complete the first phase of the training graduate to the "Readiness-to-Work" modules. The modules meet three afternoons a week. Participants attend the modules until they successfully interview for a supported work/job placement. The modules curriculum focuses on the critical skills needed for "Keeping a Job." The resource developer is responsible for this phase of the skill development training (Anthony, Danley & Howell, 1984).

"Choosing a Job" focuses on exploring values related to working, assessing traits as a worker, and understanding job interest areas. For some individuals, the amount of money earned in a job is most important, and for others the desire to be productive is key. The preemployment trainer and individual participants also identify the level of skills and behaviors that can detract or enhance a participant's ability to become employed. For example, one participant was consistently late for the start of class and the return from break. The trainer and participant planned that "prompt return from the break" would be the first skill to be mastered, followed by "punctuality" for the start of the class. For other participants, what is most needed is the development of work-appropriate interpersonal skills. Interventions range from conducting class social outings to identifying the frequency with which a participant will say good morning and good-bye to his classmates. By the end of this part of the curriculum, participants have identified five of their most important values related to employment. Together with the trainer, they have also decided on the skills they need to develop with regard to work. And, through exercises in *The Occupational Outlook Handbook* and *The Classification of Jobs* handbook, participants have developed particular job interests, goals, and an understanding of the skills needed to achieve these goals.

The curriculum then centers on "Getting a Job." Skill-building training focuses on continued development of interpersonal relationships, résumé development, application completion, and interview techniques. Through self-assessment exercises, class discussion, individual evaluations with the trainer, readings, and role plays, participants finish with a completed résumé, tools to complete applications, and interview skills training. Historically, participants experience a higher degree of difficulty with the second phase of the curriculum. The needed critical skill is the ability to identify verbally and in writing employment-related accomplishments and competencies while simultaneously acknowledging deficits related to employment. Support from the class, the trainer, and the person's environment is crucial during this process.

Graduation from the first phase of preemployment to the "Readiness to Work" modules depends upon the participant's ability to meet expectations that have been reiterated throughout the curriculum. Specifically, participants need to maintain a 90 percent attendance rate, complete assignments, and demonstrate a consistent ability to interact, at a predetermined frequency, with the trainer and with the group and the trainer. The modules continue to build the skills and supports needed for "Keeping a Job." Role plays are used to identify and practice the skills needed for interviews and for interactions with supervisors and co-workers. To continue motivating the participants and developing needed "world of work" skills, the curriculum also includes such activities as visits to places of work, social outings, and class exercises involving understanding personnel policies, completing tax forms, job networking, and maintaining needed supports.

Participants in the Readiness to Work modules are also interviewing for job placements developed by the ACCESS corporate representatives. By meeting with participants and reviewing each participant's level of skill, job goals, and values with the trainer and the resource developer, the representatives research and solicit private-sector employers for positions that match the participant's job goals as closely as possible. For the first four to six months of job placement, participants are TEE employees. The corporate representative who developed the job placement meets with the participant a minimum of two times a week. During these meetings, the participant and the representative continue the supported work program's version of diagnosis, planning, and intervention. For example, assessments are made regarding the skills the participant needs to develop while employed in this particular setting. Interventions range from assisting with the opening of a checking account to establishing incremental production goals. Work also focuses on the supports the participant will have when it is time to "roll over" from TEE to the host company's payroll. Follow-up services after participants graduate from ACCESS to unsubsidized competitive employment include advocacy, career counseling, job networking, and support. Jobs filled by graduates of the ACCESS program include data entry operators, administrative aides, dialysis patient assistants, dietary aides, electronic assembly, maintenance, and laboratory assistant positions. Job sites range from large insurance companies to midsize community hospitals to family-owned retail businesses.

Implementing the Psychiatric Rehabilitation Program: Strategies and Barriers

The commitment to the ACCESS program by TEE, Inc., the Alliance for the Mentally Ill, the Department of Public Welfare, and the Center for Psychiatric Rehabilitation enabled the program to overcome the barriers faced during the first year of operation. The start-up dilemmas and problems that were encountered ranged from figuring out the optimal length of preemployment training, to uncertainty around effective marketing strategies, to fears and stereotypes about people with mental illness.

Fears and worries about the ability of the psychiatrically disabled to enter competitive employment surfaced during the initial recruitment for the ACCESS program. From the outset, the program explicitly identified itself as focused on work, not treatment. With this emphasis, the staff then worked with mental health and rehabilitation agencies to identify prospective participants and their needs. Research conducted during the initial study on the viability of using the supported work model for the psychiatrically disabled clearly showed that the need existed for vocational programs. In 1984, there were approximately 6,200 clients in Massachusetts community residential and day treatment programs, but only 460 clients in vocational programs.

Service providers initially cautioned that potential applicants would have difficulty with punctuality, negotiating public transportation, and the high-stress environments found in the corporate world. Another unspoken concern by the mental health community was whether or not TEE, a supported work employment company, could effectively work with people with psychiatric disabilities.

It was clear that the ACCESS program needed to address these concerns. Reluctance by the rehabilitation and mental health communities to support the project would have drastic consequences. Few people would be referred, and those who applied to the program might not receive wholehearted support from their treatment teams. One step taken to work with the community has been a time-honored TEE, Inc., recruitment strategy. The ACCESS resource developer and director make presentations at staff meetings of potential referral organizations. During the presentations, staff can learn about the support and services provided by ACCESS and, more importantly, can ask questions about the program. The ACCESS staff also works collaboratively with the treatment team of each participant. During the initial intake interview, participants are asked to give written authorization so that, from intake on, the ACCESS staff can discuss the participants' progress with their mental health and rehabilitation supports.

Periodic mailings, annual open houses at TEE, presentations, active collaboration, and the program's success have effectively lessened the treatment community's initial reluctance. Now, referrals are made daily, and the referral sources have become strong advocates for applicants who are interested in the ACCESS program.

While ACCESS was being marketed to the community, ACCESS and TEE staff struggled for the first six months of the project to establish effective marketing strategies for the corporate community. There was uncertainty about the kinds of jobs and environments in which people with psychiatric disabilities could become successfully employed. Issues of disclosure surfaced. There were also fears about this population's ability to be consistently punctual and dependable and about how their performance, or lack thereof, would affect TEE's relationships with employers.

Effective marketing strategies have developed through trial and error, increased interaction with the ACCESS participants, and staff training around identifying participants' current skill level and functioning. By using direct skills teaching and the principles of functional assessment, the ACCESS staff are better able to identify participants' skill levels, resource needs, and job goals. By the end of the program's second full year of operation, over thirty-five Boston-area companies had worked with or are continuing to work with the ACCESS program. At the end of the first quarter of the third fiscal year, the weekly number of supported workers in job placements had increased to sixteen. And twelve participants of the program had already graduated from supported work to permanent employment in twelve private sector companies.

The overall marketing strategy has been to identify companies and positions that match as closely as possible the skills and job goals of the ACCESS participants. The marketer introduces the company to all of TEE's employment services and to a particular individual's qualifications for the open position. Interested employers learn that the ACCESS project provides service to people who have histories of psychiatric disabilities but who are now ready and motivated to work. Employers are then encouraged to discuss with each participant the nature of his or her disability. Experience has shown that this initial acknowledgment of a disability allows employers and participants to concentrate on a participant's skills and not on explanations for work history gaps. Participants have also expressed their relief in not having to avoid or "lie" about their experiences. As a result, ACCESS participants and graduates work in large and midsize insurance companies, an environmental testing laboratory, a community hospital, and a "for-profit" dialysis center. Full- and part-time jobs are filled by ACCESS supported workers. Jobs include word processors, dietary aides, electronic assemblers, and file clerks.

Program Evaluation

By the end of September 1987, the end of the first quarter of the ACCESS program's third year of operation, the following performance statistics can be given. Of the 156 people who have terminated the program during two and one-quarter years of operation, 54 completed the program and obtained competitive employment. One hundred two others left the program: 29 were referred for further training and education; 16 were terminated negatively for reasons such as walking off of the job site; 46 left the program due to reasons related to their psychiatric illness; and 11 left for reasons ranging from choosing a volunteer position to day-care problems. These data do not include the results of the three-month pilot project in the spring of 1985.

In June 1987, follow-up data were gathered on a nonrandom but representative sample of 28 of the 40 people who had, at that point, graduated into competitive employment. Of these 28, 24 remained employed at the time of data collection. The length of employment at follow-up ranged from one to twenty-one months. Of the four who were not employed, one stopped taking medication and was hospitalized; another left the job and is now in a psychosocial rehabilitation program; the third returned to the ACCESS program and entered another supported work placement. The fourth person, after one promotion and two job changes, stopped working and soon after had to be hospitalized. Half of the graduates were working in full-time positions with salaries ranging from $10,000 to $15,000 per year.

In reviewing the first two and one-quarter years of full operation, the ACCESS program can point to a number of achievements. The resource developer receives daily applicant referrals from a wide range of service providers. Marketing and job development efforts continuously yield a wide range of employment opportunities. The training and skill building curricula have been formalized, and the current structure of seven weeks of training followed by the "Readiness to Work" modules appears to have the right mix of structure and flexibility.

With this stability in program operations, the staff can now address new questions and concerns. Research grants have been applied for in order to collect and analyze data regarding the long-term effects of competitive employment for people with psychiatric disabilities. Evaluation of current program supports for graduates will address the kinds of supports needed by participants who complete the program. Time, research, discussion, and participants' needs and skills will direct the program's development of new strategies and directions as the ACCESS program, at TEE, Inc., seeks to improve the vocational opportunities available for people with psychiatric disabilities.

• • •

Emerging Directions

The vocational programs described operate within a traditional psychiatric hospital, a psychosocial agency, a vocational rehabilitation program, and a private, nonprofit employment agency. However, as different as these programs are in setting and operation, certain conclusions emerge from their common attempts to incorporate a psychiatric rehabilitation approach.

The first conclusion is that client involvement in vocational rehabilitation is both desirable and possible. All of the programs mentioned here strongly emphasize the need to anchor the rehabilitation process in the vocational goals of the client. This emphasis on the clients' vocational goals is the motivational cornerstone of the vocational rehabilitation effort and deserves the considerable investment of time and resources it requires.

The second conclusion is that vocational rehabilitation programs for persons with psychiatric disabilities must be sensitive to the wide range of vocational development needs of the client population. Because each client is unique in his or her previous vocational experience, care must be taken to develop a clear picture of vocational strengths and deficits. Program components must be derived from a comprehensive understanding of the person from a vocational, rather than a clinical, perspective. Clinical issues are relevant in that they must be understood as one aspect of the vocational rehabilitation effort.

Third, vocational rehabilitation of persons with psychiatric disabilities can be improved by incorporating a systematic psychiatric rehabilitation approach. Each of these vocational programs had an established program model before integrating the psychiatric rehabilitation approach, but all program directors found it necessary to make changes in their prevailing practice. Each program found it necessary to adapt the psychiatric rehabilitation approach to their unique setting and program. Once an effective integration of methodologies was achieved, program directors felt that there was an increase in both client satisfaction and success.

A fourth conclusion is that vocational rehabilitation of persons with psychiatric disabilities is a lengthy process, requiring a cooperative and comprehensive approach by rehabilitation, mental health, and other community resource agencies. Meeting the vocational rehabilitation needs of a person with severe psychiatric disability requires extensive resources from a variety of sources. Cooperation is required between the agency that is managing the vocational rehabilitation effort and those agencies and employers who provide the support and opportunities needed for vocational development. Effective communication and consensus of purpose between all players in the rehabilitation process are the keys to vocational success for the client.

Finally, incorporating the psychiatric rehabilitation approach into existing vocational rehabilitation programs requires patience, persistence, and skill. Change, whether in individuals or agencies, increases stress and anxiety. A thorough and complete program change requires a substantial period of time for the integration of new interventions and the utilization of new skills (Rogers et al., 1986).

SOME OPERATIONAL PRINCIPLES OF EFFECTIVE VOCATIONAL REHABILITATION

While different in setting and operation, the programs described earlier share some operational principles. These principles can be generalized to effective vocational rehabilitation practice for persons with severe psychiatric disabilities in any setting. When these principles are fully operative, clients can accomplish the vocational maturation tasks that are unique to their vocational development needs.

Principle I. Effective vocational programs provide clients with the experience and assistance they need to make vocational decisions.

Important sources of motivation are the option and the ability to make informed choices. Clients who are "placed" in work activities or vocational training programs without an opportunity to clarify values and evaluate alternatives are resistant and reluctant. Vocational rehabilitation practitioners need to involve clients in ways that fully incorporate the client's value system (Anthony, Cohen & Danley, 1988). Such involvement helps to concretize key factors which, in turn, help the counselor and the client determine how satisfied the client will be with the options being considered.

Principle II. Effective vocational rehabilitation programs assist clients in developing the skills and supports they need to be satisfied and successful as *workers*.

Many persons with severe disabilities are unsure of their desire and capacity to work. Long absences from the working world, fueled by the disincentives of the Social Security system, leave them dubious and frightened, as well as unprepared to meet the demands associated with being workers of any kind.

Effective vocational rehabilitation programs offer their participants guided opportunities to test out and develop basic work skills. Good programs help clients clarify work values and make careful decisions about the issue of risks associated with employment versus the guaranteed income of disability payments. For many clients, until greater confidence and competence are assured, the decision to work for pay and to risk losing benefits may be premature and ill-advised. Programs that offer volunteer work or transitional employment (TE) provide an opportunity for clients to test out the worker role without a long-term commitment to employment.

Principle III. Effective vocational programs assist clients in developing the specific credentials and technical skills of a preferred occupation.

Persons with psychiatric disabilities often have the capacity to learn and perform complex and difficult vocational tasks. Because problems with basic work behaviors often interfere in the application of their technical skills, their development is neglected in the vocational rehabilitation process. However, it is technical competence that is marketable in the workplace. Without specific technical abilities, persons with psychiatric disabilities are often relegated to low-paying, dead-end jobs. While there are limitations imposed by some psychiatric disabilities, many clients can work in technically complex occupations. Without technical proficiency, low-level jobs are assured; with technical proficiency, the client has greater degrees of freedom. The more highly skilled client still has an edge in obtaining employment that is meaningful and satisfying. Programs that serve developmentally disabled clients focus on developing their technical proficiency so that the skill deficits related to their disability are more tolerable. This may also be the case for persons who suffer from psychiatric disabilities.

Principle IV: Effective vocational programs assist clients in developing the skills and supports needed to be successful as *employees.*

Although different work settings have many required work behaviors in common, every environment places unique demands on an employee. Effective vocational rehabilitation practitioners assist clients in identifying, developing, and using the unique skills and supports that will ensure employment success.

Since both the person and the work environment are likely to change over time, the most effective rehabilitation programs assure that such assistance is made available to clients on an ongoing basis. The supported employment model, with the emphasis on "ongoing support in integrated work settings," offers one modality for helping persons with psychiatric disabilities maintain successful employment (Anthony & Blanch, 1987). This model operates on the premise that successful employment is possible if the client has a support system that helps compensate for the limitations associated with the psychiatric disability.

Principle V. Effective vocational programs have access to a network of environments.

A vocational rehabilitation program is comprehensive to the extent that it has access to a range of settings needed for the participants to develop and enhance their vocational maturity and marketability. Essentially, clients need environments that enable them to develop the attitudes, knowledge, and skills required to perform adequately as a worker, as a member of an occupation, and as an employee. For example, to develop as effective workers, program participants may need access to environments that help them choose whether the worker role is desirable and develop the generic competencies required of a worker, that is, the skills of getting along with others and being dependable.

Participants who can demonstrate both confidence and competence as workers may need access to environments for the development of the attitudes, knowledge, and skills required to choose, get, and keep a particular occupational role. For example, a person who wishes to become a computer operator should have the opportunity to gain the necessary firsthand knowledge of what that activity feels like. Once a clear vocational objective is established, a program participant should have access to the training environments in which to develop the knowledge, skills, and credentials required to perform the functions of their chosen occupation. Clients who demonstrate both worker and occupational skills need access to a range of employment settings commensurate with their values and competencies.

An ideal vocational rehabilitation program has access to a sufficient variety of work, educational, and training settings so that the client does not have to "fit in" or be placed in a setting simply because it is available. The types of settings available should differ from network to network depending on the interests and needs of the clients served. The network of vocational environments should also be representative of the variety of jobs and training institutions available in the particular geographic area. Therefore, it is not possible to recommend a standard continuum of vocational environments; rather, there is a need for a repertoire of settings that expands and changes with participant needs and job market fluctuations.

Principle VI. Effective vocational rehabilitation programs practice psychiatric rehabilitation, planning, and intervention strategies in relation to *each* vocational rehabilitation environment.

In the course of pursuing a long-range vocational goal, the vocational rehabilitation client may need to interact with one or more intermediate environments. For example, a client wishing to become employed as an electronics assembly technician may need to attend school and/or participate in an apprenticeship. In addition, the client may need to do volunteer work to test out the career choice or work at a part-time job to develop a positive work history and to improve dependability.

The effective vocational rehabilitation practitioner carefully applies psychiatric rehabilitation skills to help the client to select each needed environment, assess the client's needs in relation to the environmental demands, and plan for and/or provide for interventions that remedy skill and support deficits. Because many intermediate placements over several years may be needed for the client to achieve the long-range vocational goal, the vocational rehabilitation practitioner may recycle the psychiatric rehabilitation process of diagnosis, planning, and intervention several times.

SUMMARY

During the past ten years, an approach to vocational rehabilitation which incorporates psychiatric rehabilitation principles has been developed and implemented in a variety of settings. A base of knowledge has emerged from the experience of these settings. Future efforts to improve vocational outcome for persons with severe psychiatric disability will be successful to the degree effective program principles can be put into operation.

To summarize, an effective vocational rehabilitation program for the psychiatrically disabled includes: (1) a *mission* that focuses program resources on improving vocational functioning to the level required for employment in a preferred occupation; and (2) a *program* that: (a) offers opportunities for developing vocational maturity and marketability, (b) uses a psychiatric rehabilitation approach that involves clients in diagnosis, planning, and interventions, and (c) provides a network of vocational environments.

Historically, work has played an important, though varied, role in mental health treatment. Currently, there is a hopeful trend toward helping persons with psychiatric disabilities to participate as fully as possible in meaningful and gainful employment. Effective practitioners and programs are the key to this initiative. Fifty years ago, it was unusual to see a person with a severe physical handicap working in a competitive job. Today, due to major advances in medical and rehabilitation technology and attitudinal changes in society, there are more employment opportunities for persons with physical handicaps. A similar shift is occurring for persons with developmental disabilities. It is to be hoped that, with the recent advances in psychiatric rehabilitation technology, the vocational future for persons with severe psychiatric disabilities is also becoming brighter.

4
Psychiatric Rehabilitation through Education: Rethinking the Context

KAREN V. UNGER, M.S.W., ED.D.

Historical and Current Perspectives

With the onset of deinstitutionalization and the growth of the mental health centers movement, there has been a 66 percent decrease in the number of persons currently residing in state mental health hospitals (NIMH, 1977). Day hospitals and partial-care settings evolved as a means for providing clients with the support they needed for functioning in the community (Gudeman, Dickey, Evans & Shore, 1985; Acharya, Ekdawi, Gallagher & Glaister, 1982). To prevent their becoming isolated from home and work, contact and supports were maintained.

By establishing social clubs and therapeutic communities that helped clients to utilize community resources and by teaching skills of daily living, community care centers were also able to reduce the disabling effects of mental illness then brought on by long-term hospitalization (Gruenberg, 1957).

Another important factor affecting the kinds of services needed by persons with psychiatric disabilities was a change in demographics. One-third of the population of this country, or 64 million people, are between the ages of twenty and thirty-four, the age group most at risk for schizophrenia and depressive affective disorders (Egri & Caton, 1982). Many of the young persons who experience the disabling effects of mental illness have not or will not be hospitalized for long periods of time. The resulting pressures on community mental health agencies have been documented in a growing literature on the subject of young adult patients, a population that has been perceived as distinctive in its needs and patterns of service utilization (Bachrach, 1982; Egri & Caton, 1982; Pepper, Kirshner & Ryglewicz, 1981; Sheets, Prevost & Reikman (1982). Recent studies also suggest that traditional human service agencies have generally been unsuccessful in rehabilitating these chronically mentally ill young adults because they are often either unwilling or unable to use the services offered (Bachrach, 1982; Lamb, 1976; Pepper, Kirschner & Ryglewicz, 1981; Unger & Anthony, 1982).

PSYCHIATRIC REHABILITATION IN AN EDUCATIONAL CONTEXT

An accumulating body of research evidence suggests that teaching skills such as independent living, community resource utilization, and career preparation to seriously disabled young adults can improve their functioning in the community. Reviews of research have shown that psychiatrically disabled people can learn a variety of skills regardless of their symptomatology (Anthony, 1979b; Anthony, Cohen & Cohen, 1978). When these skills are properly integrated into a rehabilitation program that supports their use, they can have a significant impact on the client's independent functioning in the community (Anthony, 1979b; Anthony & Margules, 1974).

Within the past decade, however, it has become apparent that in order for the skill-training component of psychiatric rehabilitation to be used most effectively, it is important to offer it in settings that "post-deinstitutionalization" clients, often young adults, view as nonstigmatizing. Such persons have little history of lengthy hospitalizations and do not readily attend settings that clearly label them as psychiatrically disabled. Settings such as psychosocial clubs and vocational centers have become the settings of choice. In psychosocial centers, clients become "members"; in vocational centers, they are seen as "apprentice-workers" or trainees. As a further evolutionary step, academic environments have evolved where clients become "students" whose impediments to community adjustment are viewed as targets for skill development.

The formulation of "problems" as "skill deficits" implied that the impediments could be overcome through education. Skill development could assist persons with psychiatric disabilities to improve their functioning. Skill development through education, however, does not discount the importance of the environmental-support component of psychiatric rehabilitation. Rather, it emphasizes the "normalizing" of the skill-development component while still incorporating the support dimension.

Programs have emerged that stress a learning environment as the context in which the psychiatric rehabilitation approach is offered. An effective psychiatric rehabilitation program in an educational context would include a mission to teach skills in an education setting to psychiatrically disabled clients and to provide support for the use of those skills that will assist them to function more independently in their environment of choice. An ideal education setting would be in an environment that was recognized as primarily educational. The major function would be teaching skills related to the rehabilitation goals established by the student/patients. Classes would be taught in groups or to individuals. Small group activities might provide support to students as they discuss their experiences with using the new skills in outside environments. Activities within the learning setting, for example, social or recreational activities, could also serve to reinforce the new skills learned and to provide support for practicing them. Individual work could focus on the changes that resulted in students' lives as they became more independent and in control.

The two articles that follow describe the process of implementing the psychiatric rehabilitation approach in traditional (mental health centers) and nontraditional (university campus) settings. The key concept, common to both settings, is that the primary intervention is couched in an education rather than a treatment context. Traditional clinical treatment is regarded as a resource to support or facilitate the learning process and to assist in the application of the skills learned to the appropriate environment.

Case Studies

The first article by Taylor et al. describes a partial-care setting in Sussex County, New Jersey. The psychiatric rehabilitation approach, described in educational terms, is integrated into a preexisting psychosocial clubhouse that forms the basis of the day-treatment or partial-care services.

The second article describes a program in an actual educational setting. The Continuing Education Program at Boston University has implemented the psychiatric rehabilitation approach on a university campus with an emphasis on teaching participants how to choose a career goal and develop and implement a career plan. Hutchinson et al. describe how the program was developed and implemented.

Dimensions common to both programs are reflected in the mission, skill-development interventions, networking, population served, program model, and emphasis on client involvement.

Mission: The overall purpose or mission of each of the programs guides the treatment process, regardless of the methodology or environment in which treatment occurs. Authors of both case studies see their mission as helping participants to learn the skills necessary for community living. There is a commitment to learning that enables clients to increase their successful community integration.

Skill Development: Each program describes skill development as a primary intervention. The skills to be developed are those needed by the individual participants to achieve their overall living, learning, and/or working goals. Learning new skills is seen as a major component of the rehabilitation process.

Network of Services: The psychiatric rehabilitation approach emphasizes not just skill teaching but also the importance of a network of services that support the clients' use of skills. Each of the environments acknowledges the importance of resources in the rehabilitation process.

The New Jersey partial hospital component is only one of many services offered by a Center for Mental Health that provides comprehensive community-based psychiatric services. The Continuing Education Program at Boston University is not affiliated with any comprehensive treatment program. The students come from a large geographic area and are from many different catchment areas. The service networks for individual students are the result of vigorous case management efforts by program staff and the students themselves. A network of services, ideally affiliated with the university, needs to be developed. Case management is an integral part of the service delivery system in both settings.

Population Served: The population served reflects the growing number of young psychiatrically disabled persons whose primary source of treatment has been the community mental-health-service delivery system. As such, they do not have to compensate for the deleterious effects of long-term hospitalization. However, the treatment problems of the young adults are compounded by the problems of drug and alcohol abuse.

In terms of educational history, the Continuing Education Program at Boston University serves only those students who have graduated from high school. The New Jersey partial-hospitalization program serves developmentally disabled as well as psychiatrically disabled persons.

Program Model: Both programs have, as their foundation, the psychiatric rehabilitation process of diagnosis, planning, and intervention. Although the context for each is different, all components are there. In the New Jersey partial-hospitalization program, goals in all three areas of living, learning, and working may be established. At the Continuing

Education Program at Boston University the emphasis is on developing and implementing a career goal. This may include a learning goal to prepare for work by additional education or training, or a work goal.

Client Involvement: In each program the principle of client involvement in all phases of the rehabilitation process is a key concept. Individual plans and individual skill goals determine the interventions. It is assumed that all program participants can participate in their own rehabilitation process and that they can learn new skills that will help them to function more independently in their environments of choice.

A Psychiatric Rehabilitation Approach in a Clubhouse Setting: Sussex House, Newton, New Jersey

DAVID Z. TAYLOR, M.S., CRC; DIANE PIAGESI, M.A., CRC; JOHN P. MCNAUGHT, M.A., CRC; AND M. NICOLAI NIELSEN, M.D.

Sussex House is the partial-hospitalization component of the Center for Mental Health at Newton Memorial Hospital, located in Sussex County, New Jersey, a semirural bedroom community.

Sussex House began in 1979. It was developed to provide comprehensive psychosocial rehabilitation programming for individuals who, as a result of frequent or long-term hospitalizations or chronic mental illness, need a specialized program to enable them to develop the skills necessary for community living. Sussex House provides a variety of activities and experiences which minimize the obstacles that often make it difficult for these individuals to integrate into the community. Clients involved in the Sussex House program, called "members," come each day to the "club" and participate in prevocational work units that are needed to maintain the clubhouse.

From its inception, Sussex House has operated on three key principles: first, that the social and vocational aspects of psychosocial rehabilitation can be best accomplished by employing the clubhouse concept as formulated by Fountain House in the early 1950s (Beard, 1976); second, that the clubhouse members have the inherent capability to learn the skills they need, if given the opportunity and resources; and third, that any effective rehabilitation effort must include the medical and psychiatric aspects of the member's disability.

Over the course of the past several years the characteristics of members coming to Sussex House have changed. In 1979 the average daily attendance was sixteen members per day, most clients were over

the age of forty, and schizophrenia was the primary psychiatric diagnosis. Presently, the average daily attendance is thirty-five members
per day, and most clients are under forty years of age. The major goals
of Sussex House are to promote independence through skill building
and interdependence through cooperative effort. The "Clubhouse
Concept" provides the needed belongingness and an expectation that
a member's productivity helps the club. It also provides the setting in
which to make a realistic assessment of the skills and resources needed
to attain individual rehabilitation goals, a process individualized and
refined by the psychiatric rehabilitation learning approach.

Program Description

ENVIRONMENT

Sussex House members sign into their respective units upon arriving (maintenance, kitchen, clerical, or horticulture), and together plan
the day's activities. For example, a member in the kitchen prevocational unit can choose to do a variety of tasks including cooking, serving, or busing for the noontime meal. Clerical unit members may
choose from typing, filing, answering phones, and producing a news-
paper, to name a few. Each unit contributes to club functioning. The
majority of prevocational activities occurs in the morning. Social skills
are practiced when all members come together for lunch and share
their experiences from the morning's work.

Every member's afternoon schedule differs. Some continue to work
in their prevocational units while others attend specific skill-teaching
groups. Medication education, self-care, consumer education, and nu-
trition/health groups provide opportunities for members to learn and
practice needed skills as a group with individual follow-up.

DIAGNOSIS

Members begin rehabilitation at the club by participating in an orientation period in each of the prevocational units. They immediately
become productive members of the clubhouse and gain a sense of belongingness and importance. Along with this prevocational initiation,
the diagnostic process begins. The process of psychiatric rehabilitation
diagnosis at Sussex House, as described by Farkas and Anthony in
chapter 1 of this volume, has evolved over the years. What began as a
formal standardized procedure has evolved into a flexible process-
oriented approach. Members' opinions regarding their current situation, the first stage of the ORG, are now explored at almost any mo-

ment they are willing to share them. Individual time is reserved for the decision-making process to determine the member's choice of living, learning, or working environment. In these sessions, the assessments of the psychiatrist, family members, staff, boarding-home operators, and all those involved in a particular environment are shared by the clinician with the member. Their input reinforces the many sources of available support.

This process is continued by the psychiatric rehabilitation specialist, the unit supervisors, and the skill teachers in the various units and is shared in orientation evaluations. Simultaneously, the perspectives of the new member, prevocational staff, the clinician, family members, and identified significant others are pooled to formulate a clear set of values by which the member and clinician can systematically agree on overall rehabilitation goals. The member's preferences for where he or she would like to live, learn, or work provide the focus for rehabilitation efforts.

The functional assessment is an ongoing evaluation process. The member, staff, and significant others conduct an informal functional assessment, each contributing to an overall list of skills essential for maintaining the present level of functioning and a decision about what skills must be prioritized to achieve overall rehabilitation goals. Psychiatric rehabilitation specialists are critical in this process as the assessment occurs as members work in their units. Expectations for each member are determined by his or her particular rehabilitation goal. For example, a member who intends to work full-time within six months may be asked to arrive on time for unit meetings five out of five days.

PLANNING

As present levels of skill use are being evaluated, the planning phase is occurring. At the member's own pace, diagnosis is completed and the psychiatric rehabilitation plan is initiated. Based on the individual member's needs, a clinician develops a plan with the member over several sessions. Interventions are selected for the prioritized skills, which include direct skill teaching, skill programming, and monitoring the utilization of skills, depending on the level of skill use.

Finally, members and staff meet to finalize agreement on the interventions selected and to develop time frames for the established goals, which get written down into a formal treatment plan. By mutual agreement, monitoring may include other members as well as staff and significant others. All those involved sign the treatment plan to indicate their agreement and support. The plan is flexible and open to modification and revision as needed.

AGENCY PROFILE (as of October, 1987)

A. AGENCY

Name: Center for Mental Health, Newton Memorial Hospital
Location: Newton, N.J.   **Population:** 125,000 (Sussex County)
Type of Agency: Community Mental Health Agency   **Primary Sources of Agency Funding:** Contract for services with State Division of Mental Health and Hospitals, Medicaid/Medicare, sliding scale and third party insurance

Agency Size: Total number of staff: 75   Total number of clients: 2,000
Direct care staff: 55   Administration staff: 10   Support staff: 10

B. CASE STUDY PROGRAM/UNIT

Name: Partial Hospitalization (Sussex House)
Location: Sussex House, 175 High Street, Newton, N.J. 07860
Number of Programs in Unit: 1
Type of Program: Psychosocial Rehabilitation
Program Size:

Total number of staff: 10
Number of direct care only staff: 7
Number of supervisory/administrative only staff: 0
Number of support staff: 0
Mixed functions—direct care/supervisory: 2
Administrative/supervisory: 1
Number of
Ph.D./M.D.: 0*
B.S.W./B.A.: 5
M.S.W./M.A./M.Ed.: 5
High school: 0
(* − .5fte budget under OPD)

Total number of clients: 80
Male: 38   Female: 42
Average age: 39
Age Range: 18–70
Av. yrs. hosp.: 6;
Range: 3 wks.–30 years
Predominant diagnostic categories:
90% schizophrenia
8% bipolar disorders
2% personality disorders
Staff/client ratio: 1 : 11

Program Description:
Average length of stay in program: 22 months
Majority of clients are funded by: 40% Medicaid
30% Medicare   30% Self-pay
Majority of program activities are conducted: In prevocational work units (skill development groups)
Program hours of service: 8:30 A.M.–5:00 P.M.; 8:30 A.M.–9:00 P.M. (Thursdays); 8:30 A.M.–2:30 P.M. (Saturdays)
Average Length of Time to Conduct Program Activities:
DIAGNOSIS
Initial overall rehabilitation goal: 6–8 sessions over a 90-day period
Functional assessment/resource assessment: Ongoing process completed 1 week after ORG

Type: Psychiatric, Medical, Vocational/Social   Number of sessions: 1 each
   except Voc. 4–6

PLANNING
Developing the initial rehabilitation plan: 1 session
Other plans if applicable: N/A

INTERVENTIONS
Conducting direct skills teaching of one skill: 6–8 sessions over 6–8 weeks
Implementing a program for use of one skill: 4 sessions over 2 weeks
Linking up with one resource: Within 5 days

OTHER TYPES OF INTERVENTIONS
Individual therapy: referral to outpatient if needed
Group therapy: referral to outpatient if needed

INTERVENTIONS

Interventions occur where and when needed, both on an individual basis and in skill groups. Sussex House members receive direct skill teaching and skill programming interventions while at the club, at their place of residence, or on the job through the supportive employment program. As implementation of the psychiatric rehabilitation plan continues, off-site interventions increase. Formal direct skills teaching followed by skill programming gives members optimum chance for success by troubleshooting problems that might jeopardize achievement of overall rehabilitation goals. The plan keeps members and others on track. Some overall rehabilitation goals achieved by members include: staying on at the clubhouse, living in one's own room or apartment, full- or part-time employment, and graduation. Graduation from the clubhouse means members are informally discharged from the rehabilitation day program itself. Most members remain connected to the club through evening or weekend social activities at the clubhouse.

CASE ILLUSTRATION

Sussex House's approach to psychiatric rehabilitation can be demonstrated by the following case study. Tony is a twenty-seven-year-old male who had been in and out of psychiatric hospitals for the past nine years. Tony suffered from schizoaffective disorder with frequent bouts of depression leaving him feeling hopeless about himself and his future. He had tried to hold jobs and live in harmony with his parents, but always ended up fighting with the family or employees, walking off the job in anger, or leaving home.

A Sussex House clinician met Tony on a visit to the state hospital. To help Tony prepare for discharge, discussions focused on Tony's likes and dislikes about different living environments. After several meetings, Tony set his initial rehabilitation goals. They were to live at a local boarding home and attend Sussex House (to learn work skills). The formal diagnostic phase began even before Tony left the hospital, thus creating a link to the community that was followed up at the clubhouse.

Prior to discharge, the Sussex House clinician gathered information from the hospital's treatment staff regarding their perspective on Tony's skill strengths and deficits relative to his chosen rehabilitation goals. Once at Sussex House, Tony felt welcomed and needed and hopeful as he saw other members succeeding at their goals. At Sussex House he continued the dialogue begun at the hospital setting his overall rehabilitation goals. He saw the hope that was sparked while he was in the hospital emerge into concrete and reachable individual objectives. He set new goals of living in his own room and eventually working full-time in a nearby town. Tony was able to discuss with the staff what the community resources were in Sussex County, and together with his clinician and psychiatric rehabilitation specialist was able to identify the skills that were needed to attain his new goals. Several skills were easily identifiable through program involvement and activities in the prevocational unit.

Tony and his clinician started assigning priorities for the skills he needed to build in order to attain his goals. Through this process it became clear to him that he needed skills in the areas of greeting, responding, asking for help, and discussing impersonal topics. Attending the program and grooming were strengths. He now had specific skill goals to work on toward achieving his own overall rehabilitation.

A plan to help Tony perform these skills at the needed level was set with a reasonable time frame for accomplishing the goals. Tony's input was critical, reinforcing the value of his being a full participant in his rehabilitation. Interventions began at Sussex House where he learned how to greet and respond to others. Other members helped him practice discussing impersonal topics, and the clubhouse became involved in helping him implement his plan. He received a lot of support from his peers and improved in evaluating and recognizing his strengths. In the Horticulture Unit, he was taught how to ask for help by the psychiatric rehabilitation specialist. Tony worked hard at learning these skills, and after nine months he volunteered for a supportive employment job slot. He continued to work on improving his skills and three months later moved into a full-time job and his own apartment. He continues to work on his interpersonal skills at the Young Adult Program.

Implementing the Psychiatric Rehabilitation Program: Strategies and Barriers

Throughout the early stages of Sussex House, it became increasingly clear that the clubhouse program philosophy and clinical design were not sufficient to provide new staff with the diagnostic and teaching skills necessary to provide the outcomes that were expected. Although our diagnostic system was comprehensive, it did not adequately involve the member in the decision-making process. Much of the ongoing skill training was based on a staff assessment of need without fully involving the member in the process. In addition, supervisory staff were wrestling with their attempts to identify ways of helping new staff communicate more effectively with members and understand their needs.

As staff were struggling with these issues, Sussex House was requested by the New Jersey Division of Mental Health and Hospitals to participate in a project to provide technical assistance to partial-care settings. The goals of the project and those of Sussex House were the same: that is, to improve methods for rehabilitation diagnosis, treatment planning, and interventions through enhancing staff skills in identifying individual members' goals and assessing the skills and resources necessary to attain them.

An initial site assessment by this Partial Care Technical Assistance Project (PCTAP) identified "Sussex House [as] generally an effective program based on community needs for partial care services; however, the skill teaching components were general in nature and not specific to a member's particular environment." Direct skill teaching and skill programming were based not on each client's individualized functional assessment but rather on a global functional assessment. A member of the program, for example, had learned to accept supervision from the unit supervisor when necessary, in the Greenhouse. However, it was not until he was placed on a job that it was determined that he lacked the skill of asking for help from supervisors. Second, the site assessment noted that there was no systematic training process for staff. The recommendation was made that Sussex House join in the state-sponsored project to train agency staff as trainers in the skills of psychiatric rehabilitation. After successful completion of the program, the trainers would then teach their own staff the principles and skills they themselves had mastered.

Administrative and program staff, while concurring with PCTAP recommendations, had several questions before agreeing to participate in the training: (1) Did the state have the ability to mount an effective training program? (2) Was such an extensive training program necessary, given the high educational and experiential level of the staff? (3) Would the training truly meet the needs of the staff and the members? and (4) What indications were there that this approach was effective? Mutual exploration of these questions and agreement with the training principles led to a decision to participate in the project.

The training was introduced as a means of enhancing the entire staff's competence as professionals in psychiatric rehabilitation. Many house meetings and group discussions were held with members to share information about the training. Members of Sussex House viewed the training with anticipation. Already accustomed to establishing goals, they looked forward to new ways of breaking down big goals into "do-able" steps.

Five factors helped in adding psychiatric rehabilitation practices to an already existing psychosocial clubhouse model. The first was the strong belief of the program's leaders that state-of-the-art technology is necessary to maintain quality treatment at Newton Memorial Hospital. This belief dictated that programs need to be open to change. Second, the change in population characteristics from *older* to *younger* members and from members with chronic to more acute disabilities underlined the need for program modifications and augmentation. Third, the state of New Jersey had proposed Rules and Regulations for Partial Care programs that adopted the psychiatric rehabilitation approach to the operation of partial-care programs that require environmental goals, functional assessments, plans, skill teaching, and resource coordination. The fourth factor was staff acceptance of the idea of improving their skills. The last factor was member support and encouragement of the staff in their endeavor.

The first step in implementing the training plan was to select which agency staff would become trainers. It was an important decision because the motivation and skill of these individuals would be a major factor in the success of the transition. The final selection was based on many factors and included: (1) a commitment to the provision of rehabilitation services to our members; (2) a desire to continue to learn and improve one's skills; and (3) a willingness to invest extra time in working toward overall program goals. The department head and senior clinician were selected to be trainers. They became fully involved in the training program, and after a year's training began training program staff.

Several barriers had to be hurdled to accomplish the training goals fully. The staff, challenged by the new student role and expectation for change, tended to worry about implementing all the steps of psychiatric rehabilitation. As training progressed, they seemed to convince themselves that the task appeared to be overwhelming. In addition, an awareness of just how much there was to learn led to feelings of pressure to do more than they were already doing. Staff saw it as "extra." Newer staff who had just learned their roles within the clubhouse framework were confused over what psychiatric rehabilitation was; where, when, how, and by whom it would be carried out. Veteran staff were baffled by what it would require in addition to the program of our existing clubhouse. The Sussex House trainers spent time demonstrating their understanding of how staff were feeling and the reasons for those feelings, enabling dialogue to be held which eventually resolved staff concerns. The staff needed clarification that there was no pressure to have a "total psychiatric rehabilitation approach" supplanting the clubhouse model. Instead, psychiatric rehabilitation was to be a new frame of reference in which to view all that was done in the existing clubhouse. Further, staff were reassured that the new approach would be utilized and adopted only where it could be most helpful.

Two barriers remain as a challenge to program development following the total in-house training. The first has been the difficulty of clarifying staff roles around utilization of psychiatric rehabilitation—that is, determining who should be responsible for which components of the psychiatric rehabilitation process and what impact such new responsibilities would have on current job descriptions. We are still exploring this problem situation. Second, as staff try to incorporate psychiatric rehabilitation skills into their jobs, the lack of resources in the community preferred by members, particularly normal housing (Blanch et al., 1987), has been frustrating. Developing these resources would enable staff not only to help improve the quality of life of the older members but also to afford a broader, more appropriate choice in living environments for young adult members.

The psychiatric rehabilitation approach is viewed as the needed complement to the sound practices and philosophy of the clubhouse model and psychiatric treatment. Just as the entire professional staff at Sussex House had to learn about, practice, and use the clubhouse philosophy and skills, as well as psychiatric medical practices, they are now learning to use the "new tools" offered by the psychiatric rehabilitation approach. To maintain the ongoing implementation of psychiatric rehabilitation as a partner in the clubhouse model, staff meet in what are called "study groups." The study groups are a forum to review learnings, practice experiences, and continue the dialogue regarding effective implementation of the combined approaches. Study groups enable staff to focus on problem areas or dissatisfactions they are experiencing in trying to blend the "old way" with the new psychiatric rehabilitation format. The staff trainers have been obtaining support for themselves as well by going to support groups with other trainers in the state to discuss implementation and training issues.

At Sussex House, we began integrating psychiatric rehabilitation in program areas that closely matched the approach. For example, teaching in the units was modified to incorporate the structure of direct skill teaching (Cohen, Danley & Nemec, 1985a). Curricula were written for group activities. Monthly assessments of unit functioning were revised to include the concepts of rehabilitation skill development (awareness, acquisition, application, and utilization criteria). Skill goals on treatment plans were written in "skill language." We also focused on areas of program dissatisfaction, replacing old procedures and forms with revised ones incorporating psychiatric rehabilitation language, format, and process. Thus, implementation has been occurring as an evaluation of a new approach combining clubhouse and psychiatric rehabilitation.

Program Evaluation

The benefits of integrating the psychiatric rehabilitation approach with an existing psychosocial clubhouse model are many. The psychiatric rehabilitation approach gave the staff improved technical skills to enable members of this program to attain their goals. It systematized our diagnostic process, thereby improving our functional assessment capabilities and enabling the staff to develop treatment plans that were realistic and effective for producing client outcome. The new clinical documentation more than satisfactorily met newly developed state guidelines for charting in a partial-care program. The integration of the psychiatric rehabilitation approach has enabled supervisory staff to provide staff training that is thorough and totally applicable to the field of psychiatric rehabilitation. It has also enabled them to train new personnel more effectively and to evaluate their progress in the use of work skills as part of their annual review. The ability to teach staff: (1) how to be effective in the use of interpersonal skills, and (2) how to teach skills to members through the development of curriculum has led to major improvements. Most importantly, it has provided the staff with the direction and the skills necessary to experience a sense of accomplishment and competency in their jobs.

The implementation of a psychiatric rehabilitation approach helped focus Sussex House on a data collection system that evaluates rehabilitation processes and outcomes (Farkas, Nemec & Taylor, 1989). In 1985 only 15 percent of the active caseload had rehabilitation plans with individualized goals, functional assessments, and interventions. In 1986,

80 percent of the caseload had complete rehabilitation plans. Rehabilitation plan reviews by the Sussex House Quality Assurance Committee observed that client skill gains are accurately recorded and revised or new skill development objectives are found in most charts.

In 1985 the average length of stay for members in day programs was 36 months. The following year, 1986, showed a reduction to 24 months, and most recent quarterly reports reveal an average length of stay of 18 months. Of the total caseload in 1985, only 2 percent held full- or part-time jobs for more than 60 days. The September 1987 member employment report indicates 16 percent are permanently employed.

Most importantly, the members themselves demonstrate their satisfaction with the new rehabilitation focus by tabulating monthly employment reports so all members know who is working full- or part-time and how long each has been on the job. As a group, members earned (not including SSD, etc.) $4,600 in 1985, $12,400 in 1986, and $74,000 in 1987!

The revised outcome process offers much more evidence of a rehabilitation process than does counting the number of months a member stays out of a hospital. Looking ahead, Sussex House is asking for a computer and the new Lotus software program to facilitate better and more thorough data on rehabilitation outcome.

Overall, implementing psychiatric rehabilitation within the psychosocial clubhouse model has unified members and staff more than ever. Staff have developed an awareness that they have now worked out a "technical systematized approach." This has reassured them that the effort of training, practice, and utilization has been well worth it, and it has enhanced what they already valued about their profession. Members, perhaps most importantly, are experiencing an increased "partnership" in the rehabilitation process. In the club, members are using their skills to keep the club running. Now there is a system within which they can build skills to keep their own lives on course, and an increasing satisfaction with their active roles in their treatment.

Sussex House is now capable, with the integration of the "psychiatric rehabilitation process," of taking a client with a psychiatric disability through the stages of skill learning from being ready to learn, to actually learning skills, to applying them in the client's "real world," and finally to being able to use these critical skills as needed. Psychiatric rehabilitation offers Sussex House members greater opportunities to live, learn, or work where they choose, and to enjoy success and satisfaction in their lives.

A University-based Psychiatric Rehabilitation Program for Young Adults: Boston University

DORI S. HUTCHINSON, M.S.; LARRY KOHN, M.S.;
AND KAREN V. UNGER, ED.D.

In January 1985, the Center for Psychiatric Rehabilitation at Boston University opened a university-based rehabilitation program for young adults with psychiatric disabilities (Unger & Anthony, 1984). Based on the psychiatric rehabilitation approach (Anthony, 1979), the program's mission is to demonstrate the effectiveness of teaching these young adults the skills they need so that they may achieve and sustain their academic and vocational goals. The overall goal of the project is to develop a curriculum and program model, to collect outcome data, and to help mental health and educational personnel replicate the program at other universities.

Known more commonly as the Continuing Education Program (CEP), the rehabilitation program utilizes direct skills teaching as the primary intervention (Unger, Danley, Kohn & Hutchinson, 1987). Direct skills teaching is a systematic series of educational activities resulting in the competent use of new skill behaviors.

The current students in the program were recruited by sending program descriptions to the local mental health community. Acceptance to the program is based primarily on the willingness of psychiatrically disabled young adults to attend an educational program, their compatibility with other Boston University students, and their estimated desire to succeed in the job market. Since January 1985, forty students have been accepted into the program; fourteen in the first class and thirteen in each of the other two classes.

Program Description

ENVIRONMENT

The setting is Sargent College of Allied Health Professions on the Boston University campus (BU), where students are educated in a normal, nonstigmatizing learning environment. Classes are held three days a week, 2½ hours at a time, for four semesters. Students utilize other university facilities, most notably the recreational fitness center, the libraries, and the student union.

SKILLS DEVELOPMENT CURRICULUM

The content for the program consists of a series of instructional units related to career development. The first of these units is entitled "Profiling Vocational Potential." In this unit, students learn the skills that are needed to define themselves vocationally (rather than psychiatrically). They explore their personal experiences, past and present, to identify their unique qualities that will influence the outcome of their future work experience. Qualities examined include values, interests, aptitudes, competencies, and adaptabilities. The required product is a Worker Trait Profile. This is a listing of the students' most important values as well as self-ratings on different aptitudes, competencies, adaptabilities, and productivity skills. The following is an example of an occupational value that might be written into a worker trait profile: *Teamwork—the percentage of time per week I work in the same room with at least two other co-workers to complete a task.* The research then helps to clarify which occupation best matches a student's unique combination of values.

The second unit of instruction is called "Researching Occupational Alternatives." During this unit, students learn the skills needed to identify occupational interest areas, select two or more occupational alternatives, and gather relevant occupational information. Learning activities in this unit include; classroom instruction, library research, conducting information interviews, and job observations. The product for this unit is two or more occupational profiles that are detailed written descriptions of their researched occupation. The two major skills that are taught during this unit are researching information and conducting informational interviews. Students are taught how to use occupational reference material such as the *Dictionary of Occupational Titles,* the *Occupational Outlook Handbook,* and the *Guide for Occupational Exploration.* They work in the Boston University library, their own town libraries, and the Boston Public Library.

The occupational information interviews are planned meetings between individual students and someone who is employed in the occupation they are researching. The interviews can be set up by either teacher or students. The main purpose of the interview is to add to the pool of information about a specific area of interest. Students are exposed to anecdotal information and other insights that are not found in written material.

The third unit is called "Career Planning." Career planning means developing a series of experiences that the student needs in order to acquire the attitudes, knowledge, skills, and credentials necessary to

AGENCY PROFILE (as of October, 1987)

A. AGENCY
Name: Center for Psychiatric Rehabilitation
Location: Boston University, Boston, Mass. **Population:** 2,000,000
Type of Agency: Research, training in mental health
Primary Sources of Agency Funding: Federal NIMH/NIHR

Agency size: Total number of staff: approx. 50 Total number of clients: 40
Direct care staff: 3 Administration staff: approx. 11 Support staff: 16
Faculty: 20

B. CASE STUDY PROGRAM/UNIT
Name: Continuing Education Program
Location: Boston University, Sargent College

Number of Programs in Unit: 1
Type of Program: Academic/educational: career development
Program Size:

Total number of staff: 8

Number of direct care only staff: 3*

Number of supervisory/administrative only staff: 4

Number of support staff: 1

Mixed functions—direct care/supervisory: 0

Administrative/supervisory: 1

Number of
Ph.D/M.D.: 5
B.S.W./B.A.:0
M.S.W.: 3
High school: 0
*Five graduate students assist in the program.

Total number of clients: 40

Male: 20 Female: 20

Average age: 33

Age range: 21–40 yrs

Av. yrs. hosp.: 19.7 months;
Range: 0–72 months

Predominant diagnostic categories:
45% schizophrenia
43% depressive and affective disorder
12% severe borderline personality disorder

Staff/client ratio: 1 : 13*

Program Description:
Average length of stay in program: N/A
Majority of clients are funded by: 100% Federal Funds
Majority of program activities are conducted: Both groups and 1 : 1
Program hours of service: 9:00 A.M.–5:00 P.M., Monday through Friday

Average Length of Time to Conduct Program Activities:
DIAGNOSIS
Initial overall rehabilitation goal: 96 sessions over 8 months
Functional assessment/resource assessment: 72 sessions over 6 months
OTHER TYPES OF DIAGNOSIS
Type: N/A Number of sessions: N/A
PLANNING
Developing the initial rehabilitation plan: 12 sessions over 1 month
Other plans if applicable: 12 sessions over 1 month

Conducting direct skills teaching of one skill: 12 sessions over 1 month
Implementing a program for use of one skill: 12 sessions over 1 month
Linking up with one resource: 6 sessions over 12 weeks
OTHER TYPES OF INTERVENTIONS
Individual counseling: 5 hours/month/client   Group therapy: N/A

---

be ready to work in his or her chosen occupation. The classroom work focuses on designing a unique combination of work and/or school experiences that will meet a particular student's needs. The students discover areas of need through a self-assessment of their competence and credentials in relation to the requirements of their chosen occupation. Examples of career-plan experiences are internships, volunteer jobs, technical school, college, and work-study.

The fourth unit is called "Strategic Planning." Strategic planning is an assessment of the student's skill functioning in relation to his or her targeted first environment. Students are asked to develop a detailed description of their new environment. They also develop a list of their own behaviors that will be personally important to their success. From these two sources, themselves and the environment, the students are assisted in listing, describing, and evaluating their critical skills.

The fifth unit, "Preparing for Transitions," focuses on learning the skills and acquiring the resources needed to be successful. If taught in small groups, the skills are taught didactically in a college classroom, and students are asked to do homework, take notes, and submit written products or demonstrate skill acquisition that is critically evaluated.

DEVELOPING THE NECESSARY SUPPORTS

The many supports offered by the CEP ensure that the rehabilitation process occurs and that it is as rewarding and effective as possible. These supports evolved from (a) individual student needs, (b) gaps in the mental health system, and (c) a shared desire to maximize attendance and participation and to encourage progress. Although the CEP experience is greatly valued by many students, it introduces additional stress in their lives. It means conforming to a schedule, attending a large university, meeting new people, and adding transportation and material costs to tight budgets. Ongoing support makes it possible to cope with the increased pressure. A brief description of the support components follows.

Individual strategic planning is the link between the education and the rehabilitation process. The planning process begins in the classroom where students learn to assess their skill needs. Students then meet individually with staff or graduate students to arrange for the skill intervention to occur. Some examples of skill needs that have been identified are: "offering verbal support to other students," and "responding to frustrating information."

Coaching sessions are individual meetings arranged with students to assist them in understanding course content which they missed or with which they need extra help.

Individual support is contact between students and staff, either by telephone or in person, where feelings, problems, or achievements are shared.

Peer assistance uses interested students from previous classes to function as role models and support persons for incoming classes. Students are trained in interpersonal skills and direct-skills teaching methodology.

Physical and social recreation encourages students to engage each other socially outside of the classroom. This component arose as a response to a stated need of many of the students to expand their social network and their activities during their leisure time. Students in the CEP have free membership at the BU Athletic Center.

Resource linking enables the students to find the person, place, thing, or activity that will best meet a stated need. These resource needs may be identified during individual meetings or during individual informal conversations. The staff may assist the student, if desired, to contact the resource, accompany him or her to any meetings (if it is a person), or help in any way the student wants.

Outreach helps students who may be experiencing some difficulty in becoming or staying connected to the program. Students may be called on, visited, or written to by the staff. Activities include morning wake-up calls, meetings for lunch or breakfast, or visits to the hospital if a student becomes hospitalized. If a student does not attend class, an outreach activity is initiated by instructors or graduate students.

The high level of staff commitment to providing support to the students has been a key factor in helping students complete the coursework. The following student comment is typical:

I've experienced in most places that the staff is reliant on power as a means to control the population and achieve the effects they want. Here it's much more reason, in its best sense. I mean if someone has a problem—well, you listen to him. I experience the people here as much less reliant on a power relationship—much more on—do I dare say love—as a *modus operandi.*

THE PSYCHIATRIC REHABILITATION PROCESS

In terms of methodology, the instruction occurs in a group setting with ever-increasing levels of individual specification as the process moves from the diagnosis through planning and intervention. At the point when individual assessments are being done in relation to a new environment, the focus shifts from group to individual work. Diagnosis in the CEP is comprised of (a) Profiling Vocational Potential, (b) Researching Occupational Alternatives, (c) Career Planning, and (d) Part of Strategic Planning. Establishing the Overall Rehabilitation Goal (ORG), the first part of the rehabilitation diagnostic phase is, in the CEP, actually a two-phase process of moving from the broad goal of choosing an occupation to a specific goal of naming the first new environment. Profiling Vocational Potential is the unit during which the students *explore their values*. It also is a time for students to engage personally with the university, with the instructor, and with their classmates.

Exploring environments (the second step of ORG) loosely corresponds to the CEP unit of "Researching Occupational Alternatives." The adaptation that the CEP has made, is that, at this level, targeting a specific environment is not the goal. The goal is to choose one or two occupations which appear to meet the students' values and which they feel are realistic, given their key strengths and limitations and preferred length of preparation time. The third skill of establishing the ORG, *Choosing a goal*, spans researching occupational alternatives and career planning. In this section of the ORG, the CEP student must move from a broad occupational choice, through a career plan, to a readiness for an assessment in relation to the first new environment. The four-to-six-month period used to establish an overall rehabilitation goal appears to be important for two reasons. First, many of our students have either little positive work experience or a lack of work history at all. The relatively long time for ORG provides them a luxury of structured exploration that many have not had. Second, this time allows the instructors and graduate students to establish the personal relationships that are the pivotal factor in the CEP. While these relationships are important during the classroom phase they became invaluable when students enter another environment and their support needs are greatly increased.

The second part of rehabilitation diagnosis, the functional assessment, is what the CEP calls strategic planning. Strategic planning uses most of the methodology of functional assessment. The skills of functional assessment are taught to the students in a large group during the third semester. In the fourth semester, individual meetings between the student and instructor are used to continue the assessment process in relation to a present or future new environment. Planning is part of strategic planning, and is only done in relation to an environment other than the CEP. Once critical skills have been designated, the specific intervention, along with the people responsible and timelines, is written into the strategic plan.

Interventions in the CEP occur at two levels. They happen in relation to the classroom and to individual ORGs. Skill teaching in the classroom revolves around the skills of career exploration, decision making, and planning. The CEP also employs all of the support categories previously discussed, to help the students to be successful in the program. Skill interventions in relation to ORGs are done more formally and derive from the strategic plans. Skill lessons are developed using the Direct Skills Teaching method (Cohen, Danley & Nemec, 1985a) and are taught either individually or in a classroom situation. Resource coordination has not been formalized in the CEP. Although many resources are provided or arranged for the CE students, this is usually done as needed and is not part of any formalized plan at this time. It is hoped that such formal planning will soon be a part of general CEP activities.

Implementing the Psychiatric Rehabilitation Program: Strategies and Barriers

The adaptations that the CEP has made in order to put theory into practice are generally changes such as: introducing immediate interventions beyond skills teaching, renaming segments of the model, broadening the ORG process to move from the very general to the specific, for example, to make the model more "usable" in an educational environment. What is noteworthy is that there have been no deviations from the principles and philosophy of the psychiatric rehabilitation approach. The foundation of the CEP is the trusting relationships that develop between staff and students. The students are respected for who they are and are seen as active participants in their own rehabilitation. The technology of the model has been adapted in the CEP program with a minimum of difficulty because of the program's belief that the students' academic and vocational goals are attainable. This belief imparts hope and motivation to the participants.

The CEP program has been in operation for thirty-three months as of this writing. During this time, barriers to the students' participation and/or progress in the CEP have arisen as anticipated. In an attempt to increase positive outcome, the staff is beginning to examine each of these barriers in order to determine strategies for lessening their impact on the program. The major barrier is the lack of coordinated case management. The students in the CEP have needs in every area of their lives. These need areas, such as housing, therapists, social security advocacy, and leisure activities, often interfere with their success in the CEP. Another barrier to success is a lack of resources. As the program has developed in the Boston area, many good relationships with other agencies, colleges, counseling collectives, and vocational programs, as well as with key people within the BU community, have been developed. However, developing these relationships takes staff time as does linking students with those resources.

Residential problems are a major barrier. Student home lives are often isolated and stressful due to incompatible group-living situations or living with family members. With interventions of skill teaching and intense support, positive changes such as change of environments or better communication with other people in their homes have occurred.

Financial problems are a powerful obstacle to student success in the CEP. There is a great deal of anxiety related to dealing with the Social Security Administration which comes from unclear and often ambiguous policy that differs from office to office. The CEP is working with many of the students to straighten out their financial situations and see that they receive their proper entitlements.

Another case-management-related issue is access to medication or therapy. Many students have had participation and/or progress slowed by problems with medication and therapy. Decompensation is also an obstacle for students. Because of the level of involvement with students, staff are able to help them to identify and measure their own symptoms so that supports can be increased when the psychiatric illness manifests itself.

The most important facilitator to the success of the CEP is the social networking that the staff encourages and builds. The program's effectiveness begins with the staff/student relationships but is strengthened by the student/student relationships that grow from a common enterprise. The birth and rebirth of friendships as an element in the students' lives leads to their increased attendance and progress.

The CEP is acutely aware of the barriers in its path. However, the program takes a positive approach to problem solving and remains extremely optimistic and energetic. The implementation of strategies to lessen those barriers has a profound impact on the lives of these people who have become connected to our lives and whose hopes and dreams have, in part, also become ours.

As the program evolves there are a number of learnings that are relevant to implementing it.

1. *The myth of the "UMYAC"* (unmotivated young adult chronic). The experience of the CEP staff has been that, rather than working to motivate "lazy" students, what is needed is to restrain their enthusiasm gently. Many times students wanted to leap into full-time work or a full course load at school. It appears that this is a result of (a) their development of *self*-relevant rather than "*other*-relevant" career plans, and (b) the need to make up for lost time caused by their disability.

2. *"Leap before you look."* The nature of the psychiatric rehabilitation approach evolves in direct response to student needs. When one of the students quipped, "We are the content," the staff realized that they were doing something right. This statement validated the student's perception that the program's foundation is built on a course structure that meets the unique needs of the participants rather than molding the students to a rigid preexisting structure. Examples of this are: (a) one-to-one tutorials with students unable to continue in the classroom situation, (b) peer assistants in succeeding classes, (c) student-run activities during school vacations, (d) individual meetings, (e) the planning for a transition unit that comes from shared skill deficits and a desire for continued class contact after fifteen months. None of these examples was present when the program began. They were generated from observing and listening to the students and each other and are now integral program components.

3. *The crisis of rehabilitation.* Many of the students who have been in the program for six months (roughly) or more seem to come to a point where their rehabilitation gets stuck. After reporting initial positive changes in both skills and feelings about themselves, many students reach a plateau. They experience despair and discouragement, a lessening or cessation in the use of newly learned positive behavior, and, many times, a return of psychiatric symptoms. In discussing this with the student, a general theme emerges. As people begin to define themselves vocationally and as students, they begin to leave behind the identity of their diagnosis and patienthood. The emerging identity has a very positive impact. However, this period of transition is also extremely difficult. Students have to choose to be either a patient or a student, sick or well. The choice is not as obvious as it appears. Being a patient with a *DSM-III* diagnosis is a known and often comfortable entity. The identity of being a healthy person who works or goes to school is unknown and terrifying. To choose the latter means to risk everything. Because they have "tasted" the new identity, they have farther to fall if they cannot sustain their momentum. Rehabilitation, our students have shown us, is not a linear process. It is more that of a spiral, with different stages of adjustment. Sometimes, the most help-

ful thing to do is to do nothing but be there while these crises of rehabilitation are occurring.

Program Evaluation

Currently, there are thirty-two students actively involved in the
CEP. Eleven students are from the pilot group (Alpha), which began in
January 1985. Ten students represent the first experimental group
(Beta) which began in September 1985. The remaining eleven students
comprise the second experimental group (Gamma), which started in
September 1986. An additional eight students are taking time off from
the program because other areas of their lives need attention. These
students are encouraged to become reinvolved at any time they feel
ready to participate. The first two groups, the Alpha and Beta classes,
are no longer in the classroom environment. Having finished four semesters of curriculum, they have begun the first step of their career
paths. Some highlights include:

- Two out of twenty-six students have gone on to full-time course
  work at universities studying legal advocacy and secretarial
  sciences.
- Eight out of twenty-six students have gone on to part-time course
  work at universities studying psychology, ceramic technology,
  medical records technology, art therapy, and liberal arts.
- Seven out of twenty-six students are working part-time as mental
  retardation aides, clerical assistants, personal care attendant, jani-
  tor, and sales clerk.
- One out of twenty-six students is working full-time as a "nanny" in
  private child care.

These students continue to receive support from staff either through
individual meetings and/or telephone calls. They are in the process of
forming an alumni group and plan to meet biweekly to socialize and
share in each other's trials and tribulations.

The Continuing Education Program has been designed and developed to meet the needs of severely psychiatrically disabled young
adults who have career aspirations. The students have willingly participated in a university-based rehabilitation program because it is in
an educational context rather than being a traditional treatment intervention. The fact that the program occurs in a natural, nonstigmatized
environment has made the students' participation more meaningful
and rewarding to them. Since they are perceived as and are treated as
normal college students, they slowly, over time, shed their image of
themselves as psychiatric patients. They see themselves in a different

light, and this new self-perception has tremendous impact upon their lives. The combination of skill learning and comprehensive support has enabled the students to become more courageous and hopeful. Psychiatric rehabilitation is a long-term process. It requires a high level of staff optimism, commitment, and hope that rehabilitation is indeed possible, if the psychiatrically disabled student is to succeed.

• • •

Emerging Directions

The most common characteristic of the programs described in the previous section is their commitment to and utilization of the psychiatric rehabilitation approach. At Sussex House, this meant modifying the current treatment modality. For the Continuing Education Program, the psychiatric rehabilitation approach was the original treatment intervention. However, in both environments many of the processes for implementation were similar. The key concept for successful implementation was not only that service delivery staff be trained in the skills of psychiatric rehabilitation but also that all staff support the mission and underlying principles. Program policies and procedures must also support the psychiatric rehabilitation approach.

At Sussex House reorientation to a different method of providing services was a major undertaking. Staff not only had to learn new skills, but they also had to develop a process for integrating these skills into the existing clubhouse model.

The implementation of the psychiatric rehabilitation approach within an education context requires commitment at every level of the organization. Moving from a traditional medical model to a rehabilitation model means that major institutional change must occur which affects both staff and program design and implementation. Training is often seen as the major effort of institutional change. However, it is only the first step. Institutional change may require modification of the mission statement and philosophy of the organization as well as changes in policy, procedural, and supervisory functions. These modifications are reflected in changes in the record keeping and documents of the organization. It is important for staff at all levels to realize that redesigning the program and learning new skills do not mean the old ways and skills are not valued. Rather, the integration of previous experience and skills with the new facilitates positive change.

At the Continuing Education Program, only staff who were competent and experienced in the practice of psychiatric rehabilitation were hired. Because of the affiliation with the Center for Psychiatric Rehabilitation and Sargent College of Allied Health Professions, which offers a graduate degree specialization in psychiatric rehabilitation, trained persons were available. The challenge programmatically was to adapt the psychiatric rehabilitation approach to a career development program in a non–mental health setting. One of the most significant learnings in both programs has been that both staff and clients/ students value the learning process and report unanticipated levels of satisfaction with their roles in rehabilitation. Additionally, both report positive outcomes at the program, staff, and client/student levels.

REHABILITATION IN AN EDUCATIONAL SETTING: A NEW CONTEXT

As fewer persons with psychiatric disabilities spend less time in hospitals, it becomes increasingly important that community-based treatments meet their perceived needs. The treatment must also be provided in a setting that they will utilize. The evolution of the club-house model and the utilization of storefront settings have been attempts to provide more natural settings. An additional setting that shows great promise is an education setting. The use of the education setting has the additional benefit of helping participants to view themselves as students rather than patients. This change toward a more positive self-image facilitates the rehabilitation process (Unger, 1987).

Historically, one of the first programs to be provided in an education setting was the Personal Education course offered through San Mateo Union High School, in California (Lamb, 1976). The adult-education program content varied from semester to semester based on student preference. Although positive results were reported, there were no controlled studies to validate the program's impact.

The Reading Area Community College in Reading, Pennsylvania (Heffner & Gill, 1981), had a more comprehensive curriculum. Some follow-up data are reported. No effort has been made, however, to link the outcomes (such as employment rates) to the skills-based intervention.

Several other skills-based postsecondary programs have been reported. These include LaGuardia Community College in New York and George Brown College in Toronto, Canada. The LaGuardia-Transitional Mental Health Worker project was designed to test whether or not former psychiatric patients could be trained to function as mental health workers. Project students enrolled in human service courses, as did other students. Follow-up data reports compare the performance of project students with that of other human service students and the rate of rehospitalization in relation to continued attendance. Favorable results were reported (Stein, 1981).

The Toronto program at George Brown College, Rehabilitation

Through Education, teaches community living skills. The program has a large enrollment (sixty students) and reports positive results. Again, no controlled studies exist to link the skills-based program to the results (Schwenger, 1981).

The learning environments of all of these programs emphasize the roles of student and teacher. These are common roles in the non–mental health world and are familiar to the general population. Being a student does not carry the stigma of patient. Learning new skills is a positive and growth-producing activity that implies that improvement in functioning is not only possible but expected.

Education is also an activity that has become a lifelong process as more adults enroll in continuing education courses. When displaced workers need to learn new skills for new jobs, or homemakers return to the job market, education is often the means to reenter the work force. For some, education is used for life enhancement. Photography, art, cooking, investment, and stress management are all course topics offered by education institutions. Education is viewed as the way to improve the quality of one's life. Rehabilitation in educational settings is a natural outgrowth of this phenomenon.

APPLYING THE PSYCHIATRIC REHABILITATION MODEL IN AN EDUCATION SETTING

Rehabilitation in an academic or educational setting is based on rehabilitation values and principles (Anthony, 1979). A program mission will emphasize learning with support as the primary means for improving functioning. A model program will emphasize the involvement of the student or learner in the process of setting and fulfilling a living, learning, or working goal.

Involving the more severely disabled student in exploring and setting such goals may be difficult since it requires that the teacher have creative interpersonal skills and teaching methods to engage the person actively. The teacher constantly works to demystify the learning process so that the activities related to exploring goals have meaning for the student. Direct Skills Teaching (Cohen, Danley & Nemec, 1985) provides a methodology for not simply telling students what they need to learn but for demonstrations and opportunities to practice the new skills. Psychiatrically disabled persons often have difficulty generalizing skills to new environments. It is important that opportunities for practicing the new skills where they will be used are provided.

Identifying and then tracking the skills that will help students to function in their personal settings help to motivate students. Because their classroom work is tied directly to a goal they have chosen to achieve, they see the reason for their effort. For psychiatrically disabled students, this point of view may make the difference between learners who are involved and willing to do the work necessary to realize their goals and those who "drop out" or drift away.

The degree of support necessary in an educational setting is also determined by generic rehabilitation values and principles. Increased dependency can lead to improved client functioning. Students often require a great deal of personal support and counseling when they first come to a new educational setting. The psychiatrically disabled student, in making the transition from patient to student, often needs even more support to provide the security necessary to begin and continue the learning process. The change in roles, although welcome, is not easy. It is important that students have the opportunity to test out and understand experientially what the implications of the role shift are. Because the shift in role from patient to student is a very all-encompassing and dramatic one, the process of change must be attended to. The content of the classroom work, as well as the classroom environment itself, can provide the mechanisms for change. Participation in an educational process in a normal environment can, in itself, be rehabilitative in nature.

Once the student has acquired the knowledge, attitudes, and skills needed to decide upon a goal, an assessment of needed skills and resources and an overall plan have to be established. The assessment process, by necessity, may require individual work with students. It may be important, as Hutchinson et al. suggest, for both the skill and resource needs of the students that future environments be explored by them and/or their teachers so the environmental demand can be clearly assessed. Another possibility is to do the assessment in the environment where the skills are needed, as Taylor et al. did. The principle of an individualized assessment in the chosen environment is critical.

The planning phase of psychiatric rehabilitation process can occur either individually or in group, or the planning process can be taught in the classroom and applied individually with the help of a case manager or instructor.

In an educational setting the skills development and support development intervention are designed to provide the students with the knowledge, attitudes, and skills necessary to achieve their goals. Students may be grouped in classes based on the kinds of goals—living, learning, or working—that are established. The Continuing Education Program (Hutchinson et al.) concentrates on working or learning goals. Classroom instruction relates to establishing and meeting these goals. The living environment goals not addressed in the classroom may be addressed by a case worker or an instructor from the program on an

individual basis. In the Sussex House Program, the skill teaching interventions may relate to living, learning, or working goals.

To provide relevant classroom instruction to help students meet
their goals, the educational setting has to be willing to develop its
coursework in relationship to the stated overall goals of its students.
Developing courses in "Understanding Social Security Insurance (SSI)"
is only relevant if students currently in the program regularly use the
SSI system. Offering courses in "Exploring work values," as occurs in
the Continuing Education Program, is relevant because the students
attend explicitly for the purpose of developing a career plan. All courses
taught should be related to the students' functional assessment.

The model of a rehabilitation program in an educational setting is
only now beginning to take shape. The early development of this idea
is occurring in environments commonly viewed as treatment or rehabilitation settings (Taylor et al.), as well as more typical educational
settings (Hutchinson et al.). In the years ahead, rather than bringing
the clients to the treatment/rehabilitation setting, it would seem appropriate to bring the practitioners and the clients to the educational setting. In that environment, clients would more naturally experience
themselves as learners. The learning component of the rehabilitation
approach would be more real and potent. The process of psychiatric
rehabilitation lends itself easily to an application in educational settings. The challenge will be to develop a program structure, staffing
pattern, and program context that allow such an approach to take hold
in an educational environment.

5

Integrating Psychiatric Rehabilitation into Mental Health Systems

MIKAL R. COHEN, PH.D.

Historical and Current Perspectives

A service system is a combination of services organized to meet the needs of a particular client population (Sauber, 1983). Persons with long-term psychiatric problems have multiple residential, vocational, social, and educational needs. Between 1800 and 1950, these multiple needs were met within state institutions (originally called insane asylums, then state hospitals, and now mental health or psychiatric institutes). State institutions functioned as sanctuaries where persons with mental illness could be taken care of during their illness or, if necessary, throughout their lives. Although active treatment was emphasized, the de facto mental health mission for this population was custody. Rehabilitation was offered as an ancillary service within the hospital, addressed primarily toward providing activities. The mental health service system was organized to support the state institution, not the individual client.

THE CHANGE FROM A HOSPITAL-BASED SYSTEM

With the discovery of psychotropic medication, chemotherapy treatment became a preferred mode of treating the long-term psychiatrically disabled within institutions. The use of chemotherapy to reduce symptomatology, along with a number of other factors including changing federal reimbursement policies, a raised consciousness about patients' rights, and the high costs of institutional care, helped make the social reform of deinstitutionalization possible (Brown, 1982; Rose, 1979; Williams, Bellis & Wellington, 1980). By the late 1970s the resident population of state psychiatric hospitals had dramatically declined (Bassuk & Gerson, 1978).

Deinstitutionalization radically changed the way in which the long-term psychiatrically disabled are served. A variety of community settings have been developed as an alternative to centralized, state hospital care. Today, many persons with prolonged psychiatric problems are receiving chemotherapy treatment while functioning in residential, vocational, educational, and social settings in the community. Many other persons with psychiatric disabilities have rejected these settings and are not engaged in mental health services at all. Neither the state hospital-based system nor the community-based system has been very successful in helping persons with severe psychiatric disability achieve their rehabilitation goals (Anthony, Buell et al. 1972; Anthony, Cohen & Vitalo, 1978; Anthony & Nemec, 1984).

In addition, the change in location of services from the hospital to the community has created decentralized, diverse services. The diversity of services complicates the organization of these services in the mental health system. Previously, the mental health system was organized around the state hospital, but the current diversity of services requires an interdependent organization of multiple community services (Gittleman, 1974).

Another difficulty in defining the mental health service system for the long-term psychiatrically disabled stems from the varied, multiple needs of the client population (Scott & Black, 1986). Many different service systems claim responsibility for the individual needs of persons with long-term psychiatric disabilities (e.g., vocational rehabilitation, social security). The diverse needs of persons with severe psychiatric disabilities for housing, health care, economic, educational, vocational, and social supports dictate coordination among many existing service systems. The mental health service system, however, is the primary system responsible for preventing individuals who need services from being ignored or "falling through the cracks." The challenge is to define a mental health system that can consistently assure that the diverse needs of all who need services are met (Reinke & Greenley, 1986).

COMMUNITY SUPPORT SYSTEMS

The concept of a community support system (CSS) was developed as one response to the multiple services needed by the long-term psychiatrically disabled in the community (Turner & Shifren, 1979). The functions of a CSS include identifying clients in need of service; providing for crisis intervention; providing comprehensive psychosocial rehabiliation, housing supports, family supports; facilitating the use of formal and informal helping systems; and providing advocacy services (Test, 1984). Proponents of the CSS initiative have described and implemented state planning strategies that have encouraged the development of local psychiatric rehabilitation programs. Although immensely helpful in influencing the development of new psychiatric rehabilitation programs, the CSS concept has not provided a blueprint for how to integrate rehabilitation into mental health systems.

THE PSYCHIATRIC REHABILITATION APPROACH

Concurrent with the beginnings of community support systems, the psychiatric rehabilitation approach was receiving increased attention (Farkas & Anthony, 1989). The psychiatric rehabilitation approach is a conceptual way to organize the process of rehabilitation with the severely psychiatrically disabled. The goal of the psychiatric rehabilitation approach is to develop the client skills and supports necessary for clients to be successful and satisfied in their chosen environments.

The rehabilitation process is defined in three phases: rehabilitation diagnosis, rehabilitation planning, and rehabilitation interventions. Within each phase, specific elements are also defined. The approach integrates the knowledge gained from multiple research studies and the experience of psychosocial rehabilitation programs around the country. The approach is valuable in that it is clearly defined and therefore lends itself to replication and study.

USING THE PSYCHIATRIC REHABILITATION APPROACH TO UNDERSTAND SYSTEMS

The psychiatric rehabilitation approach has been used as a framework to analyze, describe, and investigate three units within the mental health service system: the personnel responsible for helping rehabilitate the psychiatrically disabled; the programs that structure the various rehabilitation environments; and the system that organizes the diverse environments into service configurations in a specified geographic area.

The attitudes, knowledge, and skills of personnel involved in psychiatric rehabilitation have been described and translated into training programs for dissemination (Anthony, Cohen & Farkas, 1985; Cohen, Danley & Nemec, 1985b; Cohen, Farkas & Cohen, 1986; Cohen, Nemec, Farkas & Forbess, 1988). The mission and process of diagnosis, planning, and intervening within a network of environments has been described for rehabilitation programs and translated into a way of conducting program consultation (Anthony, Cohen & Farkas, 1982, 1987; Farkas, Cohen & Nemec, 1988). The target population, philosophy, policies, and administrative functions of the mental health system can now be described in a way that supports the integration of psychiatric rehabilitation personnel and programs into mental health services.

HOW TO INTEGRATE REHABILITATION
INTO MENTAL HEALTH SERVICES

A mental health authority that decides to integrate psychiatric rehabilitation into its service system defines its philosophy and policies for serving persons with severe psychiatric disabilities in a way that supports psychiatric rehabilitation. In addition, it performs its administrative functions guided by its psychiatric rehabilitation philosophy and policies. The system begins its integration with specification of the target population for psychiatric rehabilitation. In the broadest context this target population consists of anyone recovering from psychiatric impairment *who is not functioning at the level at which he or she would like to function.* Specific mental health systems may need to differentiate the population they can serve further by describing demographic criteria such as residential status, age, or income. In addition, in times of funding shortages systems may need to specify the severity of impairment in their statement of target population (Bachrach, 1980). In the ideal system, however, anyone who can and wants to benefit from rehabilitation, regardless of the level of his or her impairment, is the target for rehabilitation.

The foundation of the service system is the articulation of its philosophy and policies. Mental health can begin to integrate a psychiatric rehabilitation approach into its service system by articulating a philosophy supportive of psychiatric rehabilitation. A philosophy that supports rehabilitation states beliefs about ideal rehabilitation outcomes. The statements of mission and desired outcomes emphasize helping the long-term psychiatrically disabled to function successfully in the residential, educational, vocational, and social environments of their choice with the most amount of independence possible. Rehabilitation values such as independence, competency, freedom of choice, right to support, right to personal satisfaction, normalization, empowerment, individualization, and accountability guide the statement of philosophy.

Policies translate philosophy into guidelines for practice. Policies are formally stated in legislation, regulations, rules, and procedures and are implemented through service delivery. Policies that support rehabilitation state the desired courses of action that influence rehabilitation practice (Erlanger & Roth, 1985). Policies on high-priority client populations (e.g., the lowest functioning), entitlements (e.g., decent housing), ongoing supports (e.g., for as long as is needed), high-priority programming (e.g., vocational rehabilitation), required program elements (e.g., skill teaching), and mandatory record keeping (e.g., required functional assessment) are important to support rehabilitation.

A mental health system is administered by a mental health authority (e.g., state department of mental health) that has administrative functions or responsibilities that support service delivery (Barton & Barton, 1983). A mental health system that integrates rehabilitation into its services performs its administrative functions to support psychiatric rehabilitation. These functions include planning, funding, management, program development, human resource development, coordination, evaluation, and advocacy. Table 5.1 lists the eight administrative functions. Each of these functions can be performed in a way that is consistent with the philosophy and policies that support psychiatric rehabilitation.

The planning function of a mental health authority involves designing the service system. Assessing client, personnel, and program needs; setting goals and priorities for meeting needs; and designing new and/or enhanced services are parts of the planning function. A system plan that supports psychiatric rehabilitation identifies the overall goals that persons in its target population would most like to achieve (e.g., attend school, work competitively, live independently), assesses client competencies and supports, and develops or enhances services that develop client skills and supports.

The funding function of a mental health authority involves obtaining and dispensing dollars to support services. A mental health authority that supports psychiatric rehabilitation obtains money that can be used to fund rehabilitation services (e.g., obtains flexible funding, reallocates hospital funds to rehabilitation services, and/or markets rehabilitation to legislators and other funding sources), and dispenses money to services in a way that allows rehabilitation to happen (e.g., adequate expenditures per client).

The management function of a mental health authority involves supervising the operation of services (White, 1981). Contracting, monitoring, and quality assurance are parts of the management function. A mental health authority that supports psychiatric rehabilitation

TABLE 5-1   Administrative Functions of Mental Health Authorities

Planning	Human Resource Development
Funding	Coordination
Management	Evaluation
Program Development	Advocacy

writes and monitors contracts based on rehabilitation indicators such as evidence that every client has chosen an overall rehabilitation goal and is involved in rehabilitation diagnosis, rehabilitation planning, and rehabilitation interventions (Miller & Wilson, 1981).

The program development function of a mental health authority involves providing consultation to program administrators. A mental health authority that supports psychiatric rehabilitation provides consultation on designing rehabilitation environments, structuring programs around the rehabilitation process, and developing operating guidelines compatible with psychiatric rehabilitation philosophy.

The human resource development function of a mental health authority involves selection and training of personnel. A mental health authority that supports psychiatric rehabilitation makes hiring decisions for rehabilitation services based on the presence or absence of rehabilitation attitudes, knowledge, and skills; writes job descriptions based on the tasks required to rehabilitate clients; and funds both in-service and preservice training programs that develop rehabilitation attitudes, knowledge, and skills in its trainees (Field, Allness & Knoedler, 1980; Jeger & McClure, 1980).

The coordination function of a mental health authority involves assuring interagency collaboration. Development of interagency agreements, joint training opportunities among agencies, and guidelines for linkage among agencies are parts of a system's coordination function. The coordination function facilitates cooperation among different components within the service system and among itself and the other service systems that serve its client population. For example, a mental health system that supports psychiatric rehabilitation works together with the vocational rehabilitation system to support persons with psychiatric disabilities in pursuing their vocational goals (Cohen, 1981).

The evaluation function of a mental health authority involves analysis of management information and researching client outcomes. Determining what data to collect, setting up data collection methods and procedures, and drawing conclusions from the data are parts of a system's evaluation function (Schulberg, 1981). A system that supports psychiatric rehabilitation evaluates rehabilitation process and outcomes. The data which are collected document rehabilitation goals, client competencies (e.g., strengths and deficits in client skills), rehabilitation plans (e.g., skill development objectives), and rehabilitation interventions (e.g., residential, vocational, educational, and social outcomes and client satisfaction). The data collection incorporates a variety of perspectives (e.g., the perspective of the clients, personnel, and family members). The conclusions that are drawn from the data should connect client variables, program variables, and outcomes.

The advocacy function of a mental health authority involves protecting the rights of the client population (Willets, 1980). Negotiating for more favorable eligibility criteria for entitlements and promoting community acceptance are examples of a system's advocacy function. A system that supports psychiatric rehabilitation advocates for normalized treatment; for residential, educational, vocational, and social opportunities; and for the right of persons with long-term psychiatric problems to choose living, learning, working, and social environments.

ENVIRONMENTAL CONTEXT OF THE MENTAL HEALTH SYSTEM

The mental health system functions within an environmental context that includes other delivery systems as well as political and economic factors (Scott, 1985). Figure 5.1 displays the way the mental health system is built around the client population and rehabilitation personnel and programs; is supported by mental health authorities; interacts with other service systems; and is influenced by its environmental context. The environmental context either supports or creates barriers to psychiatric rehabilitation. In the United States the environmental context includes national values such as democracy (in contrast with the establishment of authoritarian policy) and states rights that encourage the delivery system to be individualized by each state and locality according to the needs and wishes of its residents. The political climate of the system changes with various elected officials and their administrations. The health of the economy influences the availability of funding to support the service system. At the state and federal levels, politics and the economy influence the amount of financial resources and the mandates for how the resources are allocated. Public opinion greatly influences the environmental context in which a service delivery system functions.

In the United States today the environmental context is mixed in its support of psychiatric rehabilitation. Conservative political philosophy which encourages individual rather than societal responsibility for meeting basic needs is strong. Economic problems such as the large federal deficit and high unemployment in many states limit the money available to rehabilitate disabled people. Public opinion reflects increasing discomfort with the visible suffering of persons with severe psychiatric disabilities. Homelessness creates pressure on politicians and ultimately on the mental health system to institutionalize homeless persons with mental illness regardless of their individual needs and goals. The mental health system is also being required to prove the effectiveness and cost benefit of all approaches to serving persons with psychiatric problems. Psychiatric rehabilitation can demonstrate its worth based on the values of cost effectiveness as well as decency to

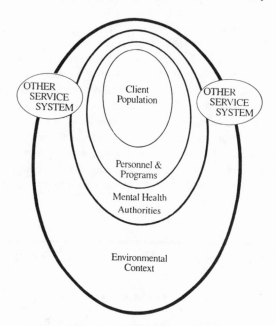

FIGURE 5-1   Cross-sectional view of the mental health system.

the client population. Vocational productivity and normalized housing are two of the outcomes rehabilitation works to achieve.

Case Studies

Within this environmental context, a growing network of clients, service providers, mental health authorities, and academics who believe in rehabilitation are working to demonstrate rehabilitation outcomes. Their efforts to educate the public about the positive aspects of the deinstitutionalization initiative, to research effective rehabilitation programs, to develop and creatively fund rehabilitation programs, to learn and teach new rehabilitation knowledge and skills, and to integrate rehabilitation philosophy and policy into mental health systems are largely responsible for the growth of psychiatric rehabilitation.

The case studies in this chapter share the story of some of the individuals who are committed to integrating psychiatric rehabilitation into mental health systems. The case studies describe the struggling efforts of individual administrators who have integrated psychiatric rehabilitation within their mental health systems. Pierce and Blanch describe the effort in Vermont to introduce psychiatric rehabilitation into day treatment programs throughout the state. The Vermont system began with the statement of a rehabilitation mission. The mental health authorities developed rehabilitation policies for day treatment consistent with the mission, and then changed the way the system conducts its planning, human resource development, management, fiscal, and coordination functions. Fishbein and Cassidy describe New Jersey's efforts to support psychiatric rehabilitation in New Jersey's partial-care programs. They emphasize the importance of integrating rehabilitation into policymaking, planning, program development, and human resource development. The two case studies in this chapter provide a basis for hope that mental health systems can integrate psychiatric rehabilitation into their services.

A Statewide Psychosocial Rehabilitation System: Vermont

JOHN E. PIERCE, M.ED., AND ANDREA K. BLANCH, PH.D.

Vermont is a small and relatively poor rural state. In 1984 the population was slightly over 500,000, and per capita income was 84 percent of the national average.

Historically, mental health services in Vermont have given a high priority to people with long-term disabilities. In 1985 Vermont ranked eighth highest among all the states in per capita expenditures for mental health services, with 77.3 percent of the total mental health budget supporting services for adults with long-term needs. Furthermore, Vermont has made a clear commitment to providing services in community settings; in 1985 Vermont was ranked number three in the proportion of funds spent in the community (52 percent of the total Department of Mental Health [DMH] budget) and number one in per capita expenditures for community-based programs ($22.92). Ninety-four percent of all Vermonters with serious, long-term mental health problems are currently served in community programs.

System Description

Vermont's mental health service delivery system includes the Vermont State Hospital (VSH), which had an average daily census of approximately 190 and about 480 admissions in 1986. VSH serves primarily as a backup for community programs; the median length of stay for people discharged from VSH during the same year was just under forty days.

Ten private, not-for-profit community mental health centers (CMHCs) provide services throughout the state under performance contracts with DMH. In many areas of the state, the CMHC is virtually the only mental health resource; only in the Burlington area is there a large number of private providers. CMHC programs include Adult Services (outpatient and consultation and education), Children's Services (outpatient, consultation, and education and residential), Emergency Services (available 24 hours per day), and Community Rehabilitation and Treatment (CRT) programs for people with long-term disabilities (residential and day programs, case management, and family education).

Implementing Psychosocial Rehabilitation

The primary locus of psychosocial rehabilitation in Vermont is in the CMHC Community Rehabilitation and Treatment programs. CRT clients often have significant functional impairments and long histories of psychiatric disability. All ages are represented, with about one-third of all CRT clients less than 35 years old, one-third between 35 and 49, and one-third 50 or older. Clients are poor, with 90 percent having an average annual family income at intake of less than $10,000. A large majority (71 percent) have been given a diagnosis of schizophrenia or affective disorder.

CRT clients live in supervised or semisupervised residential programs, in community care homes, or in their own homes or apartments. Most have been hospitalized at least once; in one sample, CRT clients had an average of four previous hospitalizations, and an average of 56.8 total months in a psychiatric hospital.

SETTING THE STAGE FOR THE PSYCHOSOCIAL
REHABILITATION APPROACH

On a statewide level, rehabilitation is supported through administrative guidelines and regulations and through a series of technical assistance and training activities. In an attempt to create community services that form an overall rehabilitative system, numerous policy documents and administrative procedures have been revised to emphasize rehabilitation goals and outcomes. Technical assistance and training activities have been situated primarily within local CMHC programs and the University of Vermont (UVM). The goal is to have the capacity for ongoing in-service training in rehabilitation available within each local community, with research, technical assistance, and undergraduate and graduate level training available at UVM and/or at other state colleges.

The current rehabilitation system in Vermont is a product of a conscious effort on the part of the Department of Mental Health to introduce and support rehabilitation and a long history of services and philosophy which were consistent with a rehabilitation approach. Rehabilitation efforts in Vermont began in the 1950s, when a joint Vocational Rehabilitation-Mental Health project moved 367 long-term VSH residents through a halfway house into community living situations (Eldred, Brooks, Deane & Taylor, 1962). Two decades later there was substantial growth in residential and day programs that purported, at least in part, to teach independent living skills. During this period, expenditures for community-based services rose from 5.7 percent to 36.5 percent of the total DMH budget, and the state hospital census dropped from 800 to 300. The rationale for this rapid relocation of people to community settings included the belief that all people (given necessary skills training and supports) can function successfully in environments of their choice. Furthermore, longitudinal research had shown that most of the "chronic" patients who left VSH in the 1950s were still living in the community, making productive contributions to family and community life, and showing little residual symptomatology (Harding, Brooks, Ashikaga, Strauss & Landerl, 1983).

The most recent attempt to expand and improve rehabilitation services began with the repeal of federal community mental health center legislation in 1981 and the concomitant cut in federal funding (a 35 percent reduction in Vermont's case). At that time, community programs, especially nonmedical programs, were particularly vulnerable to funding cuts that could ultimately exacerbate the disproportionate allocation of resources to institutional care for relatively few long-term severely disabled clients (the group with the clearest legal entitlement to service). The specter of a system increasingly dedicated to institutional care for a relatively small number of clients in turn threatened strongly held beliefs in a comprehensive community mental health system.

INTRODUCING THE TECHNOLOGY

The introduction of rehabilitation technology in Vermont was a deliberate attempt to increase the capacity of community providers to help clients become increasingly independent (thereby reducing long-term care costs), and simultaneously to shift both clients and resources from the state hospital to the community. There were three main targets for change during this process: the Department of Mental Health, the University of Vermont, and service providers. It was critical that central office administrators understand the rehabilitation approach so that we could modify our own activities and procedures accordingly; considerable technical assistance and training were therefore directed at DMH staff during the first few years. Likewise, it was important to the long-range success of the project that the state's key educational institutions begin to alter their curricula and training programs. As a first step in this direction, a Rehabilitation Training Project was established at the UVM Psychology Department.

The overall strategy adopted for changing the service delivery system was to focus clearly on desired client outcomes, offer a variety of training and technical assistance resources, and create as many incentives as possible for participating. The hope was that at least a few local programs would adopt (or adapt) an innovative approach and begin to demonstrate the desired outcomes.

Since research on the diffusion of social innovations suggests that new approaches are most likely to be implemented successfully when providers themselves play a major role in designing the innovation (e.g., Tornatzky, Fergus, Avellar, Fairweather & Fleiscer, 1980), an attempt was made *not* to define the specific "model" desired by DMH, despite considerable pressure from providers to do so. Thus, during the initial stages, information about a broad range of rehabilitation "models" was presented, including the psychiatric rehabilitation approach used by the Boston University Research and Training Center, the PACT program in Wisconsin, the Hutchings Psychiatric Institute in Syracuse, the Fountain House model from New York City, and others.

At the same time that this "awareness training" was occurring, DMH was emphasizing a broad set of rehabilitation principles and three critical outcomes that the service system was expected to produce: increased numbers of clients living independently, decreased dependence on VSH, and increased numbers of clients getting and keeping meaningful and remunerative work. During this period DMH also developed and put into motion a new funding strategy (based on a waiver of federal Medicaid rules) that was intended (1) to pay for previously nonreimbursable rehabilitation services, and (2) to reimburse intensive interventions at a higher rate than less-intensive support services. This funding strategy eventually failed due to new interpretations of client eligibility from the federal Health Care Financing Administration. However, it provided a clear financial incentive for developing rehabilitation services, demonstrated in a concrete manner that DMH was committed to a rehabilitation approach, and provided a mechanism for DMH to begin introducing rehabilitation goals and terminology into funding and documentation requirements.

Vermont next entered a period of assessment and planning. Many providers were still uncertain about the value of the rehabilitation approach and had many questions about its implications for their existing programs and organizations. At this point DMH offered to pay for on-site program assessments for each CMHC. Feedback on the assessments went directly to CMHC staff and program directors; results were not released to DMH.

Eight out of ten CMHCs were assessed by consultants from Boston University, one used a team of consultants from UVM, and one did not participate. Through these assessments, CMHC program managers gained increased understanding about rehabilitation and began to see ways in which their own services and programs could move toward a rehabilitation model. The consultants, in turn, gained an understanding of individual programs and service systems that helped them tailor subsequent training and technical assistance activities to the needs of each site.

Five out of nine participating CMHCs decided to continue with on-site staff training and technical assistance from Boston University, two developed consultative relationships with the UVM Rehabilitation Training Project, and two participated in training provided by another Vermont rehabilitation practitioner. These activities were paid for by DMH, but all planning and negotiations were conducted directly between the CMHC and the chosen consultants.

At the end of eighteen months, most participating programs had made a firm commitment to the rehabilitation approach, and had begun to show some evidence of internal change (e.g., the development of prevocational work units, increased client involvement, a vocational assessment procedure, etc.). Outside consultants, however, were unable to provide the ongoing supervision and feedback necessary for in-depth clinical skills training. It was therefore decided to sponsor a "Training of Trainers" sequence in order to establish at least one (preferably two) staff at each interested CMHC as "Rehabilitation Trainers." Four CMHCs and the Rehabilitation Training Project at UVM participated in this Training of Trainers sequence conducted by Boston University Research and Training Center.

Supporting Implementation

The development of external supports for the rehabilitation approach was important both for continued program development and as psychological support for providers faced with the task of continuing direct services while simultaneously modifying programs. Consistent support from above was critical: any evidence of lagging interest on the part of state administrators was quickly interpreted as evidence that the effort was a "passing fad."

In Vermont, the failure of one key financing strategy (the Medicaid waiver previously described), changes in top leadership, and federal and state funding cuts all threatened the continued development of re-habilitation programs. However, the use of flexible federal grant funds to pay start-up expenses for rehabilitation programs and to support on-site staff training helped to maintain the momentum. In addition, an intensive lobbying effort by consumers, advocates, and providers led to the allocation of state general funds specifically for vocational "pilot projects," thus providing an initial source of stable funding for rehabilitation programs.

External support was also provided by the Rehabilitation Training Project at UVM, which continued to disseminate information and technical assistance, organize conferences and training events, and offer rehabilitation-oriented courses. Additional evidence of ongoing support came from internal changes at DMH, such as new rehabilita-tion and employment specialist staff positions and revised treatment plan guidelines, performance contract language, and site visit proce-dures. Perhaps the most important support, however, resulted from the success of the new programs themselves. Several programs ap-plied for and received Vocational Rehabilitation Establishment Grants and within a short period of time began to gain statewide recognition as innovative and successful services.

Measures of Progress

Prior to the introduction of rehabilitation programming, few men-tal health providers believed that people labeled "chronically mentally ill" could work competitively. Moreover, employment issues were con-sidered the responsibility of Vocational Rehabilitation and not of the mental health system. As the mental health system began to adopt the rehabilitation approach, however, it became generally accepted that anyone who wanted to could get and keep a job, if he or she had the necessary skills training and supports. Initially, opportunities were limited to traditional service jobs such as clerical, maintenance, and food service, but expectations have grown as clients have begun to work successfully. A similar shift has occurred in expectations about living situations, and more and more people are living successfully in the community, with support from expanding residential (e.g., co-operative apartment) and rehabilitation programs.

POLICIES, PROGRAMS, AND PERSONNEL

At the administrative level, the Department of Mental Health has adopted an overall rehabilitation mission that is clearly reflected in the state plan, performance contract language, central office staffing, and quality indicators used in program evaluation. In addition, there is increased consumer and family involvement at all levels of policy-making, including opportunities for client and family participation in site visits and a new Consumer Advisory Council. The department's relationship with the Division of Vocational Rehabilitation Services has also improved, with a joint committee currently overseeing planning, funding, and evaluation of vocational services for mental health clients.

At the program level, most CMHCs currently use some form of individualized assessment/planning/intervention to help clients reach specified goals. Eight out of ten currently have prevocational and vocational components designed specifically to help clients get and keep paying jobs. The remaining two centers will begin programs in 1987 with targeted funding from the Division of Vocational Rehabilitation and DMH.

In terms of personnel, 60 of the current 195 full-time equivalent CRT staff work in vocational (20) or day (40) programs. Of these, 83 percent have bachelor's or master's degrees, and at least half have received some formal training in rehabilitation. In-service rehabilitation training opportunities for staff include college courses in rehabilitation offered at UVM, joint training with Vocational Rehabilitation offered through the New England Psychiatric Rehabilitation Training Program, workshops at Fountain House in New York City, and comprehensive rehabilitation in-service training programs taught by graduates of the Training of Trainers sequence.

CLIENT OUTCOMES

Two of the three client outcome measures targeted by DMH have shown substantial change. The number of clients living successfully in the community has grown substantially, and increasing numbers of clients are setting vocational goals and getting jobs. Reliance on institutional care has not decreased, due in large part to reduced or level funding of community programs for several consecutive years. While admissions to VSH have decreased by 25 percent over the past three years, the census has increased by 10 percent.

The change in vocational outcomes has perhaps been most dramatic. During 1985, over half (51 percent) of all day treatment clients in Vermont participated in prevocational or vocational training, and almost one-third (30 percent) received individualized vocational assessments. These activities are beginning to yield real jobs for clients: statewide, 17 percent of day-treatment clients held wage-paying jobs outside of the CMHC during 1986.

Change has not been uniform across community mental health centers, however. As of October 1985, only six out of ten day-treatment programs had a clear vocational emphasis (based on the percentage of clients receiving vocational assessments and/or participating in pre-vocational or vocational training). Programs with a vocational empha-sis showed a significantly higher level of client participation, with 25 percent of all CRT clients attending day treatment, compared to 21 per-cent in the nonvocational programs. They also showed more clients in wage-paying jobs outside of the agency (22 percent versus 6 percent), although the percentage of clients employed in wage-paying jobs *within* the agency (i.e., in work activities or sheltered workshops) was no different (28 percent in both cases). In addition, clients from the vocationally oriented programs were more successful in maintaining employment outside the agency, at both six months (15 percent versus .5 percent) and 12 months (10 percent versus 0 percent). Finally, voca-tionally oriented programs made more referrals to VR services (21 per-cent versus 7 percent) and received more referrals from VR (9 percent versus 0 percent). All comparisons were significant at the .05 signifi-cance level, using chi square analyses.

At the time when these data were gathered, six programs had pre-vocational and some vocational programming, but only two had any direct means for helping people to get and keep competitive jobs. In the last year, several programs have further expanded their vocational capacity, and key indicators of success have already climbed far above 1985 levels.

Despite this progress, programs in Vermont have just begun to im-plement the rehabilitation approach. The majority of CRT clients still receive no assistance in setting or moving toward their own rehabilita-tion goals. No programs yet have the capacity to do comprehensive functional assessments or effective skills teaching and programming interventions for all or most of their clients. Few have adopted a re-habilitation approach uniformly across CRT program components (residential, day programs, mental health treatment, and case man-agement), and nowhere in Vermont has the emergency care system been fully integrated with rehabilitation programs. Clearly, much re-mains to be done.

Conclusions

Vermont's experience with rehabilitation over the past five years has shown that changing the mental health system is an unpredictable process. Agencies did not appear to follow any consistent progression toward a rehabilitation approach. In one CMHC, larger organizational issues (unionization) appeared to delay program development, but once the issues were resolved, rehabilitation was quickly adopted. Similarly, staff turnover in key middle-management positions appeared in one case to hinder and in another case to facilitate change. Because of this unpredictability, and because changes in staff awareness and program structure do not necessarily translate into client outcomes, it seems essential to maintain a clear focus on outcome measures rather than monitoring process variables.

Vermont's experience suggested that the organizational position of an "advocate" for rehabilitation is not as important as the organization's readiness to try something new. Early training and technical assistance efforts focused heavily on executive and program director staff. In many cases, however, supervisory and line staff who participated in training became the critical leaders, often moving into management positions in their own or other agencies. Thus, although the support of organizational leadership was often helpful, it was in the long run productive for the department to support and nourish enthusiasm for rehabilitation wherever it was located.

Flexibility in the choice of strategies was also critical. DMH adopted a formal stance of supporting rehabilitation outcomes and principles and leaving the choice of specific program models to providers. By encouraging diversity and choice, DMH hoped that providers would develop ownership of their new programs and that services would be tailored to individual communities. Despite this stance, there was considerable tension between DMH and the CMHCs regarding issues of autonomy and control, and DMH was often perceived to be inflexible in its demands.

The Vermont experience illustrated that negative or coercive strategies are unlikely to induce lasting change. For example, tremendous energy was wasted when DMH attempted to introduce a standard statewide assessment tool. Similarly, although honest self-appraisal is critical to any change effort, providers often reacted defensively to criticism, and strategies that emphasized positive feedback (or prevented negative feedback from reaching DMH) were generally the most successful. Most effective of all were strategies that did not directly involve DMH but relied instead on information sharing, support, and even competition among providers themselves.

Vermont's experience also illustrated that linking financial policies to desired outcomes and principles is critical. Basing payment policy on unstable sources of funds may cause problems, but not having a rehabilitation-oriented financial policy is worse. In Vermont, program development and training grants helped providers pay start-up costs and recoup staff time lost from otherwise reimbursable work, while linking funding with rehabilitation conveyed the message that rehabilitation is not a transient fad. The proof of DMH commitment to rehabilitation financial policies was especially important to the executive and program director levels of the organization, where an atmosphere of support (or at least permission to try something new) is key.

Finally, experiences in Vermont suggest that the process of change is slow and variable, and that changing goals and standards may sometimes obscure progress. Apparent setbacks may therefore not always require immediate attention; a better strategy may sometimes be to wait until conditions are again conducive to change. Furthermore, since it is the nature of a goal-oriented system that standards for success will rise as previous goals are met, it is critical for a change agent to provide constant feedback on how far the system has come, as well as on how far it has yet to go.

A System Perspective on Psychiatric Rehabilitation: New Jersey

STEVEN M. FISHBEIN, M.S., C.R.C., AND KATHLEEN CASSIDY, M.S.W.

New Jersey is a small, densely populated northeastern state of 7.3 million people. The majority of the people are located near New York City. The state includes large urban centers and extremely rural farm and pineland areas.

There are approximately 129,000 mentally disabled people equally divided between men and women currently served by the New Jersey Community Mental Health system. Forty-seven percent are 18–35 years of age; 32.5 percent are 36–65, and 4.8 percent over 65 years old. Sixty-seven percent had previous service histories which included hospitalization. Their most frequent primary presenting problems are equally represented as affective disorders (18.2 percent), bizarre behavior (16.5 percent), and marital/family difficulties (16.2 percent) (Bureau of Information Systems [815], 1986). Many need help with daily living, employment, medication monitoring, and health/medical and substance abuse services. There are also groups of consumers who have special needs such as the elderly, children, and young adults with chemical abuse problems.

System Description

The mental health system by law and regulation is built on the premise of a strong state government authority. The Division of Mental Health and Hospitals (DMH&H) within the Department of Human Services directly operates seven inpatient psychiatric facilities which include children/adolescents, geriatrics, and forensic specialty hospitals. Additionally, there are five county hospitals. During Fiscal Year 1986 (July 1, 1985–June 30, 1986), these state and county hospitals served 12,326 people and had a census of 5,372 (BIS, 1986). New Jersey's Community Mental Health services are provided through contracts with 130 private, nonprofit community organizations. Twenty-one local County Mental Health Boards provide advisory input on spending and program priorities. The system's service elements include outpatient programs (individual, group, family, and marital counseling), partial-care (e.g., day-treatment, psychosocial rehabilitation) programs, residential programs, emergency services, clinical case management, and system advocacy (e.g., legal services), in a community support systems model (Turner & Tenhoor, 1978). New Jersey currently spends about $55 million for community services and receives roughly another $50 million from sources such as Medicaid, Medicare, local governments, and United Way.

Implementing Psychiatric Rehabilitation

SETTING THE STAGE FOR THE PSYCHIATRIC
REHABILITATION APPROACH

Significant events led to changes in the delivery of mental health services, which helped set the stage for the introduction of psychiatric rehabilitation. Major reform was initiated in 1976 through the report of an appointed Mental Health Planning Committee. The report called for a merger of the systems that served those severely disabled in state hospitals and those more functional individuals in community mental health centers to provide more services for discharged severely disabled persons. In response to the published recommendations, and the public support they generated, funding and policy initiatives were implemented to expand and develop such services. A number of philosophical principles, developed in 1979, dictated that service provision occur in the "natural" community or in settings that were age and culturally appropriate (normalization); that programs were to focus on adaptive behaviors rather than simply symptoms (functional orientation); that there be a proactive stance with regard to consumers rights to service (advocacy); and finally that the service system develop in a comprehensive and coherent manner (unified services).

The third event that was conducive to the development of the psychiatric rehabilitation approach occurred in 1978. New Jersey was one of nineteen states to receive a grant from NIMH to foster the creation of community support systems. The grant was used to increase the availability and range of local community support services for the most severely disabled. This included psychosocial rehabilitation, crisis services, case management, and access to housing, entitlements, and medical services, as well as increased involvement of the consumer (Turner & Tenhoor, 1978).

In 1980, the DMH&H promulgated a major revision of its regulations, incorporating the experiences and principles of the previous community support system development. The concepts, principles, and service activities required by the regulations matched those articulated by the psychiatric rehabilitation approach (Anthony, 1979a; Anthony, 1980; Anthony, Cohen & Farkas, 1982; Anthony & Nemec, 1984). The readiness of the Mental Health System as a result of these events, and the compatibility of DMH&H and psychiatric rehabilitation values and principles, set the stage for the introduction of this approach in New Jersey.

DEVELOPING A TECHNICAL ASSISTANCE CAPACITY

The evolution of the Community Mental Health System through these and other events led to a rapid increase in the number of consumers with interests, support needs, and functional limitations much different from those persons previously served by mental health programs. The rapid influx of new clients made it difficult for programs to plan program change systematically or prepare their staff for new roles, functions, and tasks. Particularly effected were partial-care programs.

Deinstitutionalization in New Jersey depended heavily on partial-care or day-treatment programs with the number of programs and clients served over a ten-year period more than doubling (Borys & Fishbein, 1983). While not planned, this expansion caused an increased number of unsolicited requests for help from partial-care program managers on such topics as conducting a functional assessment, teaching client skills, providing vocational opportunities, and revising record keeping. Concurrently, a divisional study of partial-care programs pointed out a gap between the DMH&H's image of what should be provided and what was actually occurring. For instance, individuals with severe mental illness continued to have difficulty obtaining services, and the services provided did not appear to have an impact on client functioning (Flores, Kamus-Gould & Waizer, 1980). The division realized that moving programs toward a functionally based, rehabilitation-oriented service would require significant program development and training. It also meant that the rules and regulations would ultimately need revision to support the program changes. In order to accomplish this goal, the state initiated a strategy to develop the manpower to respond to these requests. Building a capacity to provide technical assistance by hiring a complement of consultants to impact and support program change and, later, training trainers to teach the knowledge, attitude, and skills to carry out the change began in 1981 and was called the Partial Care Technical Assistance Project (PCTAP).

In developing a Technical Assistance (TA) capacity, the division contracted with a private nonprofit agency, Bridgeway House, Inc., to host the project. This was done to facilitate the recruitment of staff with expertise in partial-care service delivery and to promote the project's credibility because Bridgeway House was itself a partial-care provider. Four consultants were hired to staff the project. The psychiatric rehabilitation approach was chosen as content for the technical assistant consultants to learn because of the match between the principles and values of psychiatric rehabilitation and those of the DMH&H. It appeared to capture the intent of the divisional rules and regulations. Also, the rehabilitation process was concrete and applicable in different settings. Articulating a clear direction was important so that consultants could work toward a consistent goal without becoming overwhelmed by the amount of information and number of daily tasks. For example, PCTAP staff conceptualized the goal of their consultation to partial-care programs as developing environments within which individuals could learn and practice the skills they needed to succeed in their chosen community settings. The Center for Psychiatric Rehabilitation helped the PCTAP staff to learn both the skills of this approach as well as the skills involved in conducting technical assistance (Nemec, 1983; Schein, 1978). PCTAP project staff learned how to assess the compatibility between a program's current operation and an "ideal" psychiatric rehabilitation program (Farkas, Cohen & Nemec, 1988). The results of such an assessment are used to make recommendations to increase the use of psychiatric rehabilitation within an agency. Partial-care providers were free to request assistance from PCTAP staff to increase the participant's commitment to the TA process.

This process tailored and individualized the TA delivery by consultants. To reduce conflicting recommendations by state personnel, monitoring and inspection visits were curtailed during an agency's participation, an aspect of the program that many providers saw as an added benefit. Partial-care program leaders, as well as division staff responsible for contracting, monitoring, and inspecting agencies, were targeted for intervention and change because, without their support, any innovation would quickly disappear (Anthony, Cohen & Farkas, 1987; Anthony & Nemec, 1984; Larsen, 1982). A statewide assessment of partial-care programs was conducted. The assessment provided a profile of how agencies assessed, planned, and intervened with their

clients (Borys & Fishbein, 1983). A technical assistance plan was negotiated between each participating partial-care program leader and
PCTAP consultant using the assessment as a base. Examples of consultant interventions included helping program leaders to: revise agency
functional assessments, revise record-keeping forms, develop skill-
teaching groups, and increase the range of program activities. The individualized TA process tended to increase the likelihood that the
recipient remained interested and received the relevant assistance
(Larsen, 1982).

PROMOTING THE TECHNICAL ASSISTANCE CAPACITY:
STRATEGIES AND BARRIERS

There were several factors that either facilitated the TA outcomes
that were hoped for or set up barriers to their accomplishment. In
many cases, these factors became learnings that have been applied to
other TA or training efforts. Readiness for change (how willing program leaders were to listen to and incorporate new learnings or innovations) was one of the most critical factors impacting on TA. One of
the strong indicators of readiness was how satisfied or dissatisfied program leaders were with their current operations. For some, adapting
ingredients of a psychiatric rehabilitation approach became the answer
to their program questions. Other leaders were quite happy with what
they were doing, and in that case introducing change became difficult
at best. Readiness for change could be influenced by many factors.
Linking funds to the adoption of a new program activity such as skills
teaching was an obvious incentive when available. Finding an advocate for psychiatric rehabilitation in a top administrator within a community mental health center helped to increase middle management's
willingness to incorporate program changes. Also, introducing initial
program modifications that were easy to accomplish, such as rewriting
a record-keeping form whose content was already approved, helped to
promote a positive attitude toward change.

Time is another critical factor in promoting change. Program innovations require time to implement. On occasion, both providers
and state personnel became impatient and expected results within unrealistic time frames. It was helpful in those instances for the parties
involved to review and clarify the goals and time frames for TA and to
adjust either the product expected or delivery dates. Program priorities
often shift from year to year, influenced by funding and political realities, as well as by gaps in service that may be identified. Agency or
state personnel change also often contributed to a shift in program development priority. In those instances, it was necessary to solicit continued support from key agency or state staff as well as to reeducate

new program leaders and identify benefits for continuation of the TA efforts underway. This was often done through individual or small group seminars on psychiatric rehabilitation, during which the benefits of the approach and its compatibility with division principles and values were pointed out. Existing conferences on psychiatric rehabilitation were utilized to involve key staff.

The efforts at implementation were guided by an overall goal for psychiatric rehabilitation that was conceptualized early in the TA process. The goal was to increase the number of psychiatric rehabilitation ingredients within appropriate programs and services (e.g., partial-care and residential services). The innovation process therefore became driven by client (in this case, the program leaders) need. Adopting psychiatric rehabilitation program components created the demand for the development of staff knowledge, attitude, and skills to carry out the new program structures.

DEVELOPING A TRAINER CAPACITY

Several agencies began to request practitioner training in the skills of psychiatric rehabilitation. These were programs that incorporated a significant number of program changes and needed staff development to operationalize the changes into daily practice.

Initially, personnel development resources were unavailable through the PCTAP, although awareness training on the principles and structures of psychiatric rehabilitation were routinely delivered. A training of trainers project in the skills of psychiatric rehabilitation was developed as a result of an acknowledgment by PCTAP and divisional staff that a training resource capacity was needed. Trainers were required first to learn and practice the skills of psychiatric rehabilitation and then to learn how to train others in these skills. The process was a lengthy one (over two years) and required a strong commitment and investment of trainer time.

Fourteen trainer candidates were selected from five partial-care and residential provider agencies, the PCTAP and the DMH&H. Nine of the fourteen candidates completed their first round of training by the spring of 1986. Four of the five original partial-care/residential agency staff received training, while a fifth agency was trained by the PCTAP and divisional trainers. Follow-up technical assistance continued in these agencies to support staff implementation efforts.

PROMOTING THE TRAINING CAPACITY: STRATEGIES AND BARRIERS

The development of a training capacity results in concrete staff outcomes, with new skills learned and demonstrated. Administrative supports and regular practice in the practitioner's setting help the skills become part of everyday practice and complete the program change process. As a state manpower strategy, there are considerations that are important to review. Practitioner skill training is labor intensive and time consuming, and trainer attrition is to be expected. The selection of training sites and trainees becomes critical so that trainee loss is minimized. Skilled practitioners become part of a valuable personnel pool. Since movement of staff within the mental health field is common, a state-level person offering support (for example, attending agency study groups and making job referrals when appropriate) helps the state system retain skilled staff. For skilled trainers, we have created a psychiatric rehabilitation trainers' support network that meets regularly to share experiences and problem-solving training and implementation issues. The network includes both community agency and Greystone Hospital trainers.

Supporting Implementation

CAPITALIZING ON OPPORTUNITIES FOR IMPLEMENTATION

Having an overall direction for utilizing psychiatric rehabilitation helped its development within the state to be viewed as an evolving process. Responding to an emerging need, such as the creation of the training of trainers project, became part of an overall plan as opposed to an isolated event. Another example of this kind of response is the Northern Region Pilot Project. Launched in 1982, it represented a long-term effort to develop compatible program structures, a common language, and understanding between the community partial-care and residential agencies served by Greystone Park Psychiatric Hospital and the hospital's transitional cottage units. The project was initiated because both Greystone and a number of community agencies incorporated psychiatric rehabilitation ingredients into their programs. In addition to providing help with program and staff changes, TA staff are helping agencies to articulate written environmental expectations for clients entering and leaving their programs. This information is shared with appropriate Greystone cottage staff so that they can better prepare clients for community settings. The information sharing is expected to facilitate clients returning and integrating within those community environments.

POLICY DEVELOPMENT: SUPPORTING PROGRAM
AND PEOPLE CHANGE

There have been a number of state interventions that helped to initiate implementation of a rehabilitation approach. Articulating policy is a powerful method of developing state-level support. Policy, in the form of written rules and regulations, provides guidelines for contracting and monitoring service provision. An example of this is a revision of the *Rules and Regulations Governing Community Mental Health* for partial-care services. Written with the input of providers and division and PCTAP staff, it includes psychiatric rehabilitation concepts, principles, and outcomes. The proposed revisions organize partial care into three kinds of programs that will help clients to stabilize in, move to, and/or remain successfully in their community environments. Functional and resource assessments, as well as individualized plans, with prioritized goals and objectives, interventions, time frames, and designations of staff responsible, are required. Client skill and resource development are the primary interventions. Adoption of these revisions will likely increase the demand for TA and training. Residential services are also undergoing policy development. A new mission statement that contains many psychiatric rehabilitation principles as well as other written policy guidelines will also create an ongoing need for rehabilitation TA and training.

Measures of Progress

TECHNICAL ASSISTANCE EVALUATION

The TA provided to partial-care providers succeeded in increasing the number of agencies that have program structures calling for a connected assessment, planning, and intervention process. Fifty partial-care programs received an average of fifteen days of consultation over the past five years. In ratings conducted by PCTAP staff, thirty of these programs have incorporated some psychiatric rehabilitation procedures, record-keeping form, or activity that changed their daily method of operation. Another ten have demonstrated an openness and positive attitude toward the principles and methods of psychiatric rehabilitation but have not yet begun to implement any changes.

When pretechnical assistance assessment measures of documentation (client records) were compared to compatible posttechnical-assistance measures two years later, significant changes were noted in areas emphasized during TA (Borys & Fishbein, 1983; Delucia, Cassidy & Fishbein, 1986). Results indicate that the percentage of skill strengths and deficits as part of sampled written functionally oriented assessments increased by 47 percent. Documentation of resource strengths and deficits increased 52 percent. Time-framed treatment goals increased from 24 percent to 42 percent, and evidence of specifically prescribed interventions jumped by 42 percent.

TRAINING EVALUATION

Over 350 people in New Jersey have received introductory training in psychiatric rehabilitation in the form of workshops, in-service training, and conferences. Nine persons in community agencies have been fully trained as psychiatric rehabilitation skills trainers. These trainers have taught twenty-five individuals in the skills of psychiatric rehabilitation. The impact of the Greystone Park Psychiatric Hospital training is discussed by Craig, Peer, and Ross in chapter 2. It is noteworthy, however, that the hospital trainers have added 140 staff over the past three years trained in the skills of psychiatric rehabilitation to the pool of practitioners working with the severely psychiatrically disabled in New Jersey.

Conclusions

Experiences with creating state-level strategies to implement psychiatric rehabilitation have taught several critical principles that have been applied to technical assistance and training in other developing areas such as emergency services, psychoeducational family interventions, and chemical abuse issues. Developing an overall goal for an innovation creates a context for responding to system, program, or staff need. Without such a goal, meaningful changes become lost. An innovation can be initiated using either TA, training, or policy development. However, all three will inevitably be needed. Starting with one generates a need for the others. New Jersey began with TA and added training and policy support at the appropriate time. A program could just as successfully begin with training or policy initiatives. Clarifying the meaning of TA and training is also an important step since these two terms mean so many different things to so many different people. Technical assistance was viewed as a relationship-based, ongoing process involving program leaders rather than simply a transfer of information. Training ranged from information sharing to skill development. Such clarification can help to avoid misunderstanding. Introducing innovations is often difficult, taking time, resources, and commitment. Recognizing these facts can reduce frustration. Lastly, innovations require a readiness for change on the part of the recipient. While there are a number of ways to increase readiness, people, programs, and systems often move at their own pace and within their own time frames. The art of TA and training is to recognize the signs of readiness and be prepared to act upon them.

New Jersey has invested considerable resources in introducing and implementing psychiatric rehabilitation at a state level. The process for introducing change is rarely a smooth one. Our experience is no exception. Some mental health providers have actively resisted change or have stated their lack of interest in or need for TA. Other examples include trainees having dropped out of training programs; there have been expected objections to regulations revisions. While interventions to overcome these barriers have not always been successful, the gains at moving psychiatric rehabilitation into practice outweigh the losses. This can be seen not only in concrete outcomes but also in the growing rehabilitation culture. The common use of language such as direct skill teaching, overall rehabilitation goals, and environmental expectations is evidence of this culture. It is this atmosphere, and the state's commitment, which are helping to maintain momentum in implementing a psychiatric rehabilitation approach.

•   •   •

Emerging Directions

THE STRATEGIES FOR CHANGING THE MENTAL HEALTH SYSTEM

The preceding case studies not only demonstrate that rehabilitation can be integrated into mental health systems, but they also suggest the strategies to be used. These case studies emphasize the importance of changing the state's mental health philosophy and policies to set the stage for the introduction of rehabilitation into a service system. Pierce and Blanch write about the policy changes made by the Vermont Department of Mental Health that facilitated acceptance of a rehabilitation orientation by the state's day treatment programs. Reflection of a rehabilitation mission in the state plan, performance contract language, and hiring of central office staff; involvement of consumers and family members in policymaking and site evaluations; and emphasis in public statements on rehabilitation principles and outcomes were critical to Vermont's successful development of rehabilitation programs. Fishbein and Cassidy describe the way the state authority revised its mental health rules and regulations to reflect a rehabilitation philosophy and the way in which this created readiness for rehabilitation programming among partial-care service providers in New Jersey.

In New Jersey the state Department of Mental Health relied on program development and human resource development as critical strategies for integrating rehabilitation into their service systems. An in-depth technical assistance intervention was the cornerstone of the New Jersey system's process of change. It was used not only to make changes in individual partial-care programs but also to create system-wide awareness of rehabilitation philosophy. With increased awareness about rehabilitation, personnel in several agencies indicated a desire to learn rehabilitation knowledge and skills, thus encouraging the state to develop a statewide training capacity.

The impressive outcomes in both programmatic and personnel changes in New Jersey support the importance of investing in extensive program development and human resource development. In Vermont, human resource development also progressed in response to requests from service providers. The state took the responsive stance of offering different human resource development options to the day-treatment programs. Each program chose the sources and levels of intervention it wanted. Most chose program consultation and skills training in psychiatric rehabilitation. Although the approaches used by the state mental health authorities in New Jersey and Vermont differed in the extent to which the service providers participated in selecting the human resource development strategy, the two states ended up with very similar human resource development interventions. In addition to policymaking and human resource development, in Vermont the strategies included changing other system functions to support rehabilitation programming. The planning, management, funding, evaluation, and coordination functions all were changed to incorporate rehabilitation philosophy and policies. Pierce and Blanch emphasize the impact of changing the funding mechanisms. The presence or absence of adequate funds to support rehabilitation programming in Vermont seemed to effect the follow through of the top program administrators (e.g., the executive directors of the community mental health centers).

PRINCIPLES OF SYSTEMS CHANGE

Pierce and Blanch conclude their case study with six conclusions about systems change. They conclude that changing the mental health system to incorporate psychiatric rehabilitation is unpredictable, requires service agencies to have at least one staff member who is "ready" and willing to serve as an advocate, requires flexibility in the choice of strategies, requires financial support tied to rehabilitation outcomes, and is slow and variable. Their conclusions are consistent with the dissemination and utilization literature (Caplan, 1980; Hamilton & Muthard, 1975; Havelock & Benne, 1969; Soloff, 1972).

As with most change, a significant lag in time between the development of knowledge about rehabilitation programming and utilization of this knowledge within mental health systems is expected. Muthard (1980) and Glaser and Ross (1971) maintained that promoting cognitive awareness alone is insufficient to bring about change in practice. Jung and Spaniol (1981) summarized the knowledge from a comprehensive review of the dissemination and utilization literature and distilled fifteen principles relevant to systems change. These principles focus on the ideal product (e.g., credible, observable, relevant, advantageous, easy to use, and compatible), the ideal process (e.g., ongoing assessment, involvement of users, strategy development, and support for users), and the ideal context (e.g., readiness for change, adequate resources, and a "felt need" within the environment) of utilization. Based on an analysis of the New Jersey and Vermont experiences and the literature on systems change, the following principles of change seem particularly relevant to integrating psychiatric rehabilitation programming within a mental health system.

1. Changing the system begins and ends with a focus on the goals of the clients to be served.
2. Changing the system is facilitated by an assessment of compatibility and readiness for change (e.g., a "felt need" for change) within service settings.
3. Changing the system is facilitated by the teaching of new skills to staff and/or by supporting staff utilization of existing skills within service settings.
4. Changing the system is facilitated by peer models in the service settings.
5. Changing the system is facilitated by creating a supportive environment within service settings including selecting rehabilitation-oriented management and developing compatible program structures.
6. Changing the system is facilitated by supportive administrative functioning of the mental health authorities including supportive planning, program development, human resource development, management, coordination, funding, evaluation, and advocacy.
7. Changing the system is facilitated by adopting a rehabilitation technology that is credible, observable, relevant, compatible, understandable, and accessible.
8. Changing the system is facilitated by positive interpersonal relationships between authorities and service providers characterized by tailoring to individual agency needs and shared responsibility.
9. Changing the system is facilitated by assessment and intervention with other relevant service systems to assure their support of the rehabilitation mission.
10. Changing the system is developmental and takes sufficient time (i.e., usually two or more years).

In summary, integrating rehabilitation into mental health systems is a difficult challenge. The process of change is laborious, requiring careful definition of the target population; the system's mission for the population; and policies and procedures that support rehabilitation. All of the administrative functions of the mental health authority need to be redesigned to support psychiatric rehabilitation. The changes in New Jersey and Vermont show that although that is difficult, it is possible to accomplish. There has been a great deal of learning about how to change mental health systems to integrate rehabilitation programming, and ten principles for change have been presented.

Mental health authorities that want to incorporate rehabilitation into their service systems need to go through a similar change process. The guiding principle is that the change process must be driven by a client-oriented rehabilitation mission (i.e., a mission directed toward successful client functioning in environments of the client's choice with increased client satisfaction and independence). The change process is characterized by the following key steps:

1. State a rehabilitation mission for a clearly defined target population.
2. Write policies that translate the mission into guidelines for practice.
3. Write rules, regulations, and procedures consistent with these rehabilitation policies.
4. Define service system outcomes based on client rehabilitation goals.
5. Conduct the administrative functions of the mental health authority (e.g., planning, funding, management, program development, human resource development, coordination, evaluation, and advocacy) in a way that supports psychiatric rehabilitation.

ACKNOWLEDGMENTS

The author would like to express appreciation to the members of the Advisory Council of the Center for Psychiatric Rehabilitation, Boston University, for sharing their insights into systems planning.

6
Supports for Psychiatrically Disabled Persons

PATRICIA B. NEMEC, PSY. D., AND
KATHLEEN FURLONG-NORMAN, M.ED.

Historical and Current Perspectives

In any environment, success requires the use of certain abilities. The particular abilities needed are a function of the environment and the person's definition of success and satisfaction. Where abilities are lacking, or where abilities require supplementation, individuals rely on supports. In the psychiatric rehabilitation approach, supports are defined as persons, places, things, or activities external to an individual that make it possible for him or her to succeed in an identified environment.

The first section will further define and describe the term *supports* and relate it to three levels of involvement:

1. support through friendship and social networks;
2. support through case management and service coordination;
3. support through client and system advocacy.

This presentation differs from others in this text in that it does *not* set forth a theoretical model which prescribes program practice. Rather, the presentation and case studies that follow describe developments in the field related to providing support—a critical factor in the overall psychiatric rehabilitation approach.

SUPPORT: FRIENDSHIP AND SOCIAL NETWORKS

Friendship, the most common form of support, involves a personalized interest based on affection and esteem. It is through interactions with others that individuals define who they are. Even more so "from our earliest childhood, we have been judged and measured by our ability to make and keep friends . . . To be without friends is a cause for shame, a stigma, a symptom of personal deficiency that none of us takes lightly" (Rubin, 1985, p. 8). Difficulties in the interpersonal sphere represent one dimension by which severely psychiatrically disabled persons are defined (Goldman, 1981, 1984; Huessy, 1981; Pattison & Pattison, 1981). The need for support through friendship is therefore essential to compensate for lack of skill and other disability-related interpersonal difficulties.

Although the term *social support* is not clearly defined (Starker, 1986; Hammer, 1981), the need for social support is recognized as essential to successfully handle the stresses of daily living (Beels, 1981; President's Commission on Mental Health, 1978). Caplan (1972), an early writer on social supports, defined essential ways in which significant others provide support: "The significant others help the individual mobilize his psychosocial resources and master his emotional burdens; they share his tasks; and they provide him with extra supplies of money, materials, tools, skills, and cognitive guidance to improve his handling of his situation" (p. 5).

Social support is also provided through a support system or network. The terms *system* and *network* connote an organized, enduring pattern of relationships that is experienced by the individual in a positive way. There are natural or spontaneous support networks of informal "caregivers" such as family, friends, neighbors, and lay "counselors" like hairdressers and bartenders—people in a social or economic role who often have repetitive contact with others (Caplan, 1972).

One example of a formal social support system is the psychiatric social club. Members of the first documented social club established in a hospital setting wrote in its first magazine:

Many of us here are lonely souls who have walled ourselves off to some extent from the society of our fellows . . . We have thus deprived ourselves of the possibility of cooperative activity and of the sense of security and fulfillment that this can bring. The Sunny Side Club will enable us to take the first few steps in the direction of fuller social cooperation by giving us the opportunity of working together on its various committees or of joining in its activities. (Bierer & Haldane, 1941, p. 419)

Another example of a formal support system is a mutual help group, where those receiving help are also offering it. Mutual help groups enable their members to feel and use their own strengths and to exert control over their own lives. The group supplies support and a philosophy that helps one gain a perspective on one's own problems (Gartner & Riessman, 1982).

Natural support networks are the focus of social network therapies that have been designed to improve the flexibility and stability of a person's social network (Speck & Attneave, 1973; Morin & Seidman, 1986). For example, at one mental health program, a social network event or meeting "brings together the mentally ill client's family, friends, relatives, neighbors, co-workers, service providers, and clergy. Members of the client's network attend a series of meetings that provide practical, emotional, and psychosocial support for the client and his or her family" (Schoenfeld, Halevy, Hemley-van der Velden & Ruhf, 1986, p. 373). As part of the program, practical supports are provided, including transportation, respite, babysitting, jobs, housing, and meals away from home. Follow-up at from six months to two years showed that both number of hospitalizations and total number of days in the hospital decreased for program participants as contrasted with nonparticipants.

An additional innovative approach to establishing social support networks is taking place through the Congregational Support Program in Mental Health in New Jersey (Holcomb, 1984). Throughout the state, mental health service providers and religious leaders have worked collaboratively to assist individuals in the mental health system who need social support. Churches and synagogues have opened their doors to encourage the development of social club programs. These programs provide opportunities for members to discuss issues of mutual concern, to plan and participate in social and recreational events, and to develop further their social supports outside of the group.

SUPPORT: SERVICE COORDINATION

Both the needs of severely psychiatrically disabled persons and the services required to meet those needs have been discussed at length in the literature (Bachrach, 1979; Peterson, 1979; Talbott, 1984; Turner & Tenhoor, 1978). "Good" programs provide support through personal contact, aggressive outreach and monitoring, advocacy, and interagency referrals, while serving as stable resource bases and continuous supports for program clients (Talbott, 1984).

Much has been written about the difficulties in assisting the psychiatrically disabled to obtain needed services. Continuity and coordination of care are essential to successful psychiatric rehabilitation (Torrey, 1986; Anthony, Cohen & Vitalo, 1978; Goering, Farkas & Lancee, 1986). In addition to providing support through a one-to-one relationship with the client, case management involves assessing client needs, planning for services to meet the needs, facilitating the process of accessing the service, and monitoring service provision and advocating for change (Shifren-Levine & Fleming, 1985; Anthony, Cohen et al., 1988; Cohen, Nemec et al., 1988).

Case management is a "method of fixing responsibility for systems coordination with one individual, who works with a given client in accessing necessary services" (Shifren-Levine & Fleming, 1985). Problems in case management have arisen in attempting to help large numbers of clients negotiate the system. Case managers have often lost the focus on individualized service, particularly with the severely psychiatrically disabled. The case management function becomes more administrative or "case" oriented, and less able to involve severely disabled clients in actively selecting and linking to services (Anthony, Cohen et al., 1988).

Case managers must have a unique combination of attitudes, knowledge, and skills in order to be successful: a "growth-oriented" attitude; knowledge of the treatment and management of chronic mental illness, the use of medication and its side effects, community resources, psychosocial rehabilitation, societal attitudes toward the chronically mentally ill, the legal system, and crisis intervention; skills in interviewing, assessment, teaching, establishing rapport and maintaining relationships, good communication, community organization, advocacy, and consultation (Shifren-Levine & Fleming, 1985; Cohen, Nemec et al., 1988). Finding and keeping such special people proves to be a difficult task.

SUPPORT: ADVOCACY

The term *advocacy* means to speak in favor of an issue or to argue for a cause. Advocacy for psychiatrically disabled persons can occur at two levels:

1. advocating for an individual client as a part of linking the client to needed services, and
2. advocating to alter the mental health system to enhance service options.

Although anyone concerned about a person can serve as an advocate, advocacy is most effective when consumers advocate for themselves (Turner & Tenhoor, 1978). Consumers speaking from personal experience can educate others to understand their needs better and can achieve recognition for the knowledge they have gained through their personal experience with mental illness. For example, Budd, Harp & Zinman (1987) described one of the functions of a mutual support group as a place to develop a consumer-oriented power base to discern and choose those services that are beneficial and to make the mental health system responsive to identified needs. Mutual support groups can also provide a place to share information, to exchange ideas, and to find friends who know how to "work the system" (Budd, Harp & Zinman, 1987).

Support and encouragement for consumers to be self-advocates are essential to enable them to take an advocacy role and become empowered. Another example of how ex-patients worked collaboratively to support one another is demonstrated by Project Overcome in Minneapolis, Minnesota. This community-oriented mental health program is staffed entirely by former mental patients who operate a Speakers Bureau and also provide consultation services to various programs. The Speakers Bureau involves a team of three to four individuals who share their personal experiences by lecturing to schools, colleges, community organizations, and professionals in mental health and social services.

Families of psychiatrically disabled individuals have a high level of commitment to advocate for their loved ones. Recently, families have begun to support each other to become effective advocates through mutual self-help. A further national development for families is the formation of a national grassroots organization, the National Alliance for the Mentally Ill (NAMI). NAMI's success is fueled, according to members, by a very immediate concern: care for their mentally ill family members. It is the personal connection among family members that makes them effective and powerful as advocates (DeAngelis, 1987).

Various groups impact the system through advocacy by persuading key system personnel to implement changes in funding, regulations, and program development initiatives (Mechanic, 1986; Williams et al., 1986). The recent Rehabilitation Act Amendment of 1986 provides an example. The result of a collaborative effort of nine national organizations, the new law enables psychiatrically disabled individuals to access vocational rehabilitation services more easily. The coalition of organizations lobbied Congress for assistance to change the vocational rehabilitation service system and solicited testimony from mental health consumers and groups on the extent of the problems in this system. From that testimony and the recommendations made by the coalition of advocates, the legislation has been enacted as Public Law 99–506. The final law addresses *all* of the major concerns of the coalition and represents a significant victory for mental health advocates (Rehabilitation Act Amendments of 1986).

Case Studies

The case studies in this section discuss various ways in which support can be provided to psychiatrically disabled individuals by certain persons, that is, case managers, family members, and fellow consumers. Each example emphasizes the unique needs of psychiatrically disabled persons related to specific supports that are critical for satisfaction and success in their chosen environments. Goering et al. describe a case management program for the psychiatrically disabled, Chamberlin describes a consumer-run program, and Fisher et al. discuss the role of the family.

Goering et al. describe a community-based rehabilitative case-management program that has successfully individualized linking clients to services through rehabilitation techniques. While originally the program emphasized supporting the clients through service coordination, this alone proved inadequate. Effective support for program clients in this setting must include attention to the client's needs for a supportive interpersonal relationship and advocacy to obtain services for individual clients and to initiate system change. The focus on case management as a supportive service rather than as a brokerage function proved beneficial to program clients.

Chamberlin describes ways in which psychiatrically disabled persons can support one another. Clearly, consumers are able to support each other in the same ways nonconsumers can support them. Not only are they uniquely qualified to provide support as "friends" and helpers and to suggest ways of negotiating the system to link to needed services, but they can also advocate effectively for themselves and one another as the actual users of mental health services.

Fisher et al. describe the family's role in psychiatric rehabilitation. Families serve an important advocacy role by: (1) impacting on the system that legislates mental health services, and (2) insisting that these services be relevant to the needs of their disabled family members. Families also serve as educators, consultants, and providers in the rehabilitation process.

The Use of Rehabilitation Case Management to Develop Necessary Supports: Community Rehabilitation Services, Toronto, Ontario

PAULA GOERING, R.N., PH.D.; CORINNE HUDDART, M.S.; DONALD WASYLENKI, M.D.; AND RONALD BALLANTYNE, M.S.W.

It is commonly accepted that effective aftercare planning for discharged patients is a key element in the comprehensive rehabilitative process. When this is teamed with adequate resources and provision of supports in the community, theoretically, discharged patients should be appropriately serviced. But in fact, the elements are seldom provided in the coordinated manner necessary to achieve the desired rehabilitative results. This section describes a community-based rehabilitative case-management program focused upon service coordination for the severely disabled.

Community Rehabilitation Services is a program for long-term severely disabled psychiatric clients that was designed to address the inadequacies of traditional approaches to discharge planning and aftercare service delivery (Wasylenki et al., 1985a). Its unique structural features include: the use of community-based practitioners trained in psychiatric rehabilitation as discharge planners and case managers. Community Rehabilitation Services (CRS) came into existence in 1981. It operates as a program of Community Resources Consultants of Toronto (CRCT) and is funded by the Adult Community Mental Health Programs, Ontario Ministry of Health. The program includes a major evaluative component comparing the aftercare service use and outcome of clients in the program to that of patients dealt with in more traditional ways. The program's mission is the provision of effective community care for a population of clients deemed to be in need of community support.

The individuals who act as supports to the discharged client are community rehabilitation workers. They are continuity-of-care agents, responsible for assessing needs, facilitating access to services, and providing supportive counseling and advocacy for individual clients.

Program Description

The CRS program functions include rehabilitative assessment and planning, community service linkage and coordination, continuous interpersonal support, strengthening of individual support networks, and resource development.

ENVIRONMENTS

Community Rehabilitation workers were assigned to each of the four psychiatric inpatient settings involved in the original aftercare study. These included a large provincial psychiatric hospital, a research institute, a downtown general hospital, and a suburban hospital. Each inpatient setting was served by one credentialed community rehabilitation worker. At the provincial psychiatric hospital the credentialed worker also supervised the work of four noncredentialed workers. It is important to note that, although the workers worked with inpatient units, they were situated in a community agency (CRCT) and were not, nor were they seen as, hospital staff members.

AGENCY PROFILE (as of October, 1987)

A. AGENCY
Name: Community Resources Consultants of Toronto
Location: 120 Eglinton Ave. East, Suite 800 Toronto, Ont., Canada M4P 1E2
  Population: 2.2 million
Type of Agency: Community mental health agency   **Primary Sources of Agency Funding:** Provincial Government (Ontario Ministry of Health)
Agency Size: Total number of staff: 27   Total number of clients: 500
  Direct care staff: 22   Administration staff: 1   Support staff: 4

B. CASE STUDY PROGRAM/UNIT
Name: Community Rehabilitation Services (C.R.S.)
Location: Same

Number of Programs in Unit: 1
Program size:
Total number of staff: 15
Number of direct care only staff: 14.5
Number of supervisory/admin-
  istrative only staff: 0.5
Number of support staff: 2
Mixed functions—direct care/
  supervisory: 1
Administrative/supervisory:
Number of
  Ph.D./M.D.: 0
  B.S.W./B.A.: 4
  R.N./B.Sc.N.: 4
  M.S.W./M.A./M.Ed.: 3
  High school: 0
  Occ. therapists: 4

Type of Program: Case management
  (Comprehensive Rehabilitation)
Total number of clients: 200
Male: 124   Female: 76
Average age: 34
Age range: 19–67
Av. yrs. hosp.: 1.6; Range yrs. in
  hosp. 0.6–5.4
Predominant diagnostic categories:
  78% schizophrenia
  10% bipolar
  12% personality disorder/other
Staff/client ratio: 1:13

Program Description:
Average length of stay in program: 2.2 years
Majority of clients are funded by: 44% welfare   32% family benefits
  24% other
Majority of program activities are conducted: one to one
Program hours of service: 9:00 A.M.–5:00 P.M., Monday–Friday (flexible ac-
  cording to client need)

Average Length of Time to Conduct Program Activities:
DIAGNOSIS
Initial overall rehabilitation goal: Multiple sessions over 2–3 months, as fre-
  quently as needed
Functional assessment/resource assessment: as needed
OTHER TYPES OF DIAGNOSIS
Type: Social and Family History   Number of sessions: 3–4

Developing the initial rehabilitation plan: 2–3 sessions
Other plans if applicable: N/A
INTERVENTIONS
Conducting direct skills teaching of one skill: 4–6 sessions over 2–3 months
  (if applicable)
Implementing a program for use of one skill: 4–5 sessions over 2 months
Linking up with one resource: 4–5 sessions over 1–3 months
OTHER TYPES OF INTERVENTIONS
Individual therapy: 1–3 weekly over entire stay (if applicable)
Group therapy: N/A

CASE MANAGEMENT DIAGNOSIS AND PLANNING

Clients were selected for the program shortly after admission to hospital on the basis of scores that measured chronicity, residential instability, unemployment, and social isolation. These criteria predicted poor outcome six months and two years postdischarge in the original aftercare study, and thus defined the population most in need of the service (Goering, Wasylenki et al., 1984). Once a client was selected, a rehabilitation functional assessment was conducted and a comprehensive rehabilitation plan created.

The process of conducting an assessment and determining an overall rehabilitation goal took time and had to be completed in stages because the case managers were working with low-functioning clients who were also coping with the crisis of discharge. In the initial months, forming a relationship and getting the client established outside the hospital were the primary focuses of sessions. Resolving survival issues concerning shelter, finances, and food occupied the case manager's attention and time. Once clients were mostly settled, problem solving became balanced with regular sessions focused upon rehabilitation planning.

Much of the work with this group initially concentrated upon living environments. Each client was involved in an exploration of their satisfaction levels, future considerations, and values. The case managers guided clients in researching their options about where they wanted to live, learn, and work during the next six to eighteen months. Although this process was often interrupted by ups and downs in client functioning and attendant crises, all efforts were directed toward obtaining a clear picture of the client's chosen environments.

A client example of how a diagnosis was reached follows. Anne was a 67-year-old woman living with her 87-year-old mother in a run-down house. The intent of the referral to the case manager was to move Anne away from home. The case manager found Anne confused by what professionals and her mother had told her. She had no understanding of her own values and no experience with any other living environments. The case manager decided with her to explore options and did so by visiting each type of senior housing in the area, making over fifteen visits over a period of several months. Anne used her own reactions to these visits to define her values. "I hate wheelchairs and don't want to live with sick people." At the end of this period, she was able to state her overall rehabilitation goal clearly, that is, her intention to remain with her mother for the next eighteen months.

Functional assessments of clients were completed in stages. During the initial months the case managers developed an overall understanding of the adjustment by observing the client's functioning in the current situation. Subsequently, clients were involved in defining their strengths and deficits with regard to future environments. Typically, the functional assessment was not completed all at once. Instead, one or two skill strengths and deficits were defined, and a plan and intervention were completed before returning to the assessment of further skills.

Anne had strengths, as well as many deficits, with regard to living at home with her mother. The case manager observed difficulties with doing laundry, shopping, getting out of the house, and the like. Anne could cope with only one of these skills at a time. After learning how to do the laundry, she was able to consider other skills.

CASE-MANAGEMENT INTERVENTIONS

Even though clients were regularly involved with a number of different services after discharge, the CRS worker took primary responsibility for providing continuity of care and coordination of services. Linking and advocacy were carried out using the psychiatric rehabilitation service coordination skills. Each worker ensured that the client was receiving support in dealing with crises, coping with bureaucratic confusion, and acquiring personal and social skills. As supports were solidified the contact with the client became less frequent until only an infrequent monitoring role was maintained. The option was always present to resume an intensive supportive role if the need arose again. Caseloads for CRS workers averaged between fifteen and twenty active clients. CRS staff regularly identified shortfalls and inadequacies in the service system. These gaps in service were relayed to CRCT's consultants who were mandated to initiate change in the mental health network (Freeman, Fischer & Sheldon, 1984). CRS staff occasionally were involved themselves in community development and program coordination efforts.

Implementing Psychiatric Rehabilitation: Strategies and Barriers

Strategies for success that were devised prior to the implementation of the program were the involvement of inpatient staff in the planning and implementation of the program, the selection of experienced, enthusiastic individuals, and the provision of specialized training in psychiatric rehabilitation for the case managers.

The community rehabilitation service was implemented with the endorsement, cooperation, and participation of staff from the four inpatient settings. This process helped to resolve administrative difficulties and to facilitate the introduction of the concept as well as the rehabilitative staff into the hospitals. Representatives of the participating hospitals were members of a program advisory committee.

All staff had experience in psychiatric aftercare settings when they were hired. They also displayed the personal qualities and attitudes necessary to work with the psychiatrically disabled. Each person was energetic, hopeful, flexible, and committed.

Required competencies for the community rehabilitation workers included knowledge about case management, mental health issues, and community resources so that a clear understanding of their role in the hospital and community could develop. Because of the program's extensive links with psychiatric inpatient and outpatient settings it was particularly necessary for staff to have a working knowledge of psychiatric terminology and a comprehension of the values and culture of the traditional treatment setting. Diagnostic assessment and community service coordination skills were thought to be especially important to the accomplishment of the program goals of improved discharge planning and more balanced and sustained service use. Since so few mental health workers are trained in these rehabilitative functions, intensive in-service training in psychiatric rehabilitation was a crucial aspect of program implementation.

Four unanticipated barriers to the development of community rehabilitation workers as case management supports and the strategies used to overcome them will be described. The problems encountered were related to the following issues: obtaining sufficient training in the skills of psychiatric rehabilitation, modifying role definitions in response to system deficiencies, dealing with differences in knowledge and skills of credentialed and noncredentialed staff, and reducing staff turnover.

Although it had been decided to base the clinical practice of the case managers on psychiatric rehabilitation, there were no local programs or resources to assist with the training in specialized skills. The agency contracted with the Center for Psychiatric Rehabilitation at Boston University to provide the initial training for the eight newly hired case managers. During the first eight months of the program, four weeks of training and one follow-up session were provided. The training focused upon the skills of Community Service Coordination.

This initial training was valuable in several ways. It facilitated an understanding of a particular approach to meeting the service needs of the long-term psychiatrically disabled client that was different from that previously used by the community rehabilitation workers. They were able to incorporate the philosophy and values of psychiatric rehabilitation into their clinical practice from the beginning, and they made a good start in the development of their rehabilitation skills.

However, the training was time limited, with minimal supervision of the utilization of skills with clients in real environments. What was needed was ongoing supervision to enhance in-class learning. The barrier was a lack of funds for ongoing, direct supervision from the Center for Psychiatric Rehabilitation and the unavailability of local expertise to provide the needed assistance. The result was a feeling of frustration. The community rehabilitation workers recognized the benefits of the approach but did not feel sufficiently able to apply their newly acquired information and skills. There was also a need to learn new and different skills as role definitions changed.

The strategies used to overcome this barrier were varied. The most helpful was that one staff member decided to take advantage of the off-campus Boston University program to complete a Master of Science degree in Rehabilitation Counseling, specializing in psychiatric rehabilitation. While taking courses, this staff member was able to give awareness sessions to new staff and provide updates and case supervision that enhanced the other community rehabilitation workers' knowledge and skills. In addition, arrangements were made for some of the other staff to attend workshops in Boston, and the agency contracted with the Center to provide additional seminars in Toronto. Each of these strategies helped the program to realize and maintain its commitment to providing staff with the requisite specialized skills in psychiatric rehabilitation.

System deficiencies that necessitated changes in the role definition of the community rehabilitation workers created challenges for the program. A key objective of the program was to increase the likelihood of clients being linked to existing resources and to coordinate the clients' use of those resources. CRS had considerable success in increasing the number of links to community agencies. There were, however, a large number of client problems that could not be addressed by linking them to existing resources.

Sometimes the services required by the client population were just not available within the existing system. This problem occurred most frequently with regard to skill development interventions for those with lower levels of functioning and with regard to finding decent affordable housing. At other times the services were available but agencies were unwilling to use the case managers, insisting that they have full responsibility for the client's treatment once a client was linked. This policy was in direct opposition to the program's belief that the long-term psychiatrically disabled client needed multiple services coordinated by one individual.

As one response to these problems, the community rehabilitation workers expanded their roles to provide more direct service to "fill in the gaps." The strategy of having case managers provide skills assessments, rehabilitation planning, and skill teaching directly to clients helped to overcome system deficiencies, but it also resulted in some feelings of frustration and inadequacy since the staff had not been trained to perform these specific functions. Staff were able to perform the additional rehabilitative functions by utilizing familiar professional and personal methods but recognized that this approach was not the most effective. Providing ongoing in-service training to expand and upgrade skills was of particular importance in this area.

Another response to system deficiencies was for the community rehabilitation workers to focus more of their efforts upon advocacy and resource development. It was relatively easy for them to be involved effectively in this type of activity, because the sponsoring agency (CRCT) has a mandate and history of advocating for a more accessible system with specific programming for the severely disabled. Active and successful efforts on the part of CRCT to develop additional supportive-housing beds helped the community rehabilitation workers to deal with feelings of frustration and powerlessness that arose from repeated unsuccessful efforts to place individual clients.

A third barrier to the development of community rehabilitation workers as supports became evident after the program had been in operation for a while. Differences in the knowledge and skill levels of the two types of staff created problems. When the program began, credentialed and noncredentialed staff were hired to perform basically the same job, since it was unclear what type of worker would be required. Both types of staff were able to engage difficult clients, form long-term trusting relationships, intervene in crises, and provide ongoing support. But the credentialed staff found it easier to advocate on their client's behalf with the traditional psychiatric treatment system.

Noncredentialed staff members were handicapped by their lack of a solid working knowledge of psychiatric treatment and by not having a peer relationship with the mental health professionals with whom they frequently had to negotiate on behalf of their clients.

Staff development was made more difficult by the split in levels of knowledge and skills within the staff group. The supervisor of the noncredentialed staff had to provide continual orientation to the hospital setting and teaching of basic psychiatry in addition to rehabilitation training. The program's consulting psychiatrist responded to two types of need and interest in the monthly seminars held with the staff. The noncredentialed staff were interested in increasing their knowledge about medication, diagnostic categories, and general problem-solving techniques. The credentialed staff were requesting information about the use of rehabilitation interventions with clients and techniques to initiate system change.

The strategy utilized to overcome this barrier to the development of the community rehabilitation workers was to change the composition of the group so that there was less difference in knowledge and skills. Vacancies in the noncredentialed positions were filled with credentialed staff. This was seen as the most expedient method of reducing the amount of training and effort required, given the small size of the staff group. Another possible strategy for a larger program would be to define roles differently for the two groups and provide separate training and staff development activities, targeted specifically to their needs.

A final barrier to the development of community rehabilitation workers as supports was the high level of staff turnover that plagued the program during the first few years. Although the previously described issues may have contributed to the difficulties with maintaining staff, the most salient issue was that salary levels had inadvertently been established at an insufficient level. Salaries were less than those paid to similar positions within hospital and community agencies that did not entail as much responsibility. The strategy used to overcome this barrier was the persistent and ultimately successful efforts of the executive director to have the salaries upgraded to an appropriate level.

Program Evaluation

An independent research study to evaluate the effects of the program has been conducted by the investigators who completed the original aftercare study. The method of the study is to compare the discharge plans, aftercare service use, and outcome of clients in the program with those of matched historical controls. Data collection methods included interviews with the staff person responsible for discharge planning, and follow-up interviews with clients at 1, 6, 12, and 24 months postdischarge. Details regarding methodology and data analysis are available in research reports (Wasylenki, Goering, et al., 1985a; Goering, Farkas et al., 1986; Goering, Wasylenki et al., 1988). The results of the studies will be briefly summarized here.

Six months postdischarge, a comparison of 92 clients in the rehabilitation program with 92 matched controls demonstrated that the program was meeting a number of important needs in the provision of psychiatric aftercare (Wasylenki et al., 1985a). The program had resulted in more comprehensive aftercare needs assessments, greater numbers of referrals for aftercare services, and increased use of aftercare services by the chronically disabled population. Needs assessment, referral patterns, and service use were more balanced, as there was less reliance upon medical/therapeutic services and more use of housing, vocational, social/recreational, and financial services. At the six-month evaluation, the program had not shown a major impact upon client outcome. However, clients did report very high levels of satisfaction with and participation in the program.

Two years postdischarge a comparison of 82 clients in the program with 82 matched historical controls revealed that the program was having an impact upon several important outcomes that was not evident at the six-month follow-up (Goering et al., 1988). Clients in the program spent more time than did controls functioning in an instrumental role, for example, as worker, student, homemaker, or volunteer. They were also living in more independent housing situations and were less socially isolated. A typical client would have moved to a more independent living situation, would be socializing more, would have developed a close, confiding relationship, and would be more active in various organizations two years after entering the program. However, the client would not have achieved a reduced rate of rehospitalization.

In summary, a program that uses rehabilitation case management to develop necessary support has proven its effectiveness in changing patterns of service use and in improving the quality of client's lives. Several points have been learned about implementing such a program. Psychiatric rehabilitation is a useful framework, but its application with low-functioning clients in the postdischarge period required a flexible and tiered approach. The program required considerable continuing education efforts and on-site trainers to ensure competence in the requisite skills. In response to system deficiencies, the community rehabilitation worker role had to be expanded from its original focus upon service coordination to include more rehabilitation and resource development functions. It was more expedient to hire credentialed staff to ensure the availability of medical and rehabilitation expertise. And finally, salaries commensurate with the roles and responsibilities of staff were necessary to prevent high levels of staff turnover.

Ex-patient Groups and Psychiatric Rehabilitation
JUDI CHAMBERLIN

Ex-patient-run self-help program models of delivering services differ markedly from professionally run models. Professionally run programs assume that clients are nonfunctioning (or inadequately functioning) and develop a formal structure through which help is administered by professional caregivers. Ex-patient groups, on the other hand, usually come together informally, around perceived shared ideas or needs, and usually are loosely structured with minimal formal leadership and no formal administration. Ex-patient groups may function for months or years as informal support and advocacy networks before they become involved (if ever) in receiving money, developing a formal administrative structure, or delivering specified services. Even when such groups do develop in this direction, the kinds of structure and leadership they devise are usually innovative adaptations of their previously informal styles.

This case study focuses on the Mental Patients' Liberation Front (MPLF) of Boston, an ex-patient group that has undergone many changes while remaining true to its original ideology. MPLF was founded in 1971 by two ex-patients who were outraged at the indignities they had experienced in the name of help and treatment, and who formed a group and started holding meetings, attracting members by word of mouth.

From the beginning, the group had two major purposes: organizing politically around patients' rights issues, and acting as a support group for its membership. Some members were involved only in the political aspects of the group; others were concerned only with getting help for their personal needs; and still others were involved both in political and in support work. The type and level of involvement were seen as the individual member's choice.

Members joined and remained with MPLF because they found that it was helpful to them. The group not only attempted to help members through crises (at which it was not always successful), but it aided them through day-to-day difficulties that were often prevented from escalating into crises.

Self-Help Program Descriptions

Long before it was formally articulated, the ex-patients' movement (of which MPLF was one of the earliest groups) was developing its philosophy of helping. People were not divided into "sick" and "well," but instead were seen as being able both to give and to receive support. Similarly, people were not seen as less worthy for needing help, or more worthy for helping others. If a person was in a particularly needy period, others would rally around him or her, but this was seen as a temporary situation, not as a set of fixed roles. And, no matter how needy, people often found they were still able, at times, to give real and valuable help to others.

As members achieved success as helpers, they were able to see why much of the "help" they had received through the mental health system had not been helpful. The help that was given and accepted through the self-help group was offered on a basis of equality; both helper and helped shared a common status and condition. Professional helpers, on the other hand, operated from a superior position: they had degrees, titles, offices, and salaries, and were seen (and saw themselves) as competent and "well." Perhaps unintentionally, they often conveyed the unspoken message that their superior position was synonymous with "wellness" and that the client should not aspire to match their level of success. Further, professional helpers operated on fixed schedules: clients could see them only at specified times for a specified length of time. Such a schedule seldom matched up with the periods when the client felt most needy: frequently evenings, weekends, and holidays. Peer support was available much more on an "on demand" basis (although not *always* available exactly when needed).

Group members developed the belief, through continued relations with and support from peers, that crises and emotional ups and downs were not medical illnesses but an intrinsic part of the human condition, responsive to empathetic support from others who shared similar experiences. Also through practice, group members saw that support did not have to be delivered in a formal one-to-one session in order to be useful; often, the most helpful support took place in casual conversations or activities (such as people going out to have coffee together).

As the group was developing its practical ideology, it also became clear that a physical location to serve as a center for peer-support activities would be extremely useful. MPLF had operated for many years without such a center; it held its meetings over the years in members' houses and in the offices of several sympathetic organizations.

By the mid-to-late 1970s, models of patient-run services already existed. The first was in Vancouver, Canada. The Mental Patients' Association (MPA) was founded in 1971, the same year as MPLF and several other early ex-patient groups in the United States. Because of differing governmental policies on funding such groups, the Canadian group quite early in its history began receiving sizable federal grants (later supplemented by provincial and municipal funding) which enabled it to operate as a seven-day-a-week drop-in center, with a paid staff consisting of group members selected by their peers through an election process. In 1973–74, this author visited Vancouver and was deeply involved in MPA; in 1978, she described its operation extensively (Chamberlin, 1978). *On Our Own* was widely read within the ex-patients' movement in the United States and helped a number of groups to formulate their own plans for funded, ex-patient-run drop-in centers.

The drop-in-center model is well suited to the style of helping devised by the ex-patients' movement. By design, a drop-in center is minimally structured and informal. The MPA drop-in center, for example, was open every day (including all holidays) from 8 A.M. to midnight, and although most of the centers that have been established since by ex-patient groups (for example, in Boston, Berkeley, Baltimore, Toronto, and Portland, Maine) have less extensive hours (primarily because of funding constraints), the principle of weekend, holiday, and evening hours has been maintained. This fits in well with the pattern of members' needs and contrasts with the hours of most community-based mental health services (with the exception of hospital emergency rooms). Obviously, it is preferable for a distressed person to have the option of visiting a drop-in center to find companionship and a sympathetic ear, which are often sufficient to minimize their distress and restore a level of competent functioning.

Implementing the Self-Help Program: Strategies and Barriers

Spurred by the MPA model and by the clearly perceived needs of its own membership, Boston's MPLF began campaigning for state funding to operate its own center. At the same time, the concept of ex-patient self-help groups was gradually gaining recognition within certain segments of the mental health system. In particular, the Community Support Program (CSP), part of the National Institute of Mental Health (NIMH), began involving ex-patients in its meetings and discussions. Ex-patient speakers began to appear at CSP's national conferences (known as Learning Communities) and were vocal about their criticisms of the existing mental health system and their proposed alternatives.

Also, the President's Commission on Mental Health recognized ex-patient groups in its report by noting:

Self-help groups such as Alcoholics Anonymous have long played a role in helping people cope with their problems. Similar groups composed of individuals with mental and emotional problems are in existence or are being formed all over America. (Report to the president from the President's Commission on Mental Health, 1978)

This sentence was the commission's acknowledgment of the testimony of large numbers of ex-patients at public hearings held around the country, much of which was highly critical of the mental health system.

At the 1981 CSP Learning Community, Rose Marie Piette, a consumer advocate from Pawtucket, Rhode Island, speaking for the ex-patient peer group, stated:

We recommend that client input policies that have been developed nationally by CSP people be brought down to the local level and be expanded, the goal being the development of client-controlled programs as an alternative. This is not to say that there is not a need for staffed programs and professionals but to say that there is a need for a client-controlled alternative. (A Network for Caring, 1981, p. 18)

She went on to note that the ex-patient peer group felt that ex-patients needed to develop their own power base, "and that clients have not been asked to be involved in conferences organized by CSP in the past. It has been done now, and we are pleased to be here. . . . However, it has to be done more extensively" (A Network for Caring, 1981, p. 18). Robert Ray, a mental health professional and a CSP consultant from Chicago, then added:

I am connected with all kinds of self-help, ex-patient, and patient groups. Some are doing some partial service; some might be trying to get some housing going; others have self-help groups, including crisis lines. It is about time that we started to put some money into these things. (A Network for Caring, 1981, p. 18)

In 1983, the Learning Community adopted a resolution stating that the funding of ex-patient-run alternatives should become a CSP priority. By the 1985 Learning Community, a sizable number of ex-patients were included as participants and speakers, and Rae Unzicker, the spokesperson for the Ex-Patients' Peer Group, noted during the closing session that choice was the main theme of the peer group meeting.

It's what we want. It's simple and it's not simple at all. We want, for ourselves and for our brothers and sisters, to have the right to choose from a broad range of services including consumer run alternatives and including the choice of no service at all. And therein lies the challenge. . . . We have

begun the painstaking process . . . of developing choices. . . . We are here
for, with and because of people with real hurt. For them and for all of us
we have an exciting challenge to provide real choices. (CSP, 1985, p. 113)

In this slowly changing climate, a few funded ex-patient-run alternatives began appearing in the United States. Probably the first was
On Our Own, in Baltimore, which began operating (on a limited
schedule of two weekday evenings, and weekends from 2 to 10 P.M.)
during 1983. As the group reported in its newsletter:

On Our Own opened the door to the Drop-In Center on July 5, 1983.
Through funding received from Maryland's Mental Hygiene Administration and through money received from the Community Support System . . . we rented property.
    The idea of the Drop-In Center began long ago. On Our Own began
meeting . . . On February 6, 1981. . . . We learned that many of us worked,
were in school, day treatment programs, etc. But the evenings and weekends were very lonely. We found solace in one another. We knew what
tension, anxiety and depression really felt like. We could listen to and
understand one another. We do not consider ourselves or one another
sick, just people with feelings. (Center News, 1983, p. 1)

The article goes on to relate how the group, growing and expanding its
membership, had gotten a state grant to run a conference at which current and former patients, mental health professionals, administrators,
and others met to discuss self-help alternatives. Later the group worked
with legal advocacy groups to sponsor a course on the legal rights of
mental patients, which honed members' advocacy skills, so that ex-
patients could go into state hospitals to train both clients and staff in
patients' rights issues.
    By its activities, the On Our Own group continually showed state
officials and mental health professionals both that the group was a vocal advocate for its membership and that it was willing to work within
the system while espousing its strongly held beliefs. This became especially clear in December 1983, when On Our Own joined a class-
action suit in the United States District Court against the state of Maryland, with the aim of requiring the state to provide legal assistance to
hospitalized mental patients (as it already did for prisoners and institutionalized mentally retarded people). The lawsuit led to a 1985
settlement in which the state agreed to provide such services. Meanwhile, state funding for the drop-in center continued, and On Our
Own has expanded, both by increasing the size and days of service of
the original drop-in center and by helping in the development of other
On Our Own groups (several of which are operating their own centers) around the state.

In 1984, the Boston MPLF finally began serious discussions with officials of the Massachusetts Department of Mental Health and became the successful bidder for a proposed state-funded consumer-run project which opened in November 1985 as the Ruby Rogers Advocacy and Drop-In Center. The membership chose the name in honor of the plaintiff in the landmark right-to-refuse-treatment case, *Rogers v. Okin*. The suit, started in Federal District Court in Boston in 1975, had been a major interest of MPLF; in fact, a number of the plaintiffs were active participants in a weekly patients' rights group that MPLF sponsored within Boston State Hospital. The suit ended with a 1983 ruling that Massachusetts patients had a broad right to refuse unwanted psychotropic drugs and was considered a major victory by MPLF.

The Ruby Rogers Center operates on a seven-day-a-week schedule, with "paid participants" (the term the members prefer to "staff") on duty to resolve interpersonal disputes, promote activities and discussions, and, in general, manage the daily affairs of the center. There is also a position for a "program coordinator" (who might be considered an administrator or director), as well as an advocacy coordinator to provide one-to-one assistance with legal and other problems. All paid participants must be ex-patients and are considered part of the membership. Policy decisions are made, not by the paid participants alone, but by all interested members at weekly business meetings. This structure was designed to keep the center flexible and responsive to the members' needs.

Like other patient-run projects, the Ruby Rogers Center attracts a diverse membership, concentrating on people who have had prolonged or repeated involvement with the mental health system. Members are most likely low-income people (with many subsisting on welfare or SSI payments), who experience difficulty in finding and maintaining adequate housing, who are unemployed or underemployed, and who come to the center out of a need for companionship and understanding. It is the decision of each individual member whether to be involved in traditional mental health programs in addition to his or her involvement in the center.

The center, like other client-run programs, has been most successful in developing a sense of shared purpose and group identity among its membership. Encouraged by meeting and getting to know people like themselves, in an atmosphere of equality and mutual support, members have become more active in working for change in the system. The center has brought members to testify at legislative hearings; to attend and speak at local, regional, and national conferences; and to become involved in local coalitions (e.g., the Massachusetts Coalition for the Homeless, the Coalition for the Legal Rights of the Disabled, and others). At the center, there are frequent discussions (both scheduled and spontaneous) about patients' rights, the effects of psychotropic drugs, housing and homelessness, and other topics of real and immediate interest. One result has been a growing awareness among members that legislative lobbying as well as coalition-building skills and techniques can be utilized to advance members' causes, and workshops have been held at the center on these and related topics.

The center's advocacy efforts have assisted many members with problems with mental health, welfare, and other agencies. The advocacy program emphasizes self-help, with the advocacy coordinator, the member, and, when necessary, an attorney available through Cambridge-Somerville Legal Services, working together and sharing information. Knowledge sharing and the demystification of professional skills have always been major themes of the ex-patients' movement, and members have been helped to be their own advocates through learning rules and laws and how to apply and enforce them.

For example, in Massachusetts, both voluntary and involuntary patients, in both in- and outpatient settings, according to the *Rogers* decision, have the right to refuse psychotropic drugs. Exceptions are provided for a patient who has been determined by a judicial hearing to be legally incompetent; or for a patient who "poses an immediate threat of harm to himself or others, and only if there is no less intrusive alternative to antipsychotic drugs. . . . No other state interest is sufficiently compelling to warrant the extremely intrusive measures necessary for forcible medication with antipsychotic drugs" (*Rogers* v. *Commissioner of Mental Health*, pp. 321–22). A further exception is provided where "immediate, substantial, and irreversible deterioration of a serious mental illness" (*Rogers* v. *Commissioner of Mental Health*, p. 322), would result, with the proviso that, should the patient continue to object, the doctor must petition the court for a competency hearing. If a patient is found incompetent (at a hearing at which the patient is represented by counsel), only a judge can order continued involuntary drugging, based on an individually determined "substituted judgment" decision, in which the judge must weigh, among other factors, "the patient's expressed preferences regarding treatment" (*Rogers* v. *Commissioner of Mental Health*, p. 318). It should be clear that, in theory, Massachusetts patients are the beneficiaries of probably the most comprehensive right-to-refuse provisions in the country. However, members of the Ruby Rogers Center have numerous complaints involving forced drugging, and the center frequently receives telephone complaints from current patients about it. (Some of the people who first contact the center in this way have become, after discharge, active center participants; others have not.) The center's advocacy efforts in this area involve both informing patients about the existence and scope of *Rogers* protections, as well as negotiating with staff on behalf of (and with the assistance of) individuals who seek such assistance. On a system level, the center works with the Coalition for the Legal Rights of the Disabled to enforce *Rogers* protections, particularly in outpatient programs, where many violations have been found to occur.

Obviously, advocacy efforts also extend into other areas, including landlord-tenant issues; discrimination in housing, employment, and entitlements; efforts to obtain low-income housing; inadequate or inappropriate mental health services; and a variety of other issues for which members have sought assistance. While, clearly, not all problems can be solved through the center's advocacy efforts, at the very least the member is assured a sympathetic hearing, the presumption of belief, and access to relevant information. The availability of a backup lawyer at legal services (part of whose job description includes an active liaison with the center) has also been effective at times when lay advocacy has reached its limits.

The concept of a patient-run program, which includes advocacy that may often be adversarial with the mental health system, has made many mental health professionals wary or skeptical of independent self-help groups. However, through the history of the ex-patients' movement, there have always been sympathetic professionals (clinicians, administrators, researchers, and academics) who have played helpful and supportive roles. The key for the professional must be the recognition of the sensitivity of his or her position: to be supportive and to provide information or assistance, without being controlling or in charge. It is the group which should determine the level of professional involvement. Within these constraints, however, much genuine assistance has been provided. When groups are first starting out, professionals can be helpful by (for example) offering free meeting space; access to telephones, copying machines, and postage meters; and, through their acceptance of ex-patient activities, serving as role models to more skeptical members of the professional community. As the group becomes more established and begins to formulate specific action goals, professional roles include providing information and training about funding possibilities and procedures; providing letters of support for grant applications; and serving on advisory boards. Ex-patient groups frequently need technical assistance in such areas as bookkeeping, grant writing, record keeping, and so forth, and this has often been provided by professionals. The self-help model is maintained because it is the group which defines need and contracts (formally or informally) for its provision.

With the increasing sophistication of ex-patient groups, however, they have begun to provide technical assistance to one another. Many groups' charters, bylaws, and similar documents, as well as grant applications, have been modeled on those of more established groups. In 1986, this technical assistance function was formalized by the creation of the National Mental Health Consumer Self-Help Clearinghouse, cofunded by the National Institute of Mental Health and the National Institute on Disability and Rehabilitation Research in cooperation with the Boston University Center for Psychiatric Rehabilitation. Administered by Project SHARE of Philadelphia, this clearinghouse serves to link ex-patient groups in need of technical assistance in specific areas with those groups that have such expertise, and to fund training projects.

Self-help groups are becoming an established part of the mental health continuum, increasing the range of choices available to clients and providing a viable alternative model of helping. Professionals in the field need to learn more about these groups and the self-help model and to make this information available to their clients. Further, professionals and self-help practitioners need to communicate in an atmosphere of trust and mutual respect, recognizing their differences of philosophy and approach, while recognizing as well their shared belief in helping each individual, no matter how labeled, to achieve the maximal degree of autonomy. Professionals who have adopted the rehabilitation approach, with its emphasis on individual needs and client autonomy, have a particular responsibility to familiarize themselves and their clients with local ex-patient groups.

Self-help Programs and Psychiatric Rehabilitation

There are a number of similarities between the psychiatric rehabilitation approach and that of ex-patient self-help groups (although, of course, the psychiatric rehabilitation approach is both professional and formal). Unlike many mental health interventions, psychiatric rehabilitation depends on the cooperation and the active involvement of the client. The stress that psychiatric rehabilitation professionals put on doing things only *with* clients (and not to or for them) is one that strikes a responsive chord in people who, all too often, have been subjected to paternalistic, coercive, or compulsory interventions. Similarly, the stress on the individualization of the psychiatric rehabilitation approach compares favorably with impersonal or depersonalizing practices that are all too familiar to most clients. For these reasons, many individuals may choose to combine being members of ex-patient self-help groups with being clients of psychiatric rehabilitation professionals, and such a combination should work well.

To further understanding and cooperation, professionals can invite representatives of ex-patient groups to speak to staff and clients. Academics can invite group members to address their students. Administrators can help move reluctant bureaucracies toward funding (and then toward adequate and continued funding) of self-help alternative projects. Researchers can help devise the innovative techniques that will be necessary to evaluate such projects properly. In many areas, such contacts are already well established.

Professionals need to be aware that members of ex-patient groups are often angry and frustrated. People who have seen themselves and their peers subjected to illegal forced drugging and other violations of basic rights and human dignity (unfortunately still all too common) may find it hard to be dispassionate; this often contrasts with the professional style of objectivity and neutrality. But with the recognition that the full spectrum of helping services must include the self-help option, difficulties of communication can be overcome, and people of very different backgrounds can learn to work together toward the goals of autonomy and self-esteem for psychiatrically labeled people.

The Family and Psychiatric Rehabilitation: A Family/Professional Perspective

HARRIET FISHER; LEROY SPANIOL, PH.D.; ANTHONY M. ZIPPLE, SC.D.; AND ANN CORAPI

Professionals need new ways of looking at the family, a new perspective or paradigm. Families must be seen as part of the solution, not as part of the cause of severe mental illness. The National Alliance for the Mentally Ill, a family advocacy and support organization, has grown since the late seventies into an important resource for assisting professionals in understanding the family's role in the rehabilitation process. Families have a lot to offer the rehabilitation process. They can be an important asset to the continuity and coordination of care needed for treatment of family members suffering from mental illness. In fact, families often are the primary caretakers because the mental health system has been unable or unwilling to provide the services needed in the community to care for their disabled family members adequately (Hatfield, 1987). While families are often eager to assist their family member, they frequently lack the knowledge, skills, and support systems to be truly helpful (Spaniol, Jung et al., 1987).

Old theories take a long time to die. Many professionals have begun to go beyond such concepts as the "schizophrenogenic mother," "ne'er-do-well father," and the more recent "high expressed emotion families." Yet, many other professionals are approaching families with the same old beliefs, interventions, and blame. All too often professionals still function as though parenting or the family structure has been the cause of the mental illness. All too often the family is seen as needing therapy to prevent or to heal the mental illness of the family member with the disability. All too often the family is stigmatized by unnecessary negative labeling.

Family Roles in Psychiatric Rehabilitation

Families can serve a variety of fulfilling roles in the psychiatric rehabilitation process. Family members can serve as educators, consultants, advocates, and partners in a support system for the disabled family member, other families, professionals, and legislators.

FAMILIES AS EDUCATORS

Families can help their disabled family member understand his or her illness, diagnosis, medication, side effects, and the implications of the rehabilitation intervention. The amount of contact between families and their disabled family member is often greater than the contact professionals have. Families are in an excellent position to teach and to coach their family member in important living and management skills, yet at times families may need special help in developing these skills.

Many families have become especially knowledgeable about mental illness. In some cases they have come to know more than the professional. In any event, their knowledge is an important resource in the rehabilitation process. In addition to the technical knowledge, families know their own family member well. They know how he or she reacts to life events, to the illness, and to the interventions of the mental health system. They know their family member's strengths and weaknesses. The family's knowledge is an important adjunct to the knowledge professionals gain from their brief experience with their client. Families can teach professionals what they know about their family member and can update them about mental illness and its treatment.

It may sound presumptuous to assume that families can teach professionals about mental illness. Unfortunately, many professionals have never been trained, have been trained incorrectly, are out of touch with current developments, or are burned out (Minkoff, 1987). Fortunately, many professionals are eager to learn new skills and gain new information. They are often as frustrated as the family members with the quality of services provided to persons with severe mental illness. They can acknowledge the inadequacy of their preparation and realize that the mental health system is not providing them with the answers they need. There are other professionals who need to be more assertively confronted. Families can also teach these more resistant professionals (Zipple & Spaniol, 1987).

Families also need to educate professionals about how they experience the mental illness of their family member. Professionals need to see the family's experience as valid and as normal. Families go through a process of adjusting to having a family member with a severe mental illness. Their process is similar in many ways to the efforts of families that deal with other types of crises, such as a disabling physical disability. Families may experience denial, anger, acceptance, coping, and finally advocacy as they come to grips with this devastating illness and its impact on their loved ones. What is especially helpful to professionals is to see the family experience as the normal process of adjusting to a traumatic loss of the person they once knew. Their expectations for their loved one are shattered by his or her unremitting personality and behavioral changes. We know from the literature on loss that individuals experience tremendous depths of feelings, act quite differently from the ways in which they would normally act, and appear confused and despondent when confronted with a loss situation (Bloom-Feshbach & Bloom-Feshbach, 1987).

Professionals have often attributed the mental illness of the disabled one to the reactions they have observed in other family members. What professionals have not fully realized is that these reactions are perfectly normal, given the crisis families are dealing with. This new awareness, that is, of family adjustment to a crisis, can provide an important new perspective to professionals in working with families. Instead of seeing families as "crazy," they can see them as reacting normally to a severe loss. With this perspective come techniques to assist families to deal with their reactions at each phase of their "normal process of adjustment." The literature on stress, adaptation, and coping provides many examples of relevant techniques.

Families are important educators for vendors of mental health services. They can provide important feedback on how programs are functioning, and on how well clients are being served. Families can provide that extra source of motivation to vendors to monitor and evaluate the outcomes of their programs regularly. Families can also be an important source of imaginative ideas about program changes and program innovations. Family members have expertise in avocational and social areas of programming. These can range from subjects such as hobbies, practical projects, work skills, recreation, and artistic endeavors. Vendors can call on the family to teach their skills to the staff or to volunteer their time to assist in the programming.

FAMILIES AS CONSULTANTS

In a professional's first contact with the ill person he or she may be told that the family was cruel to him or her, never paid attention, or was too overprotective or domineering. The client may say the family has spent his or her inheritance; that he or she is adopted; that he or she is being persecuted. Only by consulting with the family will the professional know whether this information is accurate or if it is a symptom of the illness. The family's input can help to assess more fully the accuracy of the disabled member's statements and the reality of his or her family background.

Families are also important sources of information about the disabled family member's strengths, abilities, interests, and special talents. Focusing on the disabled person's deficits can be especially detrimental to his or her rehabilitation. It is more productive to develop strengths, and the family often has up-to-date information about these strengths. The focus on the disability is particularly acute in the area of mental illness. Perhaps this is because the illness is so disabling. Families as active consultants can help to refocus the rehabilitation process on what their disabled family member can do, wants to do, or needs to do to function effectively in the living, learning, work, and social environments of his or her choice.

Families can be an important resource in the development and implementation of the rehabilitation plan. Many clients continue to be involved actively with their families. Families are an important source of information on how their disabled family members are doing. Their role as consultants to the planning team can increase the likelihood that that plan will actually work. Families can give input into the content of the plan, the steps necessary to carry out the plan, and ways to monitor progress. Their wealth of information about their family member can be an important resource to the rehabilitation professional.

Families can also serve as consultants to boards of directors, community boards, and mental health advisory boards (Bernheim, 1987). They can give important input on how programs are functioning, how service linkages are working, and how clients are benefiting or not benefiting from what is happening. Board members need to hear from family members. They need to know their perspective and to include it in their decision-making and advising process.

FAMILIES AS ADVOCATES

Families, more than any other segment of society, know of the many needs of the mentally ill population that are not currently being met. Families, more than any other group, are advocating for a balanced service system including accredited hospitals, more enlightened rehabilitation programs, supported housing (quarter-way residences, half-way residences on hospital grounds and in the community, cooperative apartments, single-room-occupancy residences), and supported work opportunities (Bernheim, 1987). Families are in the vanguard of those advocating for newly proven treatment methodologies to be in widespread use. Families of the mentally ill are in total support of programs that treat their family members as individuals with something useful they can present to society. Examples of such innovative programs include Fountainhouse, vocational programs suited to an individual's skills rather than low-paying, unskilled jobs, and education programs such as the Continuing Education Program at Boston University, where students are helped to develop and implement a career plan that meets their interests and abilities.

The concerns of families, however, include more than their own family members. Families know that gains for their family member mean gains for the disabled members of all families. They know that clients and families have similar needs. They know that the efforts of each family contribute to the overall effort to change the mental health system. Thus, families who have joined together in the National Alliance for the Mentally Ill have a sense of shared effort and advocacy. They learn that they are not alone in how they feel about their family member, or in how they experience the mental health system. Other family members feel and experience the same thing. Advocacy brings families out of the closet. Advocacy makes the inherent strengths of families more available to the greater community. Advocacy links families to one another. Advocacy builds the family's sense of confidence in their ability to make a difference for their family member and other disabled persons. Advocacy strengthens the potential for healing within the family and within society.

Professionals are also the recipients of family advocacy. Families can and have advocated with professionals for improved services helpful to family members and to professionals (Bernheim, 1987). While professionals do benefit from family advocacy they often find it difficult to deal with. Advocacy takes families out of the docile, accepting role that professionals are taught to expect from them. Professionals often feel that families are too aggressive. Professionals may feel families are blaming them just as they say *they* have been blamed. In addition, professionals are not trained to deal with healthy families. They often have to find some problem with families in order to feel comfortable working with them. Professionals are going through many adjustments as they are confronted with strong-willed, well-read, and articulate families. Once professionals can begin to see the basic wellness of families and to acknowledge their important role in the rehabilitation process, professionals will calm down and get back to their basic job of providing quality services to their clients.

Professionals are clearly the benefactors of family advocacy. Professionals often feel alone in their own advocacy efforts for clients. Families can bring about changes that professionals alone could never bring about. Professionals will benefit from these changes in practice, programs, and systems. Families know that their advocacy will make a difference, and they want the needed changes with all possible haste. They are determined to change the practice of mental health by changing the ways in which professionals are trained, programs are operated, and systems are planned and managed. And they know they will. Professionals need to join in partnership with families because together they can make a better mental health system. Families need professionals. Their disabled family members need professionals. The professionals need families.

The National Alliance for the Mentally Ill has over 900 local chapters in every part of the country. A prime purpose of NAMI is to advocate for enlightened legislation and services for the severely mentally ill. At the national and local level there are many important support and advocacy activities. Professionals need to see NAMI and its local affiliates as resources for families they are working with. Professional activities can benefit from the support and advocacy NAMI can give.

FAMILIES AS PROVIDERS

Providing is the usual role assigned to families. They fit this role easily for it is just an extension of their many years of parenting. However, they should not be cast in this role unless it is elective. For far too many years it has been "their place." Alternatives are needed to having the parents replace the mental health system as the primary caretaker. Families can assist the treatment team, educate the treatment team, consult with the treatment team, and advocate for the treatment team. But they should not be the primary treatment givers for their disabled family member. This is the professional's role.

There are many things that families can provide short of being the primary treatment givers. Families can provide some teaching and coaching of daily-living and problem-solving skills. Families can provide assistance in understanding and monitoring medication usage and its side effects. Families can provide social opportunities through family gatherings and by encouraging and supporting friendships for their disabled family member. Family groups can assist programs by organizing activities and social gatherings for the clients of these programs. Family groups can provide special activities during the many holidays. These suggestions are not intended to exhaust the possibilities for activities or services that families can provide. The important point is that families cannot become the primary support system or provider of services unless they personally choose this role. As family members, however, there are many things they can do and are doing with their family member with the disability as well as with other members of their family.

Professionals should not look upon family members as the easy-to-recruit, primary caregivers in the family home. This has too frequently been the solution to a difficult problem. The resources of the family home should be available, but they should not be the only option. For independence and age-appropriate functioning to occur, people need to be able to live away from the family home. Families also need this. They need the opportunity to separate from their children and to get on with their own lives. Families and professionals together need to look for broader solutions to the issues of service provision. Professionals cannot allow the availability of family support for the client to distract them from their own need to periodically review and update their services and systems of service with the severely mentally ill. Families do not want to take over the mental health system; they want to radically change it so that it routinely provides competent medical and rehabilitation interventions.

Families and Professionals Together

In the last analysis, families and professionals are in this together. Their mutual and sometimes independent roles are still being conceived and negotiated. What is important is that they work together as partners in the rehabilitation of the disabled family member. The commitment to the partnership is what is important, along with mutual respect, frank honesty, and a flexibility that respects the inherent ambiguity of mental illness and our efforts to deal with it. This will begin to reduce the blaming that often occurs and redirect our energies toward helping the person with the disability.

The client also is a partner in this process and has his or her own distinct role. NAMI's vision is that everyone work together cooperatively, as members of the team. This positive view will release the energies for healing in each of the members of this team, for their mutual benefit.

Families want to be looked at as a part of the solution to the many functional problems associated with severe mental illness. Families, in differing degrees, have knowledge, strengths, energy, and interests in the well-being of their disabled family member. They also have many ties to and influences with community resources. They can be useful in building a more complete and balanced continuum of services within the community, including the hospital.

• • •

Emerging Directions

Support can be provided to the psychiatrically disabled through friendship and social networks, case management and service coordination, and client and system advocacy. The preceding case studies suggest four principles pertaining to creating, offering, and strengthening supports for psychiatrically disabled persons.

The *first* principle is that support, in and of itself, is a critical rehabilitation intervention.

An effective psychiatric rehabilitation program attends to the support needs of its clients. Providing support is a program value, and evidence of this value is seen in the treatment of clients, staff, and those outside of the program who also support the clients. Supports are critical to client success in the environments where they choose to live, learn, and work. Research on case management programs such as the one described by Goering et al. indicate that, over a long period of time, case management can make a difference in client functioning, as well as in the client use of services (Goering, Farkas et al., 1988; Goering, Wasylenki et al., 1988). Much more work needs to be done to document actual outcomes for support interventions than has traditionally been reported (Farkas, Nemec & Anthony, in press). Persons with psychiatric disabilities must be supported both as people and as persons with disabilities. They must be given support in the form of friendship, services, and community acceptance.

The *second* principle is that support also must be provided to those who support the clients themselves. All three programs in this chapter emphasized the need to support or nurture those who do the supporting.

Case managers require the support of well-funded programs to which to link their clients. Goering et al. make the point that effective and comprehensive systems of service are essential. Without adequate services available for their clients, case managers are reduced to trying to provide services themselves. This endeavor can meet with minimal success at best and almost guarantees burnout among the case manager group. Organizational structures are needed which enable case managers to perform their assigned functions and which facilitate both their personal and professional development.

Families require the support of receptive professionals; mental health administrators and practitioners need to listen to the families and to structure their mental health services to meet the needs they identify. Emotional support is essential. As Fisher, Spaniol, Zipple, and Corapi (chap. 6, this vol.) explain, without adequate information, feedback, and assistance with stress management, families are unable to mobilize their own resources to benefit their disabled family members optimally.

Consumers must be supported to succeed both as individuals and as helpers to their peers. Resources must be provided to enable consumers to develop their own program—space, money, and technical assistance. Chamberlin effectively makes the point that openness is needed on the part of everyone involved in mental health service delivery: openness to the idea that consumers should have a voice; openness to the inevitability of consumer participation in their own treatment; and openness to providing additional support as needed to maintain the momentum of individuals and of the consumer movement on the road to success.

A *third* principle is that supports must be individualized. The supports offered need to be personalized to each person in need. Chamberlin points out that no matter how needy a person might feel, he or she is still individually able to help and support others.

Goering et al. emphasize some ways in which rehabilitation programs and mental health systems can promote individualization, thereby enabling the case manager to provide or obtain needed supports for his or her clients. Timelines must include adequate periods for assessment and planning as well as providing rehabilitation interventions. Staff-client ratios must permit one-to-one attention.

Individualization may also include the extensive involvement of the client's family. The Fisher et al. article emphasizes that families look for assistance on treatment coordination, referrals, practical advice, information on mental illness, and assistance with stress management to enable themselves to help in the care of their individual family member.

The *fourth* and final principle is that support includes making opportunities available as well as offering assistance, encouragement, and advocacy. Opportunities must exist for clients to become active participants in their own rehabilitation and to foster their own personal growth. Opportunities for consumer involvement in program operation also foster personal growth and the acceptance of responsibility. Consumer involvement in program and policy development increases the likelihood that the supports provided will be those which are most needed. Chamberlin and Fisher et al. address the need for avenues for client and family involvement and the important emerging role of families and consumers in the areas of education, service provision, and political advocacy. Clearly, the future direction for enhancing the success and satisfaction of people with psychiatric disabilities must emphasize development and the provision of support.

7
The Future of Psychiatric Rehabilitation

WILLIAM A. ANTHONY, PH.D., AND
MARIANNE D. FARKAS, SC.D.

Putting Theory into Practice

Psychiatric rehabilitation practice has highlighted different issues in many different areas (residential, vocational, educational, systems, and supports). These learnings provide the backdrop for a discussion about the future of rehabilitation.

RESIDENTIAL REHABILITATION PROGRAMS

In the effort to develop residential rehabilitation programs for persons with psychiatric disabilities, Alternatives Unlimited, ReVisions, and Greystone Psychiatric Hospital all came face-to-face with the problems arising from earlier approaches to residential care. In the initial stages of the rehabilitation process, residents are given choices about where they would like to live. When such decision making is taken seriously it becomes very clear that the client's preferences are often for long-term stable housing situations rather than for the time-limited, treatment-oriented residential settings in which most are currently housed. To take client preferences truly into account (one of the basic values of the rehabilitation approach), it is necessary to separate the issue of where clients live from the kind of treatment or rehabilitation they are able to receive.

A second learning comes from the difficulties the residents have in living successfully in their housing of choice. The ability of residential programs to develop systematic steps to help residents transfer what they have learned in one setting to the next setting seems tied, in part, to the range of housing options accessed by the residential programs.

In other words, the more varied the housing options, the more likely it is that the program can teach residents the skills they need in the actual environment in which they hope to remain. Success in rehabilitation terms, however, is not only a function of skill use, but also a function of the availability of ongoing support. Obviously, if a residential program has only a time-limited mandate, then long-term ongoing support becomes a major problem.

The third learning for the field of residential rehabilitation, derived from the efforts of the programs described in this book, is that the role of the hospital in residential services is still very controversial. It seems clear, from the Greystone experience, that hospitals *can* deliver rehabilitation (as can any setting) if the values of the organization, the skills, knowledge, and attitudes of the staff, and the program structures are congruent with a psychiatric rehabilitation approach. The controversy is over whether or not hospital programs *should* deliver rehabilitation services. This controversy has not yet been resolved. The continuing stigma and the past history of psychiatric hospitals, in conjunction with the current need for them to exist *somewhere* in the array of services for the psychiatrically disabled person, make the immediate resolution of this controversy unlikely. In sum, the field of residential rehabilitation is now at the point of recognizing the need to: develop a range of housing options that reflect resident preferences and functioning; separate the issues of housing from the type of rehabilitation or treatment services a resident receives; develop opportunities for residents to practice learned skills in the "real world" settings where they will be needed; and develop mechanisms for ongoing long-term support as needed.

VOCATIONAL REHABILITATION

The four programs described in the vocational rehabilitation section (Social Rehab Center, New York Hospital, Laurel Hill Center, and TEE) run the gamut of settings from a private psychiatric hospital, to a psychosocial center, to competitive employment sites. Each of them, however, grappled with the problems of helping persons who often have very little vocational experience learn how to choose, get, and keep their preferred job. As in the field of residential rehabilitation, the challenge has been to help people achieve their goals in "real world" settings while providing the needed rehabilitation services or supports. A second learning from the experiences of the field is that client involvement in choosing, getting, and keeping a preferred job is not only desirable but also possible. As both the New York Hospital program and TEE point out, the greatest barrier to this involvement is often the attitudes of the mental health professionals who have not previously thought of this population as having vocational potential. Work has been seen by the mental health system, for the most part, as only a therapeutic pastime. A third learning, as illustrated by Laurel Hill, the Social Center, and New York Hospital, is that vocational rehabilitation is a lengthy process that requires a comprehensive approach and a great deal of cooperation from many systems. As the programs described in the vocational section discovered, the greater the types of work and levels of responsibilities that exist as options for persons with psychiatric disabilities, the greater the number of types and levels of vocational goals that are chosen. People's ideas of the type of workers they are and the type of work to which they can aspire have a great deal to do with the number and quality of past vocational experiences they have had and the type of support they can count on over time. Vocational programs that are brief and focus on only one aspect of vocational development cannot succeed unless other programs exist to "fill in" the gaps. Fourth, as an outgrowth of the third learning, "progressive" vocational programs are developing a range of work options in the "real world" so that they can help find positions which match client preferences and skills, rather than trying to continue to "fit" clients into the positions that exist.

EDUCATIONAL REHABILITATION

Vocational goals have long been accepted as a legitimate part of rehabilitation efforts, if not part of mental health efforts. The current focus on educational settings as a legitimate part of rehabilitation is a newly emerging one. The fact that there are any programs that focus on the educational goals of psychiatrically disabled persons is an advance in the field. The two programs described, Sussex House and the Continuing Education program, offer something of a bridge from the past by demonstrating that education can occur in as diverse settings as a mental health day-treatment or partial-care setting and on a university campus.

A second learning in the educational arena is that a focus on learning new skills can in and of itself provoke crises that lead to some deterioration in current skill functioning. Both the semester system in the academic environments and the time-limited nature of the skill classes in a partial-care/day-treatment setting have to be modified in order to incorporate a student's fluctuations in integrating new learning. Students with severe psychiatric disabilities (not unlike students without disabilities) have peaks and valleys in their learning process. Disabled students may become more overwhelmed or discouraged by these fluctuations and may require a greater degree of support just when they seem to be doing best. The structure and timing of educational rehabilitation programs must accommodate this type of learning style.

A third learning has been that educational programs, by themselves, cannot take care of all of the comprehensive needs of students with severe psychiatric disabilities. While educational rehabilitation does seem to enable people to develop an identity beyond that of "patient" or "disabled person," students still require interventions in the other areas of their lives—residential, vocational, medical, and so forth. An educational rehabilitation program, therefore, needs a good network of student support systems (case management, housing, etc.) in order for it to operate most effectively.

Lastly, as in the residential and vocational rehabilitation areas, even as more innovative educational rehabilitation programs are being developed, the next development is emerging. "Supported learning" programs that support students in the academic programs of their choice as opposed to special educational programs are ideas that have hardly been tested. They are as yet an idea, however, whose time is rapidly approaching.

SYSTEMS

Integrating psychiatric rehabilitation into mental health systems has proven to be an even more difficult task than integrating the approach into programs. Change at a systems level is variable and unpredictable. It requires flexible strategies and at least one responsible "change agent" who has the financial support, skills, and vision to stay at it for five to ten years. It seems clear from the experiences of the state of New Jersey and the state of Vermont that current mental health systems do not have policies and overall mission statements that include rehabilitation concepts. In fact, it is relatively rare to find systems that do. The policy changes that appear to promote such a rehabilitation approach need to be those that encourage programs and personnel to set overall rehabilitation goals, conduct functional and resource assessment plans, and deliver skill and resource interventions. Just hoping for rehabilitation to happen or talking about it, without concentrated efforts to provide resources and technical expertise, does not, in fact, translate into any rehabilitation occurring. The strategy of linking outcomes to financial support from the system takes a long time but holds promise, as do the strategies of manpower development and state-level consultation on programs. It is clear that more state systems are beginning to think about the implications of at least creating housing resources based on client preference and level of functioning. Other states are beginning to develop a range of vocational settings, far beyond the traditional sheltered workshop or even transitional employment options, making it clear that the message that persons with psychiatric disabilities are first and foremost people, who have a variety of aspirations, interests, and abilities, is finally being heard at systems levels.

SUPPORT

Most treatment approaches do view themselves as providing support services. The first learning to arise out of attempts to put psychiatric rehabilitation approaches into practice is that support, in and of itself, is a critical type of intervention. Providing support to help people obtain and maintain their environments of choice implies that the support is ongoing and directly related to client goals. The case management program described by Goering et al. (chapter 6, this volume) found that it could not put time limits on its support. Limitless support does continue to pose a problem for programs that have to struggle to continue support to current clients while also taking on new ones. In some ways the experience of consumer and family members is that of case managers without time limits.

The second learning is that support for as long as needed requires that all those giving support also be supported. Family members, in particular, have made it clear that they require respite and some support to continue to provide their disabled family member with support in turn. Without that support, professional and consumer alike "burn out."

The third learning is that the development of support programs requires that the type of supports given remain flexible and tailored to the ongoing, but changing needs of the client served. The implication for programs is that support services need to be based on actual assessments of what supports are needed at any one given period of time.

The last learning is that professionals, families, and consumers all have a great deal to offer each other within the context of a psychiatric rehabilitation approach. Information sharing, full involvement in service planning, and provision of individual supports are areas in which collaboration of all "constituents" enhances the effectiveness of the delivery to the client.

The future of psychiatric rehabilitation is more assured if the field uses the learnings of previous psychiatric rehabilitation efforts. Future developments in the field will not occur if program administrators and practitioners do not venture to modify or refine their existing programs based on these learnings. In essence, there must be an ongoing commitment to program change, guided and shaped by past learnings.

Commitment to Program Change

The programs in this book demonstrate a number of factors that facilitated their ongoing adoption of a psychiatric rehabilitation approach. A program's readiness for change is a major factor in the success of any change process. Readiness can stem from either internal or external reasons. Adopting a psychiatric rehabilitation approach is much easier when the program already has a mission, structure, and environments that are already congruent with rehabilitation values. Change begins more often when the people in the programs feel sufficiently dissatisfied with the current state of affairs to want to change, and when there are resources both within and outside the program (such as funding, staff, space). Change occurs when there is committed, interpersonally skilled leadership knowledgeable about psychiatric rehabilitation programs; when there are change agents who can both plan for change and take advantage of opportunities that arise at the moment; and when there are skilled persons who can help program and system personnel gain the skills they need to do things differently. These factors for change apply to changing programs and the practitioners who deliver the program's services. For the change to be complete and become part of the established order, it needs to also affect the system. As the administrators demonstrated, change can begin from the systems level, move to programs, and eventually shape the practitioners. It can begin at the program level and then affect both the practitioners and the system, over time. There is no "right place" to begin. Neither does one person or program have to effect every level for psychiatric rehabilitation to occur. Those who wish to implement psychiatric rehabilitation begin at the level over which they have the most control and in the area in which they have the most skill and knowledge. They look for help in the areas over which they have less control; either less skill or less knowledge.

Change takes time. People create change and people change slowly. The experiences of the programs described in this book confirm the conventional wisdom: that is, it takes about six months to introduce change; six months to mobilize for change; and about another year to get some change to occur. The first change that usually occurs is a change in language (i.e., new words for old activities) and in some attitudes. Changes in actual daily practice usually take another year to three years. Then it takes three to five more years for the change to "embed" itself into the structure of the programs so that it becomes "the way we do business." As one administrator put it, "psychiatric rehabilitation is for those of us who know we are in 'it' for the long haul—because the clients are."

The Future of Psychiatric Rehabilitation

Is psychiatric rehabilitation more than a passing fad? Will the programs and systems described in this book vanish from the scene, or will they be the foundation from which future innovations are made? Is psychiatric rehabilitation more than a 1980s variation of what appear to be the innovations of the past decade, for example, sensitivity training and primal scream therapy? We, of course, think it is much more than a passing fad. To us, psychiatric rehabilitation is a field that is here to stay.

THE NEED FOR RESEARCH IN THE FUTURE

In order for psychiatric rehabilitation to continue to evolve into the future, it needs a solid research foundation. Since 1972, we have periodically published reviews of the state of rehabilitation research (Anthony et al., 1972; Anthony & Margules, 1974; Anthony & Farkas, 1982; Anthony, Cohen & Cohen, 1984; Dion & Anthony, 1987; Farkas & Anthony, 1987).

In the latest review, Dion and Anthony (1987) concluded that a psychiatric rehabilitation intervention does effect rehabilitation outcome positively. Because almost all studies combine different elements of support and skill development in many different ways, it is impossible at this time to unravel their unique contribution to outcome. In 1974, Anthony and Margules did a review of the literature and tentatively concluded that psychiatrically disabled persons can learn important skills in spite of their symptomatology, and that these skills, when combined with appropriate community supports, can have an impact on rehabilitation outcome. It appears that over a decade later the same conclusion can be advanced, based on additional data and relatively more sophisticated research designs. Yet, there still exist monumental problems in this research area. The most critical problem is the continued need for experimental research on replicable, rehabilitation interventions. Mosher and Keith (1979), Goldberg (1980), Meyerson and Herman (1983), and Keith and Matthews (1982) all have called for well-controlled process and outcome studies of a psychiatric rehabilitation approach.

However, it is encouraging to note that over time the research designs have become increasingly more refined. A number of research studies have now been published which have used random assignments to experimental and control groups (Bond, 1984; Dincin & Witheridge, 1982; Paul & Lentz, 1977; Wolkon, Karmen & Janaka, 1971; Ryan & Bell, 1985; Bond & Dincin, 1986) or matched experimental and control groups (Wasylenki, 1985; Goering, Farkas & Lancee,

1986; Vitalo, 1979; Beard, Malamud & Rossman, 1978; Hoffman, 1980; Mosher & Menn, 1978; Matthews, 1979). The positive outcomes of these studies seem in no way different from the outcomes generated by quasi-experimental designs.

In spite of the fact that the field's data base still rests on a number of nonexperimental studies, these studies still do have value. They have provided the empirical and conceptual foundation for the experimental studies that have begun to appear. They have seized the data that were available and used the studies to fashion more specific interventions that can now be researched experimentally. Much of this previous research can be considered exploratory, examining the practical significance of interventions prior to the experimental test. When viewed from this perspective, the psychiatric rehabilitation field is prepared and poised for the additional, critical, experimental work that will be undertaken in the future.

In addition to the research foundation, the field of psychiatric rehabilitation has "staying power" for two other reasons: (1) the emergence of a technology on which psychiatric rehabilitation programs are grounded, and (2) the accompanying changes in the mental health "culture" which now support continued development of the psychiatric rehabilitation field.

PSYCHIATRIC REHABILITATION PROGRAMS
AND PSYCHIATRIC REHABILITATION TECHNOLOGY

As illustrated in this book, the emerging technology of psychiatric rehabilitation is being incorporated into a number of mental health and rehabilitation programs around the country. Prior to the development of a rehabilitation technology, programs that called themselves psychiatric rehabilitation programs were often defined by what they were *not*, rather than by what they were. Thus, rehabilitation programs would characterize themselves as, for example, *not* providing long-term psychotherapy, *not* exclusively relying on drug treatment, and *not* "curing" illness, etc. When asked what they were in fact providing, however, the answers became more vague. They included "community based," provided "continuity of care," and were "group membership oriented." Now, of course, programs that are based on a psychiatric rehabilitation technology can describe their individual programs in much greater detail. The client outcome mission of the program can be articulated. The philosophy, principles, and values underlying the program can be made explicit. The diagnostic, planning, and intervention components of the particular program can be operationalized.

Because of this specificity, the details of the program can be described to consumers in more understandable terms. The program itself has a better chance of evaluating its outcomes and changing the program based on this evaluation. Furthermore, programs can be more effectively replicated when the technology on which they are based can be explicated.

Programs such as those described in this book are in fact helping to define the future of psychiatric rehabilitation. In addition, they are helping to modify the very mental health culture in which they will be operating.

PSYCHIATRIC REHABILITATION PROGRAMS AND THE MENTAL HEALTH CULTURE

The adoption of psychiatric rehabilitation technology is a gradual process. As exemplified in this book, programs progress through a series of evolutionary steps in their effort to integrate the skills and techniques of psychiatric rehabilitation into their programs.

This step-by-step evolutionary process is the normal way in which new technology is incorporated into any field. Technology rarely evolves through breakthroughs; more often the course is steady, year-to-year improvement. That is the course we envision for the field of psychiatric rehabilitation.

However, even this slow, steady progress is uncertain if the mental health culture is not supportive of a psychiatric rehabilitation approach. By mental health culture we mean the attitudes and values of the persons who provide direction to the mental health field. Fortunately, the culture as represented by such persons (i.e., policy-makers, administrators, consumers, practitioners) is becoming more accepting of the psychiatric rehabilitation approach.

A culture has a strong influence on the adoption of any technology. Acceptance of the technology is due not necessarily to the value of the innovation itself, but rather to the readiness of the culture to accept it. The best example outside of the field of mental health is the differential adoption of Western technology by Japan and China. The major reason for the difference between the acceptance of Western technology in Japan and China is a cultural readiness to incorporate it.

There are a number of indicators of changes in the mental health culture that are increasing the probability of psychiatric rehabilitation becoming a permanent fixture in the mental health field. One major change involves the outcome goals that are becoming acceptable for state and local departments of mental health. Now residential and vocational goals are becoming legitimate mental health goals. Mental health professionals are starting to accept the idea that they should assist in the vocational and residential functioning of a person with a psychiatric disability. Policymakers are beginning to act as if they understand that these are not just appropriate areas of interest for vocational rehabilitation or welfare or the housing authority, but critical areas in which mental health professionals should be involved. Increasing numbers of state mental health directors are concerned about the vocational and residential functioning of persons who are severely psychiatrically disabled. That is a major switch from a decade ago. Psychiatric rehabilitation can grow in a culture that looks at those types of outcomes as critical.

Another relevant cultural change is that persons with psychiatric disabilities are beginning to be seen by the mental health culture as persons first and disabled persons second. That cultural change happened years ago in the area of physical disabilities, when persons with physical disabilities said, "Wait a minute, I'm not a 'wheelchair person,' I'm a *person* who's using a wheelchair." Suddenly, the consumers of mental health services are saying, "I'm not mentally ill. I'm a person who has a mental illness, or some psychiatric problems, or some emotional problems." The *person* is being emphasized. The person with a disability is somebody who has aspirations just like anyone else—for a job, for a place to live, for friends, for people to turn to in a crisis. The field is starting to learn that persons who have psychiatric disabilities are not disabled twenty-four hours a day; at many times they are not disabled at all. They are people first. This change in thinking is consistent with the philosophy and values of psychiatric rehabilitation.

Another change in the mental health culture is that the environment is now being recognized as a major factor in a person's recovery. No longer is it just the person who is assessed and treated. We're not just focusing on the client's strengths and deficits and believing that, if we can change them, then they will recover. The environment in which the person functions is being seen by the mental health culture as an important determinant of client outcome. Not only do we have to assess the person, but we have to assess the environment too—the person's immediate environment as well as the larger environment of, for example, the social security system or the welfare system. These relevant systems can present various disincentives to the person's rehabilitation. When the mental health culture starts to see the environment as a barrier and as a potential facilitator, it is becoming very consistent with a rehabilitation philosophy and a rehabilitation orientation.

Similar to this focus on the environment, community supports are being seen as critical in the mental health culture. In physical rehabilitation support has always been seen as critical. Physical rehabilitation supports are very concrete. They include crutches and wheelchairs, canes, and ramps. Now we're seeing that support is critical if we're trying to rehabilitate persons with psychiatric disabilities. If we're trying to reach rehabilitation goals—vocational, independent living, or educational—supports are critical. It is now a more natural thing to ask in mental health circles, "What are the supports?" And we have terms now—"supportive work," "supportive housing," "supportive learning," "consumer-run alternatives"—that provide peer supports, companion programs, support networks. Support has become an accepted kind of intervention. We still have a lot to learn about how to provide that support, but it's becoming a natural type of intervention in the mental health culture. That change bodes well for the future adoption of psychiatric rehabilitation technology.

The mental health culture is now more apt to listen to the needs and wants of the consumer, because consumers have demanded that they listen. This was not necessarily something that the mental health culture wanted to do, but it is something it was forced to do. One thing that many consumers want is better rehabilitation approaches. A survey of family members that Leroy Spaniol did at the Center for Psychiatric Rehabilitation gathered data on what family members want (Spaniol & Zipple, 1988). One of their strongest desires is for better vocational and social rehabilitation services. Consumer surveys of ex-patients agree. So as we start to listen to consumers, they will demand more and better rehabilitation programs.

What else has changed in the mental health culture? Currently, consumers are demanding that the mental health professionals describe the helping process in more understandable ways. They aren't as in awe as they once were of professionals who make everything so mysterious and esoteric. Consumers and their families want the helping process explained in a way that they can understand and be involved in. Fortunately, this can be done. As the mental health culture grows in the direction of using more comprehensible language it will be consistent with what psychiatric rehabilitation is trying to do. The necessity of explaining "informed consent" in a way that is clear and the starting of family education approaches are examples of ways in which we're beginning to describe the helping process in a more understandable way.

Finally, the mental health culture is starting to focus more of its attention on function and not just on symptomatology. The rehabilitation conceptual model of impairment, disability, and handicap allows for an integration of symptom and function. Symptoms of the *impairment* may lead to some type of *disability* so that the person can't function as well. An inability to function leads to some type of *handicap* due to this lack of functioning, resulting in failure to get a job, for example. Just to focus on impairment is no longer tolerated. Even if the symptoms are reduced, the field must focus on how the person is functioning and in what role they are able to function. The mental health culture has begun to operate from this rehabilitation perspective.

THE MENTAL HEALTH CULTURE AND
THE MENTAL HEALTH SYSTEM

In the past the mental health culture has focused on system goals rather than on client outcome goals. Previous mental health goals, such as "continuity of care," "community based treatment," and "de-institutionalization," were all system goals rather than client outcome goals. Such system goals reflect a mental health culture that does not value psychiatric rehabilitation programs highly. In contrast, a system that builds itself around client goals (e.g., increasing the opportunity for persons to function in a successful and satisfied way in the environment of their choice) is naturally supportive of the development of psychiatric rehabilitation programs.

The key to designing systems that support psychiatric rehabilitation programming is to listen to the consumers of the service. The primary source of policymaker learning should be the service recipients and their families, not the professionals and their theories. The "lock them up" mentality and the "turn them loose" mentality are similar in that the services clients want are provided in neither place. When you ask clients what they want, their answers indicate that they want what most people want—a decent place to live, a job, friendships, and support in times of crises—indeed, goals toward which rehabilitation programs are intended.

Rehabilitation programs for persons with psychiatric disabilities will continue to improve wherever the local, state, and national systems commit themselves to rehabilitation outcomes for their clients. Policies that drive systems must be explicit about their overriding rehabilitation mission or goal and the accompanying philosophy and values that anchor this goal.

A system that adopts a rehabilitation mission will change its values and philosophy from:

1. trying to create least restrictive environments to trying to create the *person's most preferred environment*.
2. constructing a continuum of care to arranging a *repertoire of resources*.
3. designing types of buildings to designing *types of supports and services*.
4. professionals placing clients to *clients choosing places*.
5. providing "make work" in make-work environments to *developing real work in real-work environments*.

6. figuring out where people should be put to figuring out *what supports and services people want.*
7. believing that the direction in which we proceed comes from our books and their theories to believing that *the direction comes from the people we serve and their families.*
8. a predominant focus on cost containment to a *renewed focus on life enhancement.*
9. a deinstitutionalization era mentality with its stress on increasing the opportunity for freedom in a person's life to a rehabilitation orientation with its concern for *increasing the opportunity for life in that person's freedom.*

From a rehabilitation perspective, the deinstitutionalization era is dead, and the rehabilitation era is beginning. If a system is successful in developing rehabilitation programs, fewer people will be living in hospitals—and a goal of deinstitutionalization will be accomplished. However, such a goal can be achieved from the philosophical base of rehabilitation rather than from the policies of deinstitutionalization. In contrast to the deinstitutionalization mentality, rehabilitation is an idea about which all persons can be enthusiastic. In this new era of rehabilitation we can stop talking about closing buildings; we can start talking about opening people's lives. We can stop talking about how buildings function, and we can start talking about how people function.

In retrospect, there was a part of deinstitutionalization that was easy. All we did was open the doors to the institution and give people a prescription for their medicine when they left. Now comes the hard part. The hard part is opening up the doors of the community and helping people develop a prescription for their lives. That's rehabilitation—and that's something about which persons can be enthusiastic.

THE HUMAN DIMENSION OF CHANGE: A FINAL WORD

The dimension that allows the necessary program and system change to occur requires skilled, dedicated, and knowledgeable people. Quintessentially important is their unshakable belief in the clients' ability to change. That is ingrained into their belief system—persons with severe psychiatric disabilities have the capacity to grow and to change. They expect improvement in functioning and they often get it. And they expect no less of themselves.

It is the people who believe in client growth who also believe in their own growth. If clients are expected to struggle through the change process then so, too, are the programs and systems that serve them, and the practitioners who work in them.

This book has been about changes; about program and system

leaders who think that a rehabilitation approach represents a better way to help persons with psychiatric disabilities. The field of psychiatric rehabilitation will continue to evolve and grow into the future as long as the people who plan for it, program for it, and practice it continue to evolve and grow. Psychiatric rehabilitation represents hope for the future. It gives up on no one person. While its current programs and systems are limited by the present state of our knowledge, its basic philosophy is that of hope for changes—a hope for the further development of the field as well as for those whom it serves. The bottom line is that if we don't expect the systems and the programs and people who comprise the psychiatric rehabilitation field to change, how can we expect those whom it serves to change?

Contributors

William A. Anthony, Ph.D., Director, Center for Psychiatric Rehabilitation; Professor, Sargent College of Allied Health Professions. Center for Psychiatric Rehabilitation, Boston University, 730 Commonwealth Ave., Boston, Massachusetts, 02215.

Ronald Ballantyne, M.S.W., Chief Administrator, Whitby Psychiatric Hospital, Whitby, Ontario, Canada L1N 559.

Dave Basel, M.S., Director of the Vocational Division (SWEEP), Laurel Hill Center, 2621 Augusta, Eugene, Oregon 97403.

Andrea K. Blanch, Ph.D., Assistant Professor, Psychology Department, University of Vermont; New York State Office of Mental Health, 44 Holland Ave., Albany, New York 12229.

Mary Alice Brown, M.S., Executive Director, Laurel Hill Center, 2621 Augusta, Eugene, Oregon 97403.

Paul J. Carling, Ph.D., Director, Center for Change Through Housing and Community Support. Department of Psychology, University of Vermont, Burlington, Vermont 05405–0134.

Kathleen Cassidy, M.S.W., Special Assistant to Deputy Director, New Jersey Division of Mental Health and Hospitals, CN700, Trenton, New Jersey 08625.

Judi Chamberlin, Member, Mental Patients' Liberation Front of Boston; Program Coordinator, Ruby Rogers Center; Training Assistant, Center for Psychiatric Rehabilitation. Center for Psychiatric Rehabilitation, Boston University, 730 Commonwealth Ave., Boston, Massachusetts 02215.

Mikal Cohen, Ph.D., Associate Executive Director, Center for Psychiatric Rehabilitation. Boston University, 730 Commonwealth Ave., Boston, Massachusetts 02215.

Ann Corapi, Executive Board Member, Alliance for the Mentally Ill of Massachusetts. 30 Newman Way, Arlington, Massachusetts 02174.

Thomas J. H. Craig, M.D., M.P.H., Clinical Director, Center for Mental Health; Clinical Associate Professor of Psychiatry, University of Medicine and Dentistry of New Jersey. Newton Memorial Hospital, 175 High St., Newton, New Jersey 07860.

Karen S. Danley, Ph.D., Branch Director, Vocation Rehabilitation Initiatives, Center for Psychiatric Rehabilitation; Research Assistant Professor, Department of Rehabilitation Counseling, Sargent College. Center for Psychiatric Rehabilitation, Boston University, 730 Commonwealth Ave., Boston, Massachusetts 02215.

Marianne D. Farkas, Sc.D., Director, Graduate Specialization Programs; Research Associate Professor, Rehabilitation Counseling, Sargent College; Director of International Rehabilitation, Center for Psychiatric Rehabilitation. Center for Psychiatric Rehabilitation, Boston University, 730 Commonwealth Ave., Boston, Massachusetts 02215.

Steven M. Fishbein, M.S., C.R.C., Director of Training, Bureau of Program Support, New Jersey Division of Mental Health and Hospitals, CN700, Trenton, New Jersey 08625.

Harriet Fisher, Executive Board Member, Alliance for the Mentally Ill of Massachusetts. 16 Litchfield Ave., Norfolk, Massachusetts 02096.

Paula Goering, R.N., Ph.D., Associate Director, Research of the Continuing Care Division; Senior Mental Health Consultant, Social and Community Psychiatry of the Clarke Institute of Psychiatry; Assistant Professor, Department of Psychiatry, Faculty of Nursing, University of Toronto. Clarke Institute of Psychiatry, Toronto, Ontario, Canada M5T 1R8.

R. Scott Graham, M.A., Executive Director, ReVisions, Inc., and Vice-President of the Maryland Association of Psychosocial Services. ReVisions, Inc., P.O. Box 21059, Catonsville, Maryland 21228.

Katherine J. Harrison, LICSW, Program Director, ACCESS program. Transitional Employment Enterprises, Inc., Morgan Memorial Goodwill Industries, 1010 Harrison Ave., Boston, Massachusetts 02111.

Corinne Huddart, M.S., Rehabilitation Consultant, 37 First St., Uxbridge, Ontario Canada L0C 1K0.

Dori Stauss Hutchinson, M.S., Instructor, Continuing Education Program. Center for Psychiatric Rehabilitation, Boston University, 730 Commonwealth Ave., Boston, Massachusetts 02119.

Larry Kohn, M.S., Director, Continuing Education Program. Center for Psychiatric Rehabilitation, Boston University, 730 Commonwealth Ave., Boston, Massachusetts 02215.

Elisa Lang, M.Ed., M.A., C.R.C., Director, Therapeutic Activities; Lecturer of Therapeutic Activities, Department of Psychiatry at Cornell Medical College. Therapeutic Activities Department, New York Hospital—Cornell Medical Center, Westchester Division, 21 Bloomingdale Road, White Plains, New York 10605.

John P. McNaught, M.A., Associate Director, Center for Mental Health, Newton Memorial Hospital, Newton, New Jersey 07860.

Vera Mellen, M.A., Director, The Social Center for Psychiatric Rehabilitation, 2810 Dorr Ave., Fairfax, Virginia 22031.

Dean Mynks, M.A., Senior Associate, Technical Assistance Services. Center for Psychiatric Rehabilitation, Boston University, 730 Commonwealth Ave., Boston, Massachusetts 02215.

Patricia B. Nemec, Psy.D., Clinical Assistant Professor, Department of Rehabilitation Counseling, Boston University, 1 University Road, Boston, Massachusetts 02215.

Debra B. Nevas, B.S., Senior Research Assistant. Center for Psychiatric Rehabilitation, Boston University, 730 Commonwealth Ave., Boston Massachusetts 02215.

M. Nicolai Nielsen, M.D., Vice President for Mental Health Services. Center for Mental Health, Newton Memorial Hospital, Newton, New Jersey 07860.

Kathleen Furlong-Norman, M.Ed., Director, Technical Assistance Resource Center. Center for Psychiatric Rehabilitation, Boston University, 730 Commonwealth Ave., Boston, Massachusetts 02215.

Shirlee M. Peer, R.N., B.S.N., M.A., (Retired) Assistant Hospital Administrator, Transitional/Cottage Unit. Greystone Park Psychiatric Hospital, Greystone Park, New Jersey 07950.

Virginia Perelson, M.Ed., Community Support Director. Mental Health Services, 1516 Atwood Ave., Johnston, Rhode Island 02920.

Diane C. Piagesi, M.A., CRC, Senior Clinician, Sussex House; Member, Board of Directors, New Jersey Psychiatric Rehabilitation Association. Sussex House, Center for Mental Health, Newton Memorial Hospital, 175 High St., Newton, New Jersey 07860.

John E. Pierce, M.Ed., Director of Planning and Program Development. Vermont Division of Mental Health, 103 South Main St., Waterbury, Vermont 05676.

Dennis H. Rice, M.Ed., Executive Director, Alternatives Unlimited, Inc. 36 Douglas Road, Whitinsville, Massachusetts 01588.

Priscilla Ridgway, M.S.W., Research Associate. Center for Psychiatric Rehabilitation, Boston University, 730 Commonwealth Ave., Boston, Massachusetts 02215.

John J. Rio, M.A., C.R.C., Consultant, Therapeutic Activities Department, the New York Hospital—Cornell Medical Center, Westchester Division; Bridgeway House Mental Health Technical Assistance Center in Princeton, New Jersey. 501 Pelham Road, New Rochelle, New York 10805.

E. Sally Rogers, Sc.D., Director of Research. Center for Psychiatric Rehabilitation, Boston University, 730 Commonwealth Ave., Boston, Massachusetts 02215.

Michael D. Ross, A.B., Ph.D., Chief Executive Officer. Marlboro Psychiatric Hospital, Station A, Marlboro, New Jersey 07746.

Michael F. Seibold, M.A., Director of Vocational Services. Alternatives Unlimited, Inc. 36 Douglas Road, Whitinsville, Massachusetts 01588.

LeRoy Spaniol, Ph.D., Associate Executive Director, Center for Psychiatric

Rehabilitation; Research Associate Professor in the Department of Rehabilitation Counseling, Sargent College. Center for Psychiatric Rehabilitation, Boston University, 730 Commonwealth Ave., Boston, Massachusetts 02215.

David Z. Taylor, M.S., C.R.C., Coordinator of Transitional Services, Center for Mental Health; Training Associate with the New Jersey Partial Care Technical Program. Center For Mental Health, Newton Memorial Hospital, 175 High St., Newton, New Jersey 07860.

Jean M. Taylor, B.S., Director of Training. ReVisions, Inc., Catonsville, Maryland 21228.

Karen Unger, M.S.W., Ed.D., Director of the Education Initiatives Branch. Center for Psychiatric Rehabilitation, Boston University, 730 Commonwealth Ave., Boston, Massachusetts 02215.

Donald A. Wasylenki, M.D., Director of the Continuing Care Division, Clarke Institute of Psychiatry; Associate Professor, Department of Psychiatry, University of Toronto. Clarke Institute of Psychiatry, Toronto, Ontario, Canada M5T 1R8.

Anthony Zipple, Sc.D., Associate Director, Psychiatric Rehabilitation Specialization Program; Assistant Professor, Department of Rehabilitation Counseling, Sargent College. Sargent College of Allied Health Professions, Boston University, 1 University Road, Boston, Massachusetts 02215.

References

Acharya, S., Ekdawi, M. Y., Gallagher, L., & Glaister, B. (1982). Day hospital rehabilitation: A six year study. *Social Psychiatry, 17*, 1–5.

Allen, R., & Velasco, F. (1980). An inpatient setting: The contribution of a rehabilitation approach. *Rehabilitation Counseling Bulletin, 23*, 108–17.

Allyon, T., & Azrin, N. (1965). The measurement and reinforcement of behavior of psychotics. *Journal of Experimental Analysis of Behavior, 8*, 357–83.

American Psychiatric Association Task Force on Community Residential Services. (1982). *A Typography of Community Residential Services*. Washington, D.C.: American Psychological Association.

Anthony, W. A. (1977). Psychological rehabilitation: A concept in need of a method. *American Psychologist, 32*, 658–62.

———. (1979a). *The Principles of Psychiatric Rehabilitation*. Baltimore: University Park Press.

———. (1979b). The rehabilitation approach to diagnosis. *New Directions in Mental Health, 2*, 25–36.

———. (1980). A rehabilitation model for rehabilitating the psychiatrically disabled. *Rehabilitation Counseling Bulletin, 24*, 6–129.

———. (1982). Explaining psychiatric rehabilitation by an analogy to physical rehabilitation. *Psychological Rehabilitation Journal, 5*, 61–65.

———, & Blanch, A. (1987). *Supported Employment for Persons Who Are Psychiatrically Disabled: An Historical and Conceptual Perspective* (Monograph). Boston: Boston University, Center for Psychiatric Rehabilitation.

———, Buell, G. J., Sharratt, S., & Althoff, M. W. (1972). Efficacy of psychiatric rehabilitation. *Psychological Bulletin, 78*, 447–56.

———, Cohen, M. R., & Cohen, B. (1983). The philosophy, treatment process, and principle of the psychiatric rehabilitation approach. *New Directions for Mental Health Services: Deinstitutionalization, 17*, 67–69.

———, Cohen, M., & Cohen, B. (1984). Psychiatric rehabilitation. In J.

Talbott (ed.), *The Chronic Mental Patient: Five Years Later.* New York: Grune and Stratton.

———, Cohen, M. R., & Danley, K. S. (1988). The psychiatric rehabilitation approach as applied to vocational rehabilitation. In J. A. Ciardiello & M. D. Bell (eds.), *Vocational Rehabilitation of Persons with Prolonged Mental Illness.* Baltimore: Johns Hopkins University Press.

———, Cohen, M. R., & Farkas, M. D. (1982). A psychiatric rehabilitation program: Can I recognize one if I see one? *Community Mental Health Journal, 18,* 83–96.

———, Cohen, M. R., & Farkas, M. D. (1987). Training and technical assistance. In A. Meyerson (ed.), *The Clinical, Legal, and Administrative Aspects of Psychiatric Disability.* Washington, D.C.: American Psychiatric Association Press.

———, Cohen, M. R., & Farkas, M. D. (1988). Professional pre-service training for working with the long term mentally-ill. *Community Mental Health Journal,* Winter.

———, Cohen, M., Farkas, M. D., & Cohen, B. F. (1988). Case management: More than a response to a dysfunctional system. *Community Mental Health Journal* 24(3), 219–28.

———, Cohen, M. R., & Nemec, P. (1986). Assessment in psychiatric rehabilitation. In B. Bolten (ed.), *Handbook of Measurement and Evaluation in Rehabilitation.* Baltimore: Paul Brookes.

———, Cohen, M., & Vitalo, R. (1978). The measurement of rehabilitation outcome. *Schizophrenia Bulletin, 4,* 365–83.

———, Danley, K. S., & Howell, J. (1984). Vocational rehabilitation of the psychiatrically disabled. In N. Mirabi (ed.), *The Chronically Mentally Ill: Research and Services.* Jamaica, N.Y.: SP Medical and Scientific Books.

———, & Dion, G. (1986). Psychiatric rehabilitation: A research review. *Rehabilitation Research Review.* Washington, D.C.: Catholic University, Data Institute, NARIC.

———, & Farkas, M. D. (1982). A client outcome planning model for assessing psychiatric rehabilitation interventions. *Schizophrenia Bulletin, 8,* 13–36.

———, & Jansen, M. (1984). Predicting the vocational capacity of the chronically mentally ill: Research and policy implications. *American Psychology, 39,* 537–44.

———, Kennard, W. A., Forbess, R., & O'Brien, W. (1986). Psychiatric rehabilitation: Past myths and current realities. *Community Mental Health Journal, 22,* 249–64.

———, & Liberman, R. P. (1986). The practice of psychiatric rehabilitation: Historical, conceptual and research base. *Schizophrenia Bulletin, 12,* 542–59.

———, & Margules, A. (1974). Toward improving the efficacy of psychiatric rehabilitation: A skills training approach. *Rehabilitation Psychology, 21,* 101–5.

———, & Nemec, P. B. (1984). Psychiatric rehabilitation. In A. S. Bellack (ed.), *Schizophrenia: Treatment, Management and Rehabilitation*. New York: Grune and Stratton.

———, Pierce, R., Cohen, M., & Cannon, J. (1980). *Diagnostic Planning: Psychiatric Rehabilitation Practice Series* (Book 1). Baltimore: University Park Press.

Apte, R. Z. (1968). Halfway houses: A new dilemma in institutional care. *Occasional Papers on Social Administration* (no. 27). London: G. Bell & Sons.

Arce, A. A. (1983). *Statement before the Committee on Appropriations, in U.S. Senate Special Hearing on Street People*. Washington, D.C.: U.S. Government Printing Office.

Avirom, U., & Segal, S. P. (1973). Exclusion of the mentally ill: Reflection on an old problem in a new context. *Archives of General Psychiatry, 29,* 126–31.

Bachrach, L. (1976). A note on some recent studies of mental hospital patients released into the community. *American Journal of Psychiatry, 133,* 73–75.

———. (1978). A conceptual approach to deinstitutionalization. *Hospital and Community Psychiatry, 29,* 573–78.

———. (1979). Planning mental health services for chronic patients. *Hospital and Community Psychiatry, 30,* 387–93.

———. (1980). Overview: Model programs for chronic mental patients. *American Journal of Psychiatry, 137,* 1023–36.

———. (1982a). Program planning for young adult chronic patients. In B. Pepper & H. Ryglewicz (eds.), *The Young Adult Chronic Patient* (p. 254). San Francisco: Jossey-Bass.

———. (1982b). The young adult chronic patient: An analytical review of the literature. *Hospital and Community Psychiatry, 33*(3), 189–297.

———. (1983). New directions in deinstitutionalization planning. *New Directions for Mental Health Services, 17,* 93–106.

———. (1984). The homeless mentally ill and mental health services: An analytical review of the literature. In H. R. Lamb (ed.), *The Homeless Mentally Ill*. Washington, D.C.: American Psychiatric Association.

———. (1986a). Deinstitutionalization: What do the numbers mean? *Hospital and Community Psychiatry, 37,* 118–21.

———. (1986b). The future of the state mental hospital. *Hospital and Community Psychiatry, 37,* 467–74.

Backer, T. E., Liberman, R. P., & Kuehnel, T. G. (1986). Dissemination and adoption of innovative psychosocial interventions. *Journal of Consulting and Clinical Psychology, 54,* 111–18.

Bandura, A. (1969a). *Principles of Behavior Modification*. New York: Holt, Rinehart and Winston.

———. (1969b). Social Learning theory of identificatory processes. In D. Goslin (ed.), *Handbook of Socialization Theory and Research*. Chicago: Rand McNally.

Barton, W. E., & Barton, G. M. (1983). *Mental Health Administration: Principles and Practices* (vols. 1 & 2). New York: Human Sciences Press.

Bassuk, E. L. (1980). The impact of deinstitutionalization of the general hospital psychiatric emergency ward. *Hospital and Community Psychiatry,* *30,* 254.

———. (1983). Addressing the needs of the homeless. *Boston Globe Magazine,* November 6.

———, & Gerson, S. (1978). Deinstitutionalization and mental health services. *Scientific American, 238*(2), 46–53.

Baxter, E., & Hopper, K. (1981). *Private Lives/Public Spaces: Homeless Adults of New York City.* New York: Community Service Society.

———, & Hopper, K. (1984). Troubled in the streets: The mentally disabled homeless poor. In J. A. Talbott (ed.), *The Chronic Mental Patient: Five Years Later.* New York: Grune and Stratton.

Beard, J. H. (1976). Psychiatric rehabilitation at Fountain House. In J. Meislin (ed.), *Rehabilitation Medicine and Psychiatry.* Springfield, Ill.: Charles C. Thomas.

———, Malamud, T. J., & Rossman, E. (1978). Psychiatric rehabilitation and long term rehospitalization rates: The findings of two research studies. *Schizophrenia Bulletin, 4,* 622–35.

———, Propst, R. N., & Malamud, T. J. (1982). The Fountain House model of psychiatric rehabilitation. *Psychosocial Rehabilitation Journal, 5,* 47–59.

Beels, C. C. (1981). Social support and schizophrenia. *Schizophrenia Bulletin, 7,* 58–72.

Bell, R. L. (1970). Practical applications of psychodrama: Systematic role playing teaches social skills. *Hospital and Community Psychiatry, 21,* 189–91.

Bennis, W. G., Benne, K. D., Chin, R., & Corey, K. E. (eds.). (1976). *The Planning of Change* (3d ed.). New York: Holt, Rinehart and Winston.

Berhneim, K. F. (1987). Family consumerism: Coping with the winds of change. In A. B. Hatfield & H. P. Lefley (eds.), *Families of the Mentally Ill: Coping and Adaptation.* New York: Guilford Press.

Bierer, J., & Haldane, F. P. (1941). A self-governed patients' social club in a public mental hospital. *Journal of Mental Science, 87,* 419–26.

Blanch, A. K., Carling, P. J., & Ridgway, P. (1987). Normal housing with specialized supports. Paper presented Sept. 27, New Jersey State Residential Conference.

Bloom-Feshbach, J., & Bloom-Feshbach, S. (1987). *The Psychology of Separation and Loss.* San Francisco: Jossey-Bass.

Bond, G. R. (1984). An economic analysis of psychosocial rehabilitation. *Hospital and Community Psychiatry, 35,* 356–62.

———, & Boyer, S. L. (in press). The evaluation of vocational programs for the mentally ill: A review. In J. A. Ciardiello & M. D. Bell (eds.), *Vocational Rehabilitation of Persons with Prolonged Mental Illness.* Baltimore: Johns Hopkins University Press.

———, & Dincin, J. (1986). Accelerating entry into transitional employment in a psychosocial rehabilitation agency. *Rehabilitation Psychology, 31,* 143–55.

Borys, S., & Fishbein, S. M. (1983). *Partial Care Technical Assistance Project:*

Pretest Results (Research and Evaluation Report). Division of Mental Health and Hospitals. CN 700, Trenton, N.J. 08625.

Braun, P., Kochansky, G., Shapiro, R., Greenberg, S., Gudeman, J. E., Johnson, S., & Shore, M. F. (1981). Overview: Deinstitutionalization of psychiatric patients—A critical review of outcome studies. *American Journal of Psychiatry, 138,* 736–49.

Brown, P. (1982). Approaches to evaluating the outcome of deinstitutionalization: A reply to Christenfeld. *Journal of Psychology, 10,* 276–81.

Budd, S., Howie the Harp, & Zinman, S. (eds.) (1987). *Reaching Across: Mental Health Clients Helping Each Other.* Riverside: California Network of Mental Health Clients.

Budson, R. (ed.) (1981). *New Directions for Mental Health Services: Issues in Community Residential Care* (no. 11). San Francisco: Jossey-Bass.

Bureau of Information Systems. (1986). *Unified Services Transaction Form: Caseload, Service Area & Frequency Reports for Fiscal Year 1986.* Division of Mental Health and Hospitals. CN 700, Trenton, N.J. 08625.

Campbell, M. (1981). The three-quarterway house: A step beyond halfway house toward independent living. *Hospital and Community Psychiatry, 32,* 500–501.

Cannady, D. (1982). Chronics and cleaning ladies. *Psychosocial Rehabilitation Journal, 5,* 13–16.

Cannon, M. S. (1975). *Halfway Houses Serving the Mentally Ill and Alcoholics, United States, 1973* (Survey and Reports Branch, Division of Biometry, NIMH). Washington, D.C.: U.S. Government Printing Office.

Caplan, G. (1972). *Support Systems.* Keynote address to Conference of Department of Psychiatry. Newark: Rutgers Medical School and New Jersey Mental Health Association.

Caplan, N. (1980). What do we know about knowledge utilization? In L. A. Braskamp & R. D. Brown (eds.), *New Directions for Program Education* (no. 5). San Francisco: Jossey-Bass Publications.

Carkhuff, R. R. (1969). *Helping and Human Relations* (vols. 1 & 2). New York: Holt, Rinehart and Winston.

———. (1983a). *The Productive Teacher.* Amherst, Mass.: Human Resource Development Press.

———. (1983b). *The Art of Helping* (5th ed.). Amherst, Mass.: Human Resource Development Press.

———, & Berenson, B. G. (1976). *Teaching as Treatment: An Introduction to Counseling and Psychotherapy.* Amherst, Mass.: Human Resource Development Press.

———, & Berenson, B. G. (1977). *Beyond Counseling and Therapy.* New York: Holt, Rinehart and Winston.

———, Berenson, B. G., & Pierce, R. M. (1976). *The Skills of Teaching: Interpersonal Skills.* Amherst, Mass.: Human Resource Development Press.

———, & Berenson, D. H. (1981). *The Skilled Teacher: A systematic Approach to Teaching Skills.* Amherst, Mass.: Human Resource Development Press.

Carling, P. J. (1978). Residential services in a psychosocial rehabilitation context: The Horizon House model. In *New Directions in Mental Health Care: Cooperative Apartments*. Adelphi, Md.: National Institute of Mental Health (Mental Health Study Center).

———. (1981a). *Choreography with an Uncertain Score: Federal Collaboration in Housing and Mental Health*. Rockville, Md.: National Institute of Mental Health (Community Support Program).

———. (1981b). Nursing homes and chronic mental patients: A second opinion. *Schizophrenia Bulletin, 7*(4).

———. (1984a). *The National Institute of Mental Health Community Support Program: Emerging Issues: A Report of the NIMH/CSP Program Review*. Rockville, Md.: National Institute of Mental Health (Office of State and Community Liaison).

———. (1984b). *Housing Status and Needs of the Chronically Mentally Ill Population: A Briefing Paper*. Rockville, Md. National Institute of Mental Health (Office of State and Community Liaison).

———. (1984c). *Meeting the Housing and Residential Service Needs of Persons with Psychiatric Disabilities: A Report on the National Institute of Mental Health Housing Technical Assistance Workshop*. Boston: Boston University, Center for Psychiatric Rehabilitation.

———. (1984d). *Developing Family Foster Care Programs in Mental Health: A Resource Guide*. Burlington: University of Vermont.

———, Daniels, L., & Randolph, F. (1985a). *A Feasibility Study to Examine the Development of a Regional Community Mental Health System as an Alternative to Vermont State Hospital*. Boston: Boston University, Center for Psychiatric Rehabilitation.

———, Daniels, L., & Ridgway, P. (1985b). Meeting the housing needs of persons with psychiatric disabilities: Comments on the state-of-the-art. Paper presented at Virginia State-Of-The-Art Conference on Deinstitutionalization, Richmond.

———, & Ridgway, P. (in preparation). *Meeting the Housing Needs of Psychiatrically Disabled Persons through Community Residential Rehabilitation: Concepts, Interventions and Outcomes*. Boston: Boston University, Center for Psychiatric Rehabilitation.

Carpenter, J. O., & Bourestan, N. C. (1976). Performance of psychiatric hospital discharges in strict and tolerant environments. *Community Mental Health Journal, 12*, 45–51.

Caton, C. L. (1981). The new chronic patient and the system of community care. *Hospital and Community Psychiatry, 32*, 254.

Center for Psychiatric Rehabilitation (in preparation). *Psychiatric Rehabilitation Program Consultation: Training Packages*. Boston: Boston University, Center for Psychiatric Rehabilitation.

———. (1984). *Annual Report for the National Institute of Handicapped Research*. Boston: Boston University, Center for Psychiatric Rehabilitation.

Center News. (1983). *Consumers' Report*, Sept.–Oct. Baltimore: On Our Own.

Chamberlin, J. (1978). *On Our Own: Patient-controlled Alternatives to the Mental Health System*. New York: Hawthorne Books.

Chatetz, L., & Goldfinger, S. M. (1984). Residential instability in a psychiatric emergency setting. *Psychiatric Quarterly, 56,* 20–34.

Cheek, F. E., & Mendelson, M. (1973). Developing behavior modification programs with an emphasis on self control. *Hospital and Community Psychiatry, 24,* 410–16.

Ciardiello, J. A., & Bingham, W. C. (1982). The career maturity of schizophrenic clients. *Rehabilitation Counseling Bulletin,* Dec., 3–9.

Coche, E., & Flick, A. (1975). Problem solving training groups for hospitalized psychiatric patients. *Journal of Psychology, 91,* 19–29.

Cohen, B. F., & Anthony, W. A. (1984), Functional assessment in psychiatric rehabilitation. In D. Halpern & M. Fuhrer (eds.), *Functional Assessment in Rehabilitation.* Baltimore: Paul Brookes.

Cohen, M. R. (1981). *Improving Interagency Collaboration between Vocational Rehabilitation and Mental Health Agencies: A Conference Summary Report.* Boston: Boston University, Center for Psychiatric Rehabilitation.

———, Anthony, W. A., Pierce, R., & Vitalo, R. (1980). *The Skills of Community Service Coordination* (Book 6, Psychiatric Rehabilitation Series). Baltimore: University Park Press.

———, Danley, K., & Nemec, P. (1985a). *Directory of Technical Assistance Resources for Community Support Systems.* Boston: Boston University, Center for Psychiatric Rehabilitation.

———, Danley, K., & Nemec, P. (1985b). *Psychiatric Rehabilitation Practitioner Package: Direct Skills Teaching.* Boston: Boston University, Center for Psychiatric Rehabilitation.

———, Farkas, M. D., & Cohen, B. F. (1986). *Functional Assessment: Psychiatric Rehabilitation Training Packages.* Boston: Boston University, Center for Psychiatric Rehabilitation.

———, Farkas, M. D., Cohen, B. F., & Unger, K. V. (1987). Psychiatric rehabilitation training package: Overall rehabilitation goal. Prepublication draft, Boston University, Center for Psychiatric Rehabilitation.

———, Nemec, P. B., Farkas, M. D., & Forbess, R. (1988). Psychiatric rehabilitation training package: Case management. Prepublication draft, Boston University, Center for Psychiatric Rehabilitation.

Cohen, B. F., Ridley, D., & Cohen, M. R. (1983). Teaching skills to severely psychiatrically disabled persons. In H. A. Marlowe (ed.), *Developing Competence* (pp. 96–115). Tampa: University of South Florida Press.

Coiner, R. (1986). *Vocational Rehabilitation of the Chronically Mentally Ill: A Study of the Laurel Hill Center.* Eugene, Ore.: Laurel Hill Research Institute.

———. (1987). *Predicting Vocational Success of the Chronically Mentally Ill: A Study of Variables Differentiating Laurel Hill Clients.* (Unpublished report). State of Oregon Mental Health Division.

Cometa, M. S., Morrison, J. K., & Zishoren, M. (1979). Halfway to where? A critique of research on psychiatric halfway houses. *Journal of Community Psychology, 7,* 23–27.

Coulton, C. L., Holland, T. P., & Fitch, V. (1984). Person-environment congruence and psychiatric patient outcome in community care homes. *Administration in Mental Health, 12,* 71–88.

Craig, T. J. H., Hussey, P., Parsons, P. J., & Seamans, S. (1985). A family group program in a state psychiatric hospital. *Hospital and Community Psychiatry, 36.*

———, & Ross, R. E. (1987). A staff opinion survey in a state hospital. Unpublished paper, Greystone Park Psychiatric Hospital, Morris Plains, N.J.

Crites, J. O. (1969). *Vocational Psychology.* New York: McGraw-Hill.

CSP: Choices and challenges. (1985). *Proceedings of the Seventh National Conference of the National Institute of Mental Health.* Washington, D.C.: National Institute of Mental Health.

Cummings, J., & Markson, E. (1975). The impact of mass transfer on patient release. *Archives of General Psychiatry, 32,* 804–9.

Danley, K. S., & Anthony, W. A. (in press). *Improving Vocational Rehabilitation Practice through a Psychiatric Rehabilitation Approach: A Workshop Training Package for Vocational Rehabilitation Counselors.* Boston: Boston University, Center for Psychiatric Rehabilitation.

———, Rogers, E. S., & Nevas, V. B. (1989). A psychiatric rehabilitation approach to vocational rehabilitation. In M. D. Farkas & W. A. Anthony (eds.), *Psychiatric Rehabilitation Programs: Putting Theory into Practice.* Baltimore: Johns Hopkins University Press.

Davis, A. E., Dinitz, S., & Pasamanick, B. (1974). *Schizophrenics in the New Custodial Care Community: Five Years after the Experiment.* Columbus: Ohio State University Press.

DeAngelis, T. (1987). Alliance flexing muscle. *APA Monitor, 18,* 13.

Dellario, D. J. (1985). The relationship between MH/VR interagency functioning and vocational rehabilitation outcome in the psychiatrically disabled. *Rehabilitation Counseling Bulletin,* March, 167–170.

———, & Anthony, W. A. (1981). On the effectiveness of institutional and alternative placement for the psychiatrically disabled. *Journal of Social Issues, 37*(3).

Delucia, N., Cassidy, K., & Fishbein, S. M. (1986). *Efficiency & effectiveness of New Jersey partial care programs.* (Bureau of Research & Evaluation Report.) Trenton: New Jersey Division of Mental Health and Hospitals.

Department of Health and Human Services. (1983). *Report to Congress on Shelter and Basic Living Needs of Chronically Mentally Ill Individuals.* Washington, D.C.

Dincin, J. (1981). A community agency model. In J. Talbott (ed.), *The chronic mentally ill* (pp. 212–26). New York: Human Sciences Press.

———, & Witheridge, T. F. (1982). Psychiatric rehabilitation as a deterrent to recidivism. *Hospital and Community Psychiatry, 33,* 645–50.

Dion, G. L., & Anthony, W. A. (1987). Research in psychiatric rehabilitation: A review of experimental and quasi-experimental studies. *Rehabilitation Counseling Bulletin, 3,* 177–203.

Dodson, L. C., & Mullens, W. R. (1969). Some effects of jogging on psychiatric hospital patients. *American Corrective Therapy Journal, 23,* 130–34.

Doll, W. (1976). Family coping with the mentally ill: An unanticipated problem of deinstitutionalization. *Hospital and Community Psychiatry, 27,* 183–85.

Egri, G., & Caton, C. L. (1982). Serving the young adult chronic patient in the 1980's: Challenge to the general hospital. In B. Pepper & H. Ryglewicz (eds.), *The young adult chronic patient* (pp. 25–31). San Francisco: Jossey-Bass.

Eldred, D. M., Brooks, G. W., Deane, W. N., & Taylor, M. B. (1962). The rehabilitation of the hospitalized mentally ill: The Vermont story. *American Journal of Public Health, 52,* 39–46.

Ellsworth, R. B., Foster, L., Childers, B., Arthur, G., & Kroeker, D. (1968). Hospital and community adjustment as perceived by psychiatric patients, their families, and staff. *Journal of Consulting and Clinical Psychology, 32,* 1–41.

Erickson, E. (1968). *Identity, Youth and Crisis.* New York: Norton.

Erickson, R. (1975). Outcome studies in mental hospitals: A review. *Psychological Bulletin, 82,* 519–40.

———, & Hyerstay, B. J. (1980). Historical perspectives on treatment of the mentally ill. In M. S. Gibbs, J. Lachermeyer, & J. Sigal (eds.), *Community Psychology: Theoretical and Empirical Approaches.* New York: Gardner Press.

Erlanger, H. S., & Roth, W. (1985). Disability policy. *American Behavioral Scientist, 28,* 319–46.

Eysenck, H. H. (1960). *Behavior Therapy and the Neuroses.* New York: Pergammon.

Fairweather, G. W. (ed.). (1980). The Fairweather Lodge: A twenty-five year retrospective. *New Directions for Mental Health Services* (no. 7). San Francisco: Jossey-Bass.

———. (1971). *Methods of Changing Mental Hospital Programs.* (Progress Report to the National Institute of Mental Health no. R12–178887.) East Lansing: Michigan State University.

———, Sanders, D. H., Maynard, H., & Cressler, D. L. (1969). *Community Life for the Mentally Ill.* Chicago: Aldine.

Farkas, M. D. (1981). *Outreach Case Management: Report of Practitioner Training.* Boston: Boston University, Center for Psychiatric Rehabilitation.

———, & Anthony, W. A. (1980). Training rehabilitation counselors to work in state agencies, rehabilitation and mental health facilities. *Rehabilitation Counseling Bulletin, 24,* 129–44.

———, & Anthony, W. A. (1981). *Rehabilitation; A Response to the Shortcomings of Deinstitutionalization.* (Monograph 1.) Boston: Boston University, Center for Psychiatric Rehabilitation.

———, & Anthony, W. A. (1987). Outcome analysis in psychiatric rehabilitation. In M. Fuhrer (ed.), *Rehabilitation Outcomes: Analysis Measurement* (pp. 43–56). Baltimore: Paul Brookes Publishing.

———, & Anthony, W. (1989). Psychiatric rehabilitation: The approach and its programs. In M. D. Farkas & W. A. Anthony (eds.), *Psychiatric*

Rehabilitation Programs: Putting Theory into Practice. Baltimore: Johns Hopkins University Press.

———, Anthony, W. A., Cohen, M. R., Cohen, B. F., & Danley, K. S. (in preparation). *Encouraging University Graduate Programs to Develop Psychiatric Rehabilitation Curriculum.* Boston: Boston University, Center for Psychiatric Rehabilitation.

———, Cohen, M., & Nemec, P. (1988). Psychiatric rehabilitation programs: Putting concepts in practice. *Community Mental Health Journal,* pp. 7–21.

———, Nemec, P. B., & Anthony, W. A. (1989). *Case Management Program Outcomes: Do We Know What We Are Doing?* Prepublication Draft. Boston: Boston University, Center for Psychiatric Rehabilitation.

———, Nemec, P. B., & Taylor, J. A. (1989). Assessing Psychiatric Rehabilitation Programs. Prepublication Draft, Boston University, Center for Psychiatric Rehabilitation.

———, O'Brien, W., & Nemec, P. N. (1988). Graduate level curriculum in psychiatric rehabilitation: Filling a need. *Psychosocial Rehabilitation Journal, 12,* 55–66.

———, Rogers, E. S., & Hiti, J. (1987). Revising a standardized level of functioning instrument: A general methodology. Prepublication draft, Boston University, Center for Psychiatric Rehabilitation.

———, Rogers, S., & Thurer, S. (1987). Rehabilitation outcomes for the recently deinstitutionalized patient: The ones left behind. *Hospital and Community Psychiatry, 38,* 864–70.

Field G., Allness, D., & Knoedler, W. (1980). Application of the training in community living program to rural areas. *Journal of Community Psychology, 8,* 9–15.

Fishbein, S., & Cassidy, K. (1989). A system perspective on psychiatric rehabilitation: New Jersey. In M. Farkas and W. Anthony (eds.), *Psychiatric Rehabilitation Programs: Putting Theory into Practice.* Baltimore: Johns Hopkins University Press.

Flores, D., Kamis-Gould, E., & Waizer, J. (1980). *Survey of Clients Served by State Funded Partial Care Programs: An Analysis of Program Appropriateness & Effectiveness.* (Bureau of Research & Evaluation Report.) Trenton: New Jersey Division of Mental Health and Hospitals.

Forsythe, R. P., & Fairweather, B. W. (1961). Psychotherapeutic and other hospital treatment criteria: The dilemma. *Journal of Abnormal and Social Psychology, 62,* 598–604.

Freeman, H. E., & Simmons, O. G. (1961). Feelings of stigma among relatives of former mental patients. *Social Problems, 8,* 312–21.

———, & Simmons, O. G. (1963). *The Mental Patient Comes Home.* New York: Wiley.

Freeman, S.J.J., Fischer, L., & Sheldon, A. (1980). An agency model for developing and coordinating psychiatric aftercare. *Hospital and Community Psychiatry, 31,* 768–71.

Friel, T. W., & Carkhuff, R. R. (1974). *The Art of Developing a Career.* Amherst, Mass.: Human Resource Development Press.

Frey, W. D. (1984). Functional assessment in the 80's: A conceptual enigma, a technical challenge. In A. Halpern & M. Fuhrer (eds.), *Functional Assessment in Rehabilitation*. New York: Brooke Publishing Co.

Gartner, A. J., & Riessman, F. (1982). Self-help and mental health. *Hospital and Community Psychiatry, 33,* 631–35.

Geller, J. L. (1982). State hospital patients and their medication—Do they know what they take? *American Journal of Psychiatry, 139,* 611–15.

Geller, M. P. (1982). The "revolving door": A trap or a life style? *Hospital Community Psychiatry, 33,* 388–89.

Gittleman, M. (1974). Coordinating mental health systems. *American Journal of Public Health, 64,* 496–500.

Glaser, E. M. (1972). Knowledge transfer and institutional change. Paper presented at the Western Psychological Association Convention in Portland, Ore.

———, & Ross, U. L. (1971). *Increasing the Utilization of Applied Research Results* (NIMH Grant No. 5R12MH0925–2). Washington, D.C.: National Institute of Mental Health.

Glasscote, R. M., Gudeman, J. E., & Elpers, R. (1971). *Halfway Houses for the Mentally Ill: A Study of Programs and Problems*. Washington, D.C.: Joint Information Service of the American Psychiatric Association and the National Association for Mental Health.

Goering, P., Farkas, M. D., Wasylenki, D., Lancee, W. J., & Ballantyne, R. (1988). Improved functioning for clients of a rehabilitation case management program. *Psychosocial Rehabilitation Journal, 12,* 1, 3–17.

———, Farkas, M. D., & Lancee, W. J. (1986). Predicting outcome for a rehabilitation case manager program for chronic psychiatric client. Prepublication draft, Boston University, Center for Psychiatric Rehabilitation.

———, Wasylenki, D., Lancee, W., & Freeman, S.J.J. (1984). From hospital to community six-month and two-year outcomes for 505 patients. *Journal of Nervous and Mental Disease, 172,* 667–73.

———, Wasylenki, D., Farkas, M. D., Lancee, Wm., & Ballantyne, R. (1988). What difference does case management make? A two-year follow up of a rehabilitation case management program. *Hospital and Community Psychiatry, 39,* 272–76.

Goldberg, S. (1980). Drug and psychosocial therapy in schizophrenia: Current status and research needs. *Schizophrenia Bulletin, 6,* 117–22.

Goldman, A., Gattozzi, C., & Yawke, D. (1981). Defining and counting the chronically mentally ill. *Hospital and Community Psychiatry, 32,* 259.

Goldman, H. H. (1984). The chronically mentally ill: Who are they? Where are they? In M. Mirabi (ed.), *The Chronically Mentally Ill: Research and Services* (pp. 33–44). New York: Spectrum Publications.

———, Adams, N., & Taube, C. (1983). Deinstitutionalization: The data demythologized. *Hospital and Community Psychiatry, 34,* 129–34.

———, Gattozzi, A. A., & Taube, C. A. (1981). Defining and counting the chronically mentally ill. *Hospital and Community Psychiatry, 32,* 21–27.

Goldmeier, J. (1975). *New Directions in Aftercare: Cooperative Apartment Living*. Adelphia, Md.: NIMH (Mental Health Study Center).

————, Mannino, F. V., & Shore, M. F. (eds.). (1978). *New Directions in Mental Health Care: Cooperative Apartments.* Adelphia, Md.: NIMH (Mental Health Study Center).

————, Shore, M. F., & Mannino, F. V. (1977). Cooperative apartments: New Programs in community mental health. *Health and Social Work,* 2, 119–40.

Goldsmith, J. B., & McFall, R. M. (1975). Development and evaluation of an interpersonal skill training program for psychiatric inpatients. *Journal of Abnormal Psychology,* 84, 51–58.

Goldstrum, I., & Mannderscheid, R. (1982). The chronically mentally ill: A descriptive analysis from the uniform client data instrument. *Community Support Services Journal,* 2(3), 4–9.

Greene, L. R., & De La Cruz, A. (1981). Psychiatric day treatment as alternative to and transition from full-time hospitalization. *Community Mental Health Journal,* 17, 191–202.

Greiff, I., Zipple, A. M., & McCarthy, K. (1987). Beyond shelter: Providing rehabilitation services to the homeless. *Psychosocial Rehabilitation Journal,* 9, 72–75.

Grob, S. (1983). Psychosocial rehabilitation centers: Old wine in a new bottle. In I. Barofsky and R. Budson (eds.), *The Chronic Psychiatric Patient in the Community* (pp. 265–80). Jamaica, N.Y.: SP Medical and Scientific Books.

Gruenburg, E. M. (1957). Application of control methods to mental illness. *American Journal of Public Health,* 47, 944–52.

Gudeman, J. E., Dickey, B., Evans, A., & Shore, M. (1985). Four year assessment of a day hospital-inn program as an alternative to inpatient hospitalization. *American Journal of Psychiatry,* 142: 11, 1330–33.

Hamilton, L. S., & Muthard, J. E. (1975). *Research Utilization Specialists in Vocational Rehabilitation.* Gainesville, Fla.: Rehabilitation Research Institute.

Hammer, M. (1981). Social supports, social networks, and schizophrenia. *Schizophrenia Bulletin,* 7, 45–57.

Harding, C. M., Brooks, G. W., Ashikaga, T., Strauss, J. S., & Landerl, P. D. (1983). *Aging and Social Functioning in Once-Chronic Schizophrenic Patients 21–58 Years after First Admission: The Vermont Story.* (NIMH Publication No. 29575 & the College of Medicine, University of Vermont.)

————, Brooks, G. W. Ashikaga, T., Strauss, J. S., & Breler, A. (1987). The Vermont longitudinal study of persons with severe mental illness: I. Methodology, study sample, and overall current status. *American Journal of Psychiatry,* 144, 718–26.

Harrang, G. (1967). Rehabilitation program for chronic patients: Testing the potential for independence. *Hospital and Community Psychiatry,* 18, 376–77.

Harris, M., & Bergman, H. C. (1984). The young adult chronic patient: Affective responses to treatment. In B. Pepper & H. Ryglewicz (eds.), *Advances in Treating the Young Adult Chronic Patient* (p. 260). San Francisco: Jossey-Bass.

Harrod, J. B. (1986). Letter to the editor: Families as advocates. *Hospital and Community Psychiatry, 37*, 1053.

Hatfield, A. B. (1984). *Coping with Mental Illness in the Family: The Family Guide.* Manuscript submitted for publication.

———. (1984). The family consumer movement: A new force in service delivery. *New Directions for Mental Health Services, 21*, 71–79.

———. (1987). Families or caretaker: A historical perspective. In A. B. Hatfield & H. P. Lefley (eds.), *Families of the Mentally Ill: Coping and Adaptation.* New York: Guilford Press.

———, Fierstein, R., & Johnson, D. (1982). Meeting the needs of families of the psychiatrically disabled. *Psychosocial Rehabilitation Journal, 6*, 27–40.

Havelock, R. G. (1971). *Planning for Innovation through Dissemination and Utilization of Knowledge.* Ann Arbor: University of Michigan, Institute for Social Research.

———, & Benne, K. D. (1969). An exploratory study of knowledge utilization. In W. G. Bennis, K. D. Benne, & R. Chien (eds.), *The Planning of Change* (2d ed.). New York: Holt, Rinehart and Winston.

Heffner, F., & Gill R. (1982). The role of community based service providers in rehabilitation of deinstitutionalized psychiatric patients: Does education belong in the therapeutic process? *Psychosocial Rehabilitation Journal, 5*, 5–8.

Hersen, M., & Bellack, A. (1976). Social skills for chronic psychiatric patients-rationale, research, findings and further directions. *Comprehensive Psychiatry, 17*, 557–80.

Hinterkopf, E., & Brunswick, L. K. (1975). Teaching therapeutic skills to mental patients. *Psychotherapy: Theory, Research and Practice, 12*, 8–12.

Hoffman, D. A. (1980). The differential effects of self-monitoring, self-reinforcement and performance standards on the production output, job satisfaction and attendance of vocational rehabilitation clients. Unpublished Ph.D. dissertation, Catholic University of America.

Hogan, R. (1984). It can't happen here: Community opposition to group homes. Unpublished manuscript, Rutgers University.

———. (1985a). Gaining community support for group homes. Unpublished manuscript, Purdue University.

———. (1985b). Not in my town: Local government opposition to group homes. Unpublished manuscript, Purdue University.

Holcomb, W. (1984). *Building a Support System. Manual for the Development of Church, Synagogue, and Mental Health Agency Sponsored Support Programs for Long-term Recipients of Mental Health Services.* New Jersey: New Jersey Self-Help Clearinghouse, St. Claire's Riverside Medical Center.

Huessy, H. R. (1981). Discussion: Stress, social support, and schizophrenia. *Schizophrenia Bulletin, 7*, 178–79.

Hume, K., & Marshall, C. (1980). Implementing the rehabilitation approach in mental health settings. *Rehabilitation Counseling Bulletin, 24*, 67–71.

Hursh, N. C. (1984). *Diagnostic vocational evaluation with psychiatrically disabled individuals: Preliminary results of a national survey* (Monograph). Boston: Boston University, Center for Psychiatric Rehabilitation.

Ivey, A. E. (1973). Media therapy: Education change planning for psychiatric patients. *Journal of Counseling Psychology, 20,* 338–43.

Jeger, A. M., & McClure G. (1980). The effects of a behavioral training program on nonprofessional endorsement of the "psychosocial" model. *Journal of Community Psychology, 8,* 49–53.

Jung, H., & Spaniol, L. (1981). Planning the utilization of new knowledge and skills: Some basic principles for researchers, administrators and practitioners. Unpublished manuscript, Boston University, Center for Psychiatric Rehabilitation.

Keith, S., & Matthews, S. (1984). Targeting treatment for schizophrenia: A review of group, family and milieu therapies and psychosocial rehabilitation. Prepublication draft. Rockville, Md.: National Institute of Mental Health.

Kiesler, C., McGuire, T., Mechanic, D., Mosher, L., Nelson, S., Newman, F., Rich, R., & Schulberg, H. (1983). Federal mental health policy making: An assessment of deinstitutionalization. *American Psychologist, 38,* 1292–97.

Kinder, C., Thompson, E., & Edmundson, E. (1982). Social network programs: One model of implementation. *The Management of Deinstitutionalization.* Proceedings of the 1982 Florida conference on deinstitutionalization. Tampa: University of South Florida Press.

Kint, M. G. (1978). Schizophrenia is a family affair: Problems of families in coping with schizophrenia. *Journal of Orthomolecular Psychiatry, 7*(4), 236–46.

Kirshner, M., Pepper, B., & Ryglewicz, H. (1981). The young adult chronic patient: Overview of a population. *Hospital and Community Psychiatry, 32,* 463–69.

Kohen, W., & Paul, G. L. (1976). Current trends and recommended changes in extended care placement of mental patients: The Illinois system as a case in point. *Schizophrenia Bulletin, 2*(4), 575–94.

Kohlberg, L. (1969). Stage and sequence: The cognitive developmental approach to socialization. In D. Goslin (ed.), *Handbook of Socialization Theory and Research.* New York: Rand McNally.

Kramer, B. M. *Day Hospital: A Study of Partial Hospitalization in Psychiatry.* New York: Grune and Stratton.

Krasner, L., & Ullman, L. (eds.). (1965). *Research in Behavior Modification.* New York: Holt, Rinehart and Winston.

Lamb, H. R. (1976). An educational model for teaching living skills to long-term patients. *Hospital and Community Psychiatry, 27,* 875–77.

———. (1982). *Treating the Long Term Mentally Ill.* San Francisco: Jossey-Bass.

———. (ed.). (1984). *The Homeless Mentally Ill.* Washington, D.C.: American Psychiatry Association.

———, & Goetzel, V. (1971). Discharged mental patients—Are they really in the community? *Archives of General Psychiatry, 24,* 29–34.

Lang, E. (1980). Integrating rehabilitation theory in day hospitalization. *American Rehabilitation Journal, 7*(11).

————, Richman, A., & Trout, P. (1984). Project Outreach: Volunteer transitional employment. *Psychiatric Hospital, 15*(2), 75–80.

————, & Mattson, M. (1985). The in-patient multidisciplinary treatment plan: A method for enhancing therapeutic activities approach. *Hospital and Community Psychiatry, 36,* 62–68.

Larsen, J. K. (1982). Does consultation work: Reviewing the research evidence. *Consultation,* Spring, 25–32.

Leaf, A., & Cohen, M. (1982). *Providing Services for the Homeless: The New York City Program.* New York: City of New York Human Services Administration Report.

Leff, H. S. (1984). *Resource Associated Functional Level Scale (RAFLS).* Cambridge, Mass.: North Charles Foundation.

Levine, I. S. (1984a). *Developing Community Support Service Programs: A Resource Manual for Family Groups.* Boston: Center for Psychiatric Rehabilitation, and Washington, D.C.: National Alliance for the Mentally Ill.

————. (1984b). Service programs for the homeless mentally ill. *The Homeless Mentally Ill.* Washington, D.C.: American Psychiatric Association.

Leitner, L., & Drasgow, J. (1972). Battling recidivism. *Journal of Rehabilitation,* July–August; 29–31.

Liberman, R. P., King, L. W., & DeRisi, W. J. (1976). Behavior analysis and therapy in community mental health. In H. Leitenberg (eg.), *Handbook of Behavior Analysis and Modification* (pp. 566–603). Englewood Cliffs, N.J.: Prentice-Hall.

————, Kuehnel, T. G., Phipps, C. C., & Cardin, V. A. (1984). *Resource Book for Psychiatric Rehabilitation, Elements of Service for the Mentally Ill.* Camarillo: Regents of the University of California.

Lipton, F. F., & Sabatini, A. (1984). Constructing support systems for homeless chronic patients. In H. R. Lamb (ed.), *The Homeless Mentally Ill.* Washington, D.C.: American Psychiatric Association.

Lorei, T. W., & Gurel, L. (1973). Demographic characteristics as predictors of post-hospital employment and readmission. *Journal of Consulting and Clinical Psychology, 40,* 426–30.

Lovaas, O. (1964). Clinical implications of relationships between verbal and nonverbal operant behavior. In H. Eysenck (ed.), *Experiments in Behavior Therapy.* New York: Macmillan.

McClure, D. P. (1973). Placement through improvement of client's job-seeking skills. *Journal of Applied Rehabilitation Counseling, 3,* 188–96.

Malamud, T. J. (1986). Community adjustment: Evaluation of the clubhouse model for psychiatric rehabilitation. *Rehabilitation Brief, 9*(2), 1–4.

Matthews, W. C. (1979). Effects of a work activity program on the self-concept of chronic schizophrenics. *Dissertations Abstracts International, 41,* 358B (University Microfilms no. 8816281, 98).

Mechanic, D. (1986). The challenge of chronic mental illness: A retrospective and prospective view. *Hospital and Community Psychiatry, 37,* 891–96.

Meichenbaum, D. (1966). The effects of social reinforcement on the level of abstraction in schizophrenics. *Journal of Abnormal Psychology, 71,* 354–62.

Meyerson, A., & Herman, G. (1983). What's new in aftercare? A review of recent literature. *Hospital and Community Psychiatry, 34,* 333–42.

Miller, N. (1959). Liberalization of basic S-R concepts: Extensions to conflict behavior, motivation and social learning. In S. Koch (ed.), *Psychology Study of Science* (vol. 2). New York: McGraw-Hill.

Miller, S., & Wilson, N. (1981). The case for performance contracting. *Administration in Mental Health, 8,* 185–93.

Minkoff, K. (1978). A map of chronic mental patients. In J. A. Talbott (ed.), *The Chronic Mental Patient.* Washington, D.C.: American Psychiatric Association.

———. (1987). Resistance of the mental health professionals to working with the chronic mentally ill. In A. T. Meyerson (ed.), *Barrier to Treating the Chronic Mentally Ill.* New Directions for Mental Health Services (no. 33). San Francisco: Jossey-Bass.

Morin, R. C., & Seidman, E. (1986). A social network approach and the revolving door patient. *Schizophrenia Bulletin, 12,* 262–73.

Mosher, L. R. (1984). The current status of the community support program: A personal assessment. *Psychosocial Rehabilitation Journal, 9*(3), 3–14.

———, & Keith, S. (1979). Research on the psychosocial treatment of schizophrenia: Summary report. *American Journal of Psychiatry, 136,* 623–31.

———, & Menn, A. Z. (1979). Community residential treatment for schizophrenia: Two-year follow-up. *Hospital and Community Psychiatry, 19,* 715–23.

Mowbray, C. T. (1985). Homeless in America: Myths and realities. *American Journal of Orthopsychiatry, 55*(1).

Munich, R., & Applebaum, A. (1985). The role and structure of long term hospitalization: Chronic schizophrenia. *Psychiatric Hospital, 16*(4).

Muthard, J. E. (1980). *Putting rehabilitation knowledge to use.* (Rehabilitation Monograph no. 11.) Gainesville, Fla.: Rehabilitation Research Institute.

Mynks, D. (1982). Developing and managing a psychosocial residential program. *The Management of Deinstitutionalization: Proceedings of the 1982 Florida Conference on Deinstitutionalization.* Tampa: University of South Florida Press.

National Council of Community Mental Health Centers (NCCMHC) (1984). Community residential services survey (mimeographed). Rockville: Md.: NCCMHC.

National Institute of Handicapped Research (1979). Past employment service and mentally disabled clients. *Rehabilitation Brief,* Aug. 1–4.

National Institute of Mental Health (1985). *CSP: Choices and Challenges.* Proceedings of the Seventh National Conferences of the National Institute of Mental Health. Washington, D.C.: National Institute of Mental Health.

National Institute of Mental Health, Division of Biometry and Epidemiology. (1977, June 27). *Resident Patient Rate in State Mental Hospitals Reduced to One-fourth the 1955 Rate* (Memorandum no. 6). Rockville, Md.

Nemec, P. B. (1983). Technical assistance to mental health programs: A case study. Unpublished dissertation (Psy.D. degree), Massachusetts School of Professional Psychology.

A Network for Caring: The Community Support Program of the National Institute of Mental Health (1981). Proceedings of the Fifth National Conference of the National Institute of Mental Health. Washington, D.C.: National Institute of Mental Health.

New Jersey Division of Mental Health and Hospitals (1980). *Rules and Regulations Governing Community Mental Health Services and State Aid.*

New Jersey Mental Health Planning Committee (1976). *A Manual for Reform of New Jersey's Mental Health Care System.*

Pandiani, J. A., Damkot, D., Gordon, L. R., Gramolini, R., & Kessler, R. (1982). *The Vermont alternate care assessment: Overview and technical report.* Burlington: University of Vermont.

———, Wilson, S. F., Gordon, L. R., & Carling, R. J. (1983). *Chronic Mental Health Clients in Vermont 1982–1983: A Statistical Profile.* Waterbury, Vt.: Department of Mental Health.

Pattison, E. M., & Pattison, M. L. (1981). Analysis of a schizophrenic psychosocial network. *Schizophrenia Bulletin, 7,* 135–43.

Paul, G. P. (1974). Experimental-behavioral approaches to schizophrenia. In R. Cancro, N. Fox, & L. Shapiro (eds.), *Strategic Intervention in Schizophrenia: Current Developments in Treatment.* New York: Behavioral Publications.

Paul, G. L., & Lentz, R. J. (1977). *Psychosocial Treatment of Chronic Mental Patients: Milieu vs. Social-Learning Programs.* Cambridge, Mass.: Harvard University Press.

Pelz, D. C., & Munson, R. C. (1980). A framework for organizational innovating. Unpublished paper. Ann Arbor: University of Michigan.

Pepper, B., Kirshner, M., & Ryglewicz, H. (1981). The young adult chronic patient: Overview of a population. *Hospital and Community Psychiatry, 32*(7), 463–69.

Peters, T. J., & Waterman Jr., R. H. (1982). *In Search of Excellence.* New York: Warner Books.

Peterson, R. (1979). What are the needs of the chronic mental patient? In J. Talbott (ed.), *The Chronic Mental Patient. Problems, Solutions, and Recommendation for a Public Policy.* Washington, D.C.: APA.

Piasecki, J. R., Leary, J. E., & Rutman, I. D. (1976). *Halfway Houses and Long-Term Community Residents for the Mentally Ill.* DHHS Publication no. ADM 80–1004; NIMH Series CN No. 1. Washington D.C.: Superintendent of Documents, U.S. Government Printing Office.

Pierce, J., & Blanch, A. (1989). A statewide psychosocial rehabilitation system: Vermont. In M. Farkas & W. Anthony (eds.), *Psychiatric Rehabilitation Programs: Putting Theory into Practice.* Baltimore: Johns Hopkins University Press.

Pierce, R. M., & Drasgow, J. (1969). Teaching facilitative interpersonal functioning to psychiatric patients. *Journal of Counseling Psychology, 16,* 295–98.

————, Cohen, M. R., Anthony, W. A., & Cohen, B. F. (1979). *Psychiatric Rehabilitation Practice Series: Career Counseling*. Amherst, Mass.: Carkhuff Institute of Human Technology.

Plata, M. (1981). Occupational aspirations of normal and emotionally disturbed adolescents: A comparative study. *Vocational Guidance Quarterly*, 29(4), 130–38.

Polak, P. R. (1978). A comprehensive system of alternatives to psychiatric hospitalization. In L. I. Stein, & M. A. Test, (eds.), *Alternatives to Mental Hospital Treatment*. New York: Plenum Press.

Prazak, J. A. (1979). Learning job-seeking interview skills. In J. D. Krumboltz & C. E. Thoreson (eds.), *Behavioral Counseling*. New York: Holt, Rinehart and Winston.

The President's Commission on Mental Health (1978). *Report to the President from the President's Commission on Mental Health* (vol. 1). Washington, D.C.: Superintendent of Documents, U.S. Government Printing Office.

Project Overcome. (1982). *Getting Together*. Minneapolis.

Quinn, P., & Richman, A. (1980). The contribution of a structured rehabilitation approach. *Rehabilitation Counseling Bulletin*, 24, 18–129.

Randolph, F., Carling, P. J., & Laux, R. (in preparation). *Innovative Financing Strategies in Housing and Mental Health*. Rockville, Md.: NIMH.

Rehabilitation Act Amendments of 1986 (1986). *Summary and Checklist for Action by MHA Affiliates*. Alexandria, Va.: National Mental Health Association.

Reinke, B., & Greenley, J. R. (1986). Organizational analysis of three community support program models. *Hospital and Community Psychiatry*, 37, 624–29.

Report to the President from the President's Commission on Mental Health. (1978). Washington, D.C.: Government Printing Office.

Retchless, M. H. (1967). Rehabilitation programs for chronic patients: Stepping stones to the community. *Hospital and Community Psychiatry*, 18, 377–78.

Rog, D. J., & Raush, H. L. (1975). The psychiatric halfway house: How is it measuring up? *Community Mental Health Journal*, 2, 155–62.

Rogan, D. (1980). Implementing the rehabilitation approach in a state rehabilitation agency. *Rehabilitation Counseling Bulletin*, 24, 49–60.

Rogers, C. R. (1951). *Client Centered Therapy*. Boston: Houghton Mifflin.

Rogers, E. S., Cohen, B., Danley, K., Hutchinson, D., & Anthony, W. (1986). Training mental health workers in psychiatric rehabilitation. *Schizophrenia Bulletin*, 12, 709–19.

Rogers, V. Commissioner of Mental Health, Legal Manuscript. 458 N.E. Reporter, 2d, 308, pp. 321–22.

Rose, S. M. (1979). Deciphering deinstitutionalization: Complexities in policy and program analysis. *Millbank Memorial Fund Quarterly*, 57, 529–60.

Rubin, L. B. (1985). *Just Friends: The Role of Friendship in Our Lives*. New York: Harper & Row.

Rutman, I. D., & Armstrong, K. (1985). A comprehensive evaluation of transitional employment programs in the rehabilitation of chronically mentally disabled clients. Unpublished paper. Mary E. Switzer Fellowship Project. Philadelphia: Maitrix Institute.

———, & Piasecki, J. R. (1976). *A National Survey of Community-based Residential Facilities*. Philadelphia: Horizon House Institute.

Rutner, I. T., & Bugle, G. (1969). An experimental procedure for the modification of psychotic behavior. *Journal of Consulting and Clinical Psychology, 33,* 651–53.

Ryan, E. R., & Bell, M. D. (1985). Rehabilitation of chronic psychiatric patients: A randomized clinical study. Paper presented at the meeting of the American Psychiatric Association, Los Angeles.

Safieri, D. (1970), Using an education model in a sheltered workshop program. *Mental Hygiene, 54,* 140–43.

Sauber, S. R. (1983). *The Human Services Delivery System*. New York: Columbia University Press.

Schein, E. H. (1978). The role of the consultant: Content expert or process facilitator? *Personnel and Guidance Journal, 56,* 339–43.

Schoenfeld, P., Halvey, J., Hemley-van der Velden, E., & Ruhf, L. (1986). Long term outcome for network therapy. *Hospital and Community Psychiatry, 37,* 373–76.

Schulberg, H. C. (1981). Outcome evaluations in the mental health field. *Community Mental Health Journal, 17,* 132–42.

Schwenger, C. (1981). The rehabilitation through education program at George Brown College. Unpublished personal communication.

Scoles, P., & Fine, E. (1979). Aftercare and rehabilitation in a community mental health center. *Social Work, 16,* 75–82.

Scott, W. R. (1985). Systems within systems: The mental health sector. *American Behavioral Scientist, 28,* 601–18.

———, & Black, B. L. (1986). *The Organization of Mental Health Services: Societal and Community Systems*. Beverly Hills, Calif.: Sage Publications.

Segal, S. P., & Aviram, U. (1978). *The Mentally Ill in Community-based Sheltered Care: A Study of Community Care and Social Integration*. New York: John Wiley and Sons.

Shapiro, D. (1985). Psychiatric rehabilitation: The effects of changes in a milieu. Unpublished paper presented at the 37th Institute on Hospital and Community Psychiatry. Montreal, Canada.

Shean, G. (1973). An effective and self-supporting program of community living for chronic patients. *Hospital and Community Psychiatry, 24,* 97–99.

Sheets, J. L., Prevost, J. A., & Reikman, J. (1982). The young adult chronic patient: Three year hypothesized subgroups. In B. Pepper and H. Ryglewicz (eds.), *The Young Adult Chronic Patient*. San Francisco: Jossey-Bass.

Sheper-Hughes, N. (1981). Dilemmas in deinstitutionalization: A view from inner city Boston. *Journal of Operational Psychiatry, 12,* 90–99.

Shern, D. L., Bartsch, D. A., Coen, A. S., Ellis, R. H., & Wilson, N. Z.

(1985). *A Model for Estimating Optimal Residential/Service Settings for Types of Chronically Mentally Ill Individuals.* Denver: Colorado Division of Mental Health.

Shifren-Levine, I., & Fleming, M. (1985). *Human Resource Development: Issues in Case Management.* Baltimore: State of Maryland Mental Hygiene Administration.

Soloff, A. (1972). The utilization of research. *Rehabilitation Literature, 33*(3), 66–72.

Spaniol, L., Jung, H., Zipple, A. M., & Fitzgerald, S. (1987). Families as a resource in the rehabilitation of the severely psychiatrically disabled. In A. B. Hatfield & H. P. Lefley (eds.), *Families of the Mentally Ill: Coping and Adaptation.* New York: Guilford Press.

———, & Zipple, A. M. (1988). Family and professional perceptions of family needs and coping strengths. Prepublication draft, Boston University, Center for Psychiatric Rehabilitation.

———, Zipple, A. M., & Fitzgerald, S. (1984). How professionals can share power with families: A new approach to working with families of the mentally ill. *Psychosocial Rehabilitation Journal, 18*(2), 77–84.

Speck, R., & Attneave, C. (1973). *Family network.* New York: Pantheon Books.

Starker, J. (1986). Methodological and conceptual issues in research on social support. *Hospital and Community Psychiatry, 37,* 485–90.

Stein, E. (1981). Report from the La Guardia-transitional mental health worker project. *Federation of Parents for the New York State Mental Institutions, Inc.,* 14–16.

Stein, L. (1986). Personal communication to P. Carling.

———, & Test, M. (1980). Alternatives to mental hospital treatment: I. Conceptual model, treatment programs, and clinical evaluation. *Archives of General Psychiatry, 37,* 392–97.

———, Test, M. A., & Marx, A. J. (1975). Alternative to the hospital: A controlled study. *American Journal of Psychiatry, 132,* 517–22.

———, & Test, M. A. (1985). The training in community living model: A decade of experience. In Lamb, H. R. (ed.), *New Directions for Mental Health Services.* San Francisco: Jossey-Bass.

Stelovich, S. (1979). From hospital to prison: A step forward in deinstitutionalization? *Hospital and Community Psychiatry, 30:* 618–20.

Stern, R. & Minkhoff, K. (1979). Paradoxes in programming for chronic patients in a community clinic. *Hospital and Community Psychiatry, 30,* 613–17.

Strauss, J. S., & Carpenter, W. (1972). The prediction of outcome in schizophrenics. *Archives of General Psychiatry, 27,* 739–46.

———, & Carpenter, W. (1974). The prediction of outcome in schizophrenics II. *Archives of General Psychiatry, 31,* 37–42.

———, Hafez, H., Lieberman, P., & Harding, C. M. (1985). The course of psychiatric disorder III: Longitudinal principles. *American Journal of Psychiatry, 142,* 289–96.

Stubbins, J. (1982). The clinical attitude in rehabilitation: A cross-cultural view. *World Rehabilitation Fund Monograph, 16,* New York: World Rehabilitation Fund.

Summers, F. (1981). The effects of aftercare after one year. *Journal of Psychiatric Treatment and Evaluation, 3,* 405–9.

Super, D. E. (1964). *Measuring vocational maturity for counseling and evaluation.* Washington, D.C.: National Vocational Guidance Association.

Switzer, M. E., Forward (1965). *Research and demonstration grant program* (revised). Washington, D.C.: Vocational Rehabilitation Administration, U.S. Department of Health Education and Welfare.

Talbott, J. (1979a). Deinstitutionalization: Avoiding the disaster of the past. *Hospital and Community Psychiatry, 30,* 621–24.

———. (1979b). Care of the chronically mentally ill—still a national disgrace. *American Journal of Psychiatry, 136,* 688–89.

———. (1984). The chronic mental patient: A national perspective. In M. Mirabi (ed.), *The Chronically Mentally Ill: Research and Services* (pp. 3–32). New York: Spectrum Publications.

Tessler, R. C., & Goldman, H. H. (1982). *The Chronically Mentally Ill: Assessing Community Support Systems.* Cambridge, Mass.: Ballinger Press.

———, & Manderscheid, R. (1982). Factors affecting adjustment to community living. *Hospital and Community Psychiatry, 33,* 203–7.

Test, M. A. (1976). Use of special living arrangements—A model for decision-making. *Community Living Arrangements for the Mentally Ill and Disabled: Issues and Options for Public Policy.* Rockville, Md.: National Institute of Mental Health.

———. (1981). Effective community treatment of the chronically mentally ill: What is necessary? *Journal of Social Issues, 37*(3), 71–86.

———. (1984). Community Support Programs. In A. S. Bellack (ed.), *Schizophrenia Treatment Management and Rehabilitation.* Orlando, Fla.: Grune and Stratton.

———, & Stein, L. (1978). Community treatment of the chronic patient: Research overview: *Schizophrenia Bulletin, 4,* 350–64.

Tornatzky, L. G., Fergus, E. O., Avellar, J. W., Fairweather, G. W., & Fleiscer, M. (1980). *Innovation and Social Process.* New York: Pergamon Press.

Torrey, E. F. (1986). Continuous treatment teams in the care of the chronic mentally ill. *Hospital and Community Psychiatry, 37,* 1243–46.

Turner, J.E.C., & Shifren, I. (1979). Community support systems: How comprehensive. *New Directions for Mental Health Services, 2,* 1–23.

Turner, J., & Ten-Hoor, W. J. (1978). The NIMH community support program. Pilot approach to a needed social reform. *Schizophrenia Bulletin, 4,* 319–49.

U.S. Department of Health and Human Services. (1980). *Toward a National Plan for the Chronically Mentally Ill.* Report to the Secretary by the Department of Health and Human Services Steering Committee on the Chronically Mentally Ill. Washington, D.C.

Unger, K. (in press). Rehabilitation through education: A university-based continuing education program for young adults with psychiatric disabilities. Ph.D. dissertation, Boston University. *Dissertation Abstracts International*.

———, & Anthony, W. A. (1982). Are families satisfied with services to young adult chronic patients? A recent survey and a proposed alternative. In B. Pepper and H. Ryglewicz (eds.), *The Young Adult Chronic Patient*. San Francisco: Jossey-Bass.

———, & Anthony, W. A. (1984). A university-based treatment for young adult chronic patients. In B. Pepper and H. Ryglewicz (eds.), *The young adult chronic patient revisited*. San Francisco: Jossey-Bass.

———, Danley, K., Kohn, L., & Hutchinson, D. (1987). Rehabilitation through education: A university-based continuing education program for young adults with psychiatric disabilities on a university campus. *Psychosocial Rehabilitation Journal, 10*(3), 35–51.

Vitalo, R. L. (1971). Teaching improved interpersonal functioning as a preferred model of treatment. *Journal of Clinical Psychology, 27*, 166–71.

———. (1979). An application in an aftercare setting. In W. A. Anthony (ed.), *Principles of Psychiatric Rehabilitation* (pp. 193–202). Baltimore: University Park Press.

Walker, R., & McCourt, J. (1965). Employment experience among 200 schizophrenic patients in hospital after discharge. *American Journal of Psychiatry, 122*, 316–19.

Wasow, M. (1982). *Coping with Schizophrenia: A Survival Manual for Parents, Relatives, and Friends*. Palo Alto, Calif.: Science and Behavior Books.

Wasylenki, D. A., Goering, P. N., Lancee, W. J., Ballantyne, R., & Farkas, M. D. (1985a). Impact of a case manager program on psychiatric aftercare. *Journal of Nervous and Mental Disease, 173*, 303–8.

———, Goering, P., Lancee, W., Fischer, L., & Freeman, S.J.J. (1985b). Psychiatric aftercare in a metropolitan setting. *Canadian Journal of Psychiatry, 30*, 329–35.

Weinman, B., Sanders, R., Kleiner, R., & Wilson, S. (1970). Community based treatment of the chronic psychotic. *Community Mental Health Journal, 6*, 12–21.

White, S. L. (1981). *Managing Health and Human Service Programs: A Guide for Managers*. New York: Free Press.

Willets, R. (1980). Advocacy and the mentally ill. *Social Work, 25*(5), 372–77.

Williams, D. H., Bellis, E. C., & Wellington, S. W. (1980). Deinstitutionalization and social policy: Historical perspectives and present dilemmas. *American Journal of Orthopsychiatry, 50*(1), 54–64.

Williams, P., Williams, W. A., Sommer, R., & Sommer, B. (1986). A survey of the California Alliance for the Mentally Ill. *Hospital and Community Psychiatry, 37*, 253–56.

Witheridge, T., Dincin, J., & Appleby, L. (1982). Working with the most frequent recidivists: A total team approach to assertive resource management. *Psychosocial Rehabilitation Journal, 5*, 9–11.

Wolfensberger, W. (1979). The principle of normalization and its implications for psychiatric services. *American Journal of Psychiatry*, 291–97.

Wolkon, G. H., Karmen, M., & Janaka, H. T. (1971). Evaluation of a social rehabilitation program for recently released psychiatric patients. *Community Mental Health Journal*, 7, 312–22.

Wood, D., Lenhard, S., Maggiani, M., & Campbell, M. (1975). Assertive training of the chronic mental patient. *Journal of Psychiatric Nursing and Mental Health Services*, 13, 42–46.

Wood, P. H. (1980). Appreciating the consequence of disease—The classification of impairments, disability, and handicaps. *The WHO Chronicle*, 34, 376–80.

Wright, B. (1960). *The Psychosocial Aspects of Disability*. New York: Harper and Row.

Zaltman, G., & Duncan R. *Strategies for Planned Change*. New York: John Wiley and Sons.

Zax, M. (1980). History and background of the community mental health movement. In M. S. Gibbs, J. R. Lachenmeyer, & J. Sigal (eds.), *Community Psychology: Theoretical and Empirical Approaches*. New York: Gardner, Press.

Zipple, A. M., & Greiff, I. (1986). St. Francis House: Rehabilitation support services for the homeless. Unpublished manuscript. Boston: Boston University, Center for Psychiatric Rehabilitation.

———, & Spaniol, L. (1984). *Current Research on Families that Include Persons with a Severe Mental Illness: A Review of Findings*. Boston: Boston University, Center for Psychiatric Rehabilitation.

———, & Spaniol, L. (1987). *Families that Include a Person with a Mental Illness: What They Need and How to Provide it* (A Trainer's Manual). Boston: Boston University, Center for Psychiatric Rehabilitation.

Index